P9-DCU-842

Collaborating for Project-Based Learning in Grades 9–12

Violet H. Harada
Carolyn H. Kirio
Sandra H. Yamamoto

Linworth Books

Professional Development Resources for K–12
Library Media and Technology Specialists

Library of Congress Cataloging-in-Publication Data

Harada, Violet H.
  Collaborating for project-based learning in grades 9-12 / Violet H. Harada, Carolyn H. Kirio,
Sandra H. Yamamoto.
      p. cm.
  Includes bibliographical references and index.
  ISBN-13: 978-1-58683-291-9 (pbk.)
  ISBN-10: 1-58683-291-3 (pbk.)
  1. Project method in teaching. 2. Educational technology. 3. School librarian participation
in curriculum planning. I. Kirio, Carolyn H. II. Yamamoto, Sandra H. III. Title.
  LB1027.43.H37 2008
  371.3'6--dc22
                        2007042180

Cynthia Anderson: Editor
Carol Simpson: Editorial Director
Judi Repman: Consulting Editor

Published by Linworth Publishing, Inc.
3650 Olentangy River Road
Suite 250
Columbus, Ohio 43214

Copyright © 2008 by Linworth Publishing, Inc.

All rights reserved. Purchasing this book entitles a librarian to reproduce activity sheets for
use in the library within a school or entitles a teacher to reproduce activity sheets for single
classroom use within a school. Other portions of the book (up to 15 pages) may be copied
for staff development purposes within a single school. Standard citation information should
appear on each page. The reproduction of any part of this book for an entire school or school
system or for commercial use is strictly prohibited. No part of this book may be electronically
reproduced, transmitted or recorded without written permission from the publisher.

ISBN 13: 978-1-58683-291-9
ISBN 10: 1-58683-291-3

5 4 3 2 1

Table of Contents

Table of Figures and Templates

Acknowledgments

This book was inspired by work being done at Kapolei High School in Hawaii. Since its opening in 2000 as an academy-focused secondary school, the administration, faculty, and community have envisioned Kapolei as a school where project-based, interdisciplinary learning centers on the needs and talents of its students. The authors thank the Kapolei school *ohana* (Hawaiian for family) including principal Alvin Nagasako and the other members of the administrative team, as well as all the teachers, staff, and students. Without their vision and dedicated efforts, this book would not have been possible.

We are especially grateful to our teacher-colleagues Vicky Nakasone and Elodie Arellano, and our library assistant Nancy Espiritu, who provided us with constructive feedback and critical support throughout our work. In addition, we thank Suzanne Kirio for her invaluable assistance with the graphics in this book and Sylvia Wee for editing help.

We also express our warm appreciation to Christine Weiser, Cyndee Anderson, and Marlene Woo-Lun at Linworth Publishing, Inc., for their unfailing encouragement and thoughtful advice. Their mentorship made the authoring process both pleasurable and invigorating. Finally, we thank our families for patiently supporting our late-night scrambling to meet deadlines. They have definitely been the strength behind our efforts.

About the Authors

VIOLET H. HARADA

Violet Harada is a professor of library and information science in the Department of Information and Computer Sciences at the University of Hawaii. Harada has been a secondary teacher, a curriculum writer, an elementary school librarian, and a state specialist with the Hawaii Department of Education as well as a college professor. In addition to her teaching duties, she coordinates the school library specialization for the Library and Information Science Graduate Program. Along with Joan Yoshina, she co-authored *Inquiry Learning through Librarian-Teacher Partnerships* (Linworth 2004) and *Assessing Learning: Librarians and Teachers as Partners* (Libraries Unlimited 2005). She has also worked with Sandra Hughes-Hassell on a co-edited volume, *School Reform and the School Library Media Specialist* (Libraries Unlimited 2007). In addition, Harada has published numerous articles in both scholarly and popular journals in the field and is a frequent speaker at state, national, and international library conferences.

CAROLYN H. KIRIO

Carolyn H. Kirio is a cybrarian at Kapolei High School in Hawaii where she trains, collaborates, and instructs with teacher teams in project-based learning work. Kirio served at Waianae High School as a library media specialist until she opened Kapolei High's library in 2000. In 2006 the American Association of School Librarians and Follett Learning Resources selected Kapolei's library as one of the National School Library Media Programs of the Year (SLMPY). Kirio earned her National Board Certification in 2002. She was selected as one of *School Library Journal's* "Top Ten Librarians To Watch" in 2003. The Hawaii Association of School Librarians also honored Kirio with the Golden Key Award in 1999 for her exemplary leadership in the school library profession. Kirio has a BEd in Music Education, a Professional Certificate in Secondary Education, and an MLIS in Library and Information Science. She has also been certified through Technology Training for Teachers, a Hawaii program for educators.

SANDRA H. YAMAMOTO

Sandra H. Yamamoto is also a cybrarian at Kapolei High School in Hawaii. She is heavily involved in building professional learning communities that include implementing school reform initiatives, mentoring new teachers, and facilitating professional development. She and her colleague, Carolyn Kirio, are rightfully proud of Kapolei library's recognition as one of the National School Library Media Programs of the Year (SLMPY) in 2006, an award sponsored by the American Association of School Librarians and Follett Learning Resources. Yamamoto has been a librarian at Waianae High and Pearl City High in Hawaii. Earlier in her career, she was a social studies teacher instructing secondary students in U.S. and world history, health, and career guidance. She is active in the Hawaii Association of School Librarians and has served as Scholarship Chair for five years. Yamamoto has also been a presenter at various local conferences.

Introduction

There is a silent epidemic spreading through our society. This epidemic is the serious dropout rate in our high schools. Consider the following statistics reported in a study conducted by the Peter D. Hart Research Associates (Bridgeland, Dillulio and Morison 2006) for the Bill and Melinda Gates Foundation:

- Almost one-third of our high school students do not graduate on time.
- Nearly half of our African-American, Hispanic, and Native-American students never complete high school.

While the epidemic is especially high among "low-income, minority, urban, single-parent children attending large high schools in the inner city," the problem is not unique to young people in such circumstances (Bridgeland, Dillulio and Morison 2006, 1). The quoted study conducted in 25 U.S. cities involved 467 racially and economically diverse dropouts. Participants ranging in age from 16 to 25 cited various reasons for leaving school before graduation. It was particularly disturbing that more than 47% indicated that they left school for the following reasons:

- Lack of connection to the school environment
- Perception that school was boring
- Classes were not interesting
- Feeling unmotivated (Bridgeland, Dillulio and Morison 2006, iii)

Seven in ten respondents said they were not motivated or inspired to work hard, and two-thirds indicated they would have worked harder if more effort was demanded of them (Ibid.). In fact, 70% were confident they could have graduated if they had tried. The final blow: nearly 90% of the respondents had passing grades when they chose to drop out (Ibid.).

While there are no easy answers to the dropout epidemic, the report identified "supports" that might keep students in school including the need to improve teaching and curricula to make school "more relevant and engaging" (Bridgeland, Dillulio and Morison 2006, iv). Four out of five respondents said there should be "more opportunities [in school] for real-world learning" (Ibid.). Over 80% of them said they would have continued if the learning was connected to the world outside of school (Ibid.).

The big question is how do we, as educators, design such learning opportunities? How can we motivate students to assume ownership in learning that has meaning for them? In the process of doing this, how do we help adolescents "learn to use their minds well"? (Sizer 1996, 154).

WHY PROJECT-BASED LEARNING?

As authors of this book, we believe strongly that project-based learning (PBL) is a potentially powerful means to produce relevant and rigorous learning. Although developing projects is not new in education, PBL is a more holistic instructional strategy (Railsbeck 2002). With our increasingly diverse student population, PBL takes on greater importance because it builds on students' individual strengths and allows them to explore their interests in the frame of a defined curriculum. PBL includes a wide range of specific projects; however, the following features are common to all of them:

- Real-world problems
- Firsthand investigation
- Specific goals related to curriculum, district, and state standards
- Tangible products for real audiences
- Connections among academic, life, and work skills
- Opportunities for reflective thinking and student self-assessment (Dickinson et al. 1998)

Research conducted over the last 20 years confirms that student engagement and motivation lead to higher academic achievement (e.g., Brewster and Fager 2000, Anderman and Midgley 1998, Lumbsden 1994). PBL has the potential to ignite excitement because this form of inquiry-focused learning allows students to make connections between the topics they study and their personal interests and concerns (Linn and Hsi 2000; Krajcik, Blumenfeld, Marx and Soloway 1999). Students in general develop their ability to raise complex and insightful questions (Boaler 1998). Because the topics have personal relevance for the learners, more of them are engaged in knowledge integration (Linn, Eyln and Davis 2004). Importantly, devoting time to PBL does not diminish performance on high-stakes tests (Shymansky and Kyle 1992).

PBL is not limited to students in gifted and talented classes. Schools with low-performing students have successfully implemented PBL by modifying projects, e.g., including more direct instruction, designing shorter projects, and focusing on fewer or more specific standards (Buck Institute for Education 2002).

RELEVANCE FOR SCHOOL LIBRARIES

Why should school library media specialists promote PBL? The Buck Institute for Education (2002), developers of PBL guidelines and handbooks, says that project-based learning contributes significantly to teacher collaboration because project-focused teaching encourages multidisciplinary approaches to learning. As partners in PBL, enterprising library media specialists can seize this opportunity to infuse information literacy skills into the school-wide curriculum.

Teachers and students working in PBL environments also discover that textbooks are not adequate for their questions and tasks. Frequently, even the resources located within school libraries are not sufficient for their needs. Once again, this presents library media specialists with the chance to help project teams access information through a global network linking them to vast databases, archives, and millions of users (McKenzie 1998). Librarians are also in a strategic position as information specialists to connect students and teachers with people outside the boundaries of the school. With the availability of online activity, they can bring in members of the outside community as motivators, role models, critics, and mentors.

AUDIENCE FOR THIS BOOK

This book is intended for high school instructional teams that are curious about the possibilities of PBL. It speaks to the thoughtful practitioner who wants to move away from rote learning to provide more challenging and complex work that has an interdisciplinary rather than departmentalized focus. This learning enhances rather than dilutes a standards-based curriculum.

As the authors, we take the stance that library media specialists are key partners in PBL teams. While there are countless publications on PBL for the classroom teacher, there are few books that focus on how the library media specialist contributes to PBL in a school setting. In this book, we include examples of the librarian's role in planning, delivering, and assessing for learning in PBL contexts.

ORGANIZATION OF THE BOOK

The first four chapters provide background information and frameworks for understanding and implementing PBL in high schools. To elaborate:

Chapter 1 defines PBL, describes its major characteristics, and explains the connection between inquiry learning and the features of PBL.

Chapter 2 examines PBL in the context of reform issues in today's high schools. We focus on major concerns about why students drop out, what testing is telling us about learning gaps, and how PBL might be a teaching and learning approach to help schools achieve effective curriculum reform.

Chapter 3 centers on the library media specialist and her role in PBL. We connect the learning foci of PBL with the standards of information literacy. We also challenge library media specialists to consider the skills they must possess to participate effectively in PBL teams.

Chapter 4 outlines steps in actually planning a project. We emphasize the importance of an outcome-based approach to curriculum design and stress the critical nature of team cooperation and collaboration. We also provide a checklist to assess the process of project-building initiatives.

Chapters 5 through 15 are modified examples of projects originally designed and implemented at Kapolei High School in Hawaii. For each project outline, we include the following critical features:

- Student outcomes
- Description of product or performance
- Connection with standards
- Overarching project questions
- Timeline for the project including tasks and team teaching responsibilities
- Checkpoints in the project including assessment targets and tools
- Resources used in the project
- Reflections of the instructors
- Templates and rubrics for various tasks along with samples of student work

SUMMARY

Education has to adapt to a changing world. As K-12 professionals, we must assist twenty-first-century students in acquiring the dispositions and skills they need for sustained, lifelong learning (Newell 2003). PBL embraces vital instructional practices that reflect the environment in which students currently live and learn. At the same time, PBL addresses the importance of rigorous standards, clear outcomes, and reflective accountability. In this book, we challenge teams to work through the challenges and seize the power of teaching and learning that emphasizes real-world applications.

WORKS CITED

Anderman, Lynley H., and Carol Midgley. *Motivation and Middle School Students.* Champaign: ERIC Clearinghouse on Elementary and Early Childhood Education, 1998. (ERIC Document Reproduction Service No. ED421281).

Boaler, Jo. "Open and Closed Mathematics: Student Experiences and Understandings." *Journal for Research in Mathematics Education* 29 (1998): 41-62.

Brewster, Cori, and Jennifer Fager. "Connecting the Curriculum to Real Life." *Breaking Ranks: Making It Happen.* Reston: National Association of Secondary School Principals, 2000. (ERIC Document Reproduction Service No. ED434413).

Bridgeland, John M., John J. Dillulio, Jr., and Karen B. Morison. *The Silent Epidemic: Perspectives of High School Dropouts.* A Report by Civic Enterprises in Association with Peter D. Hart Research Associates for the Bill & Melinda Gates Foundation, 2006. 30 July 2007 <http://www.gatesfoundation.org/UnitedStates/Education/TransformingHighSchools/Announcements/Announce-060302.htm>.

Buck Institute for Education. *Project Based Learning Handbook.* Novato: Author, 2002. 30 July 2007 <http://www.bie.org/pbl/pblhandbook/intro.php>.

Dickinson, Katherine P., Sengsouvanh Soukamneuth, Hanh Cao Yu, Mary Kimball, Ronald D'Amico, Rebecca Perry, Christopher Kingsley, and Susan P. Curan. *Providing Educational Services in the Summer Youth Employment and Training Program* [technical assistance guide]. Washington, DC: U.S. Department of Labor, Office of Policy & Research, 1998. (ERIC Document Reproduction Service No. ED420756).

Krajcik, Joseph, Phyllis Blumenfeld, Ron Marx, and Elliot Soloway. "Instructional, Curricular, and Technological Supports for Inquiry in Science Classrooms." *Inquiry into Inquiry: Science Learning and Teaching.* Ed. Jim Minstrell and Emily Van Zee. Washington, DC: American Association for the Advancement of Science Press, 1999. 283-315.

Linn, Marcia C., Eyln Bat-Sheva, and Elizabeth A. Davis. "Inquiry and Technology." *Internet Environments for Science Education.* Ed. Marcia Linn, Elizabeth A. Davis, and Philip Bell. Mahwah: Lawrence Erlbaum, 2004. 29-46.

Linn, Marcia C., and Sherry Hsi. *Computers, Teachers, Peers: Science Learning Partners.* Mahwah: Lawrence Erlbaum, 2000.

Lumbsden, Linda S. *Student Motivation to Learn.* Eugene: ERIC Clearinghouse on Educational Management, 1994. (ERIC Document Reproduction Service No. ED370200).

McKenzie, Jamie. "Grazing the Net: Raising a Generation of Free Range Students." *Phi Delta Kappan* 81.1 (1998): 26-31.

Newell, Ronald J. *Passion for Learning: How Project-Based Learning Meets the Needs of 21st Century Students.* Lanham: Scarecrow Press, 2003.

Railsback, Jennifer. *Project-Based Instruction: Creating Excitement for Learning.* Portland: Northwest Regional Educational Laboratory, August 2002. 30 July 2007 <http://www.nwrel.org/request/2002aug/>.

Shymansky, James A., and William C. Kyle, Jr. "The Effects of a Research Agenda: Critical Issues of Science Curriculum Reform." *Journal of Research in Science Teaching* 29 (1992): 749-78.

Sizer, Theodore R. *Horace's Hope: What Works for the American High School*. New York: Houghton Mifflin, 1996.

1 Introduction to Project-Based Learning

This chapter provides background information on Project-Based Learning (PBL) including the following: the major features and benefits of PBL; how roles change when teachers, library media specialists, and students engage in PBL; how inquiry and information literacy form the foundation for PBL; and how technology can be integrated in PBL.

BACKGROUND INFORMATION ON PROJECT-BASED LEARNING

PBL inspires provocative learning. It is a model for classroom activity that shifts away from short, isolated, teacher-centered lessons and emphasizes learning activities that are long-term, interdisciplinary, student-centered, and integrated with real-world issues and practices. In PBL, students construct meaning and practice skills through a process of inquiry that involves challenging and critical issues and topics. Consider the following scenario:

> *Seniors in a social studies class view a PBS television special on global pollution. The program delivers a disturbing message to the students: air pollution in places as distant at China affects the environmental quality in their own city. This fact challenges the students to investigate the issue. They undertake a project in which they gather information about the current situation from print and online resources. The students decide to extend beyond these sources of information to individuals, who provide diverse points of view on this complex problem. They conduct interviews and have online chats with scientists, economists, environmentalists, politicians, and business leaders. The project culminates with students collaborating on policy recommendations that they present at a virtual high school summit on global pollution that is jointly sponsored by the local department of education and the state government.*

Web sites, such as the "The Virtual Schoolhouse" (n.d.), provide a range of PBL examples similar to the one described above. Here are some of them:

- In Seattle, Washington, students in the Bilingual Orientation Center investigate how salmon breeds and the impact of the salmon industry on lives in their community. They collaborate with the Seattle Aquarium to create a series of murals based on their findings for public display.
- In Flint, Michigan, secondary school students in the Genesee Area Skill Center (GASC) Technology Center focus on why rain forests are critical in world ecology. They tackle questions such as: What threatens the rain forest habitat? How does deforestation impact life in the rain forest? What

can we do to save the rain forests? They create a simulated rain forest and devise lessons and hands-on science experiences for elementary students.

- In Kamuela, Hawaii, students at Kanu o ka 'Aina School wrestle with the question: How might we use technology to tell the unique story of our Hawaiian cultures and traditions? Using cutting edge media tools, they design and operate a multimedia production enterprise to produce marketable products relating to their Native Hawaiian cultural heritage.
- In Louisville, Kentucky, students at Southern High undertake a Bridge Project that engages them in the following deep questions: How is physics applied in the design of bridges? Why is the knowledge of math necessary when designing a bridge? How does the use of computer technology aid in bridge design? The students research different bridges and ultimately produce working scale models of them.
- In Milwaukie, Oregon, students at Milwaukie High create a "living history day." Their focal questions are: What do we know about recent wars fought by the U.S.? Who are the survivors? What can they tell us? How do we honor them? They organize a special event that hosts the Veterans of Foreign Wars for a day of panel discussions, activities, and speeches.

To succeed in these types of projects, students actively apply critical skills in project planning, collaborative problem solving, and higher-order thinking. They stretch themselves beyond the collection of facts and work toward constructing knowledge that combines facts with the analysis, synthesis, and application of this information. Teaching in PBL, therefore, requires that the instructors guide students in developing thoughtful products. These products provide evidence of students' abilities to grapple with the essential questions that frame the inquiry. The products also require students to demonstrate mastery of the content standards addressed by the project.

The roots of PBL go back at least a century to educators such as John Dewey who advocated for learning that was experiential. Teachers have been employing aspects of hands-on learning through the years (e.g., planning field trips, organizing lab investigations). PBL originates from this tradition. According to the Buck Institute for Education (2002) PBL has emerged as an effective approach to learning and teaching as a result of (1) revolutions in learning theory over the last 25 years, and (2) fundamental shifts in thinking about education in a changing world. To elaborate on these important points:

- Revolutions in learning theory: Research in both neuroscience and psychology has contributed to a better understanding about the complex dynamics of how we think and how we learn (Marzano 2003). For example, we now recognize the importance of social interaction in constructing knowledge. We also realize that new learning requires attention to past experiences and existing mental models. In addition, we are more sensitive to the importance of scaffolding how we teach content and activities to build and expand on students' existing skills.
- Shifts in thinking about education in a changing world: The evolution from an industrial age to a digital information age has forced educators to reconsider what students need to survive and thrive in a world where

change is the constant and information is generated at a mind-numbing rate (McDonald 1996). While domain knowledge remains essential, students must also have the skills to access, evaluate, and use information for lifelong, self-directed learning. In short, educators must balance *what to learn* and *how to learn* (Darling-Hammond 1997, Perkins 1992).

MAJOR FEATURES OF PBL

In research conducted by the AutoDesk Foundation (2000), teachers from 17 schools agreed that PBL reflected the following characteristics:

- Students help make key decisions within a prescribed framework.
- The focal problem or challenge has no predetermined solution.
- Students help to design the process for reaching a solution.
- Students are responsible for accessing and managing the information they gather.
- Students and instructors assess continuously.
- Students regularly reflect on what they are doing.
- A final product is expected and is assessed for quality.
- The learning environment tolerates error and experimentation.

It is clear from the above list that students are at the center of PBL. They work with instructors to determine the scope of their projects and devise plans that identify the goals and tasks to achieve their goals. The major attributes of PBL include the following:

- The issues, themes, or problems that form the core of PBL require in-depth exploration. There are no quick and easy answers; there are no sure solutions. Importantly, these issues or themes are directly related to content standards in the various disciplines. These standards provide an anchor to foundational concepts and processes in the curriculum.
- Students develop ownership in two important ways. First, they develop ownership for their projects when they select topics that are personally relevant to them. Second, students develop a new sense of responsibility as they start to take charge of their own learning. They do this by determining goals, identifying critical tasks and appropriate resources, and devising feasible timelines for accomplishing the work.
- Instructors take on the roles of facilitators and coaches. They do not relinquish control of the learning situation but share it with the students. The facilitative role affords them rich opportunities to differentiate and tailor instruction to specific student needs. They administer this assistance at the point of need. Importantly, instructors also assume the responsibility for ensuring that the projects satisfy a prescribed framework determined by the parameters of the established curriculum.
- Students use essential tools and skills that include application of technology for accessing, retrieving, and producing information. These skills range from searching online databases to using various applications for gathering data and creating presentations.

- Students collaborate with peers and adults. They establish project teams to share responsibilities and exchange ideas and points of view. They confer with instructors to assess their progress and determine next steps. They establish contact with peers in other schools and with experts in the community. As part of this process, they strengthen their skills in active listening and intelligent, coherent communication.
- Students reflect continuously as they work through their projects. Key questions they must ask themselves include: What is my goal? How well am I achieving this goal? What is working well? What problems am I having? How might I deal with these problems? What are possible solutions?
- PBL culminates in a product or performance that presents possible solutions to a problem, analyzes a dilemma from multiple points of view, or develops a theme or idea in original and thoughtful ways. This final product is evaluated for quality. As the culminating and celebratory event, it should be shared with a wider audience than the teacher.

Blumenfeld and colleagues (1991) state that students pursue solutions to "nontrivial problems" in PBL by

- Asking and refining questions
- Debating ideas
- Making predictions
- Designing plans and experiments
- Collecting and analyzing data
- Drawing conclusions
- Communicating their ideas and findings to others
- Asking new questions
- Creating artifacts

It is important to note that all of the above activities require students to examine their prior knowledge and conduct background research.

Educators frequently ask about the relationship between *problem-based learning* and *project-based learning*. The major difference is that project-based learning may or may not focus on a problem. In practice, however, these two approaches to learning are more similar than different. Both are instructional strategies that engage students in real-world tasks and open-ended problems. The instructor facilitates and coaches. Students generally work in cooperative groups for extended periods of time. They use multiple sources of information. In project-based learning and problem-based learning, assessment focuses on performance and demonstration.

BENEFITS OF PBL

Researchers have studied the effects of PBL in a range of educational settings and have found it to be generally effective in building motivation and strengthening students' abilities to solve problems (Stites 1998). PBL reflects many of the research-supported elements embedded in effective instructional design including the need to be more responsive to the diverse learning needs and interests of individual children (Tomlinson and McTighe 2006, Marzano 2003). In addition, it embraces the integration of curriculum in the different subjects, the engagement of home and community in school learning, and the involvement of students in cooperative teamwork.

Current research also promotes a shift from *memorized* learning to *memorable* learning (Marzano 2003). The former concentrates on fact gathering and recall while the latter embraces knowledge building and the demonstrated application of that knowledge. For high schools engaged in PBL, this research confirms the need to provide learning experiences that are related to themes and issues that cross disciplines. It validates cooperative and collaborative problem solving and the importance of connecting school experiences with active involvement in the life stream of the larger community.

Another benefit of PBL is the unique way that it motivates students to engage in their own learning. Within curriculum parameters, PBL offers opportunities for students to pursue their own interests and questions as they make decisions about how they will find answers and solve problems.

The Buck Institute for Education (2002) and other educators summarize the following benefits of PBL:

- It merges thinking and knowledge by helping students master both the content and the process.
- It emphasizes real-world skills including problem solving, communication, and self-management.
- It integrates disciplines by focusing on themes, issues, and deeper investigations of topics.
- It capitalizes on concerns and skills valued in the community.
- It acknowledges and meets the needs of learners with a range of learning styles and needs.

CHANGING ROLES IN PBL

In PBL, there are critical shifts from the norm in the interaction and engagement of students, instructors, families, and communities. First, students often assume both informal and formal teaching roles with their peers, younger students, and even the faculty. This change is evident when projects require applications of technology for a range of tasks. For example, students often have greater technical expertise than their instructors in using digital cameras, video camcorders, and multimedia applications. It makes sense that PBL capitalizes on their expertise and talents. By displaying their work in different formats, students inspire both teachers and peers to consider more creative forms of expression. They also instruct others in using a range of media to produce innovative work.

Second, teachers are no longer the conventional dispensers of knowledge. They discover alternative roles as coaches, facilitators, and co-learners as they hone valuable skills in questioning and developing hypotheses, and devise strategies in retrieving and evaluating information. By discussing plans, drafts, and finished products, they develop fresh perspectives on content knowledge along with their students.

Third, library media specialists are active co-facilitators as they work alongside classroom teachers to help students refine their abilities to solve information-related problems and develop strategies as critical consumers of information and discriminating producers of newly acquired knowledge. We devote Chapter 3 to a fuller description of the library media specialist's role in PBL.

Fourth, families and community members become more effectively and intensely engaged in learning situations. PBL encourages students to reach beyond the resources available in the school setting and forge links with community mentors including business leaders, scientists, and political and labor experts. The Internet and wireless technology make information truly an "anywhere, anytime" reality where learning is possible from the home as well as the school.

INQUIRY AS A FOUNDATION FOR PBL

PBL embraces a theory of constructivism, which is based on the premise that by reflecting on our experiences, we construct our own understanding of the world (Brooks and Brooks 1999). It entails a shift in learning objectives from mastery of factual information and didactic assignments to projects that stress higher-order thinking and performance-based, authentic assessments.

An inquiry approach to learning reflects the constructivist philosophy. It responds directly to the national emphasis on high standards and is bolstered by an expanding body of research about learning and the brain (Bransford, Brown, and Cocking 1999; Stripling 2003; Senge 2000). It involves students in a spiraling cycle of questioning, investigating, verifying, and generating new questions (Harada and Yoshina 2004). Pappas and Tepe (2002) describe this type of learning as "an investigative process that engages students in answering questions, solving real-world problems, confronting issues, or exploring personal interests" (27).

PBL embodies inquiry learning. It requires rigorous investigations and connections to the real world (Buck Institute for Education 2002). Exline (2004) says that inquiry is "seeking for truth, information, or knowledge…[it is] seeking information by questioning" (online). From birth, infants try to make sense of the world by inquiring. They gather information by applying the basic human senses of sight, hearing, touch, taste, and smell.

As Exline indicates, the problem is that our traditional educational system discourages the natural process of inquiry. As a result, students become less prone to ask questions as they move through the grade levels. PBL attempts to transform learning so that it nurtures students' natural inquiry process. The focus of PBL is on *how students come to know* rather than *what students know*.

Stripling (2003) succinctly outlines the inquiry process as follows:

- Connect—connect to self and previous knowledge, gain background knowledge, observe and experience to gain an overview
- Wonder—generate questions, make predictions, and develop hypotheses
- Investigate—find and evaluate information to answer questions and test hypotheses, think about the information to illuminate new questions and hypotheses
- Construct—build new understandings, draw conclusions about questions and hypotheses
- Express—communicate new ideas, apply understandings to a new context or situation

• Reflect—reflect on one's own process of learning and new understandings gained from inquiry, pose new questions

In Figure 1.1 we highlight how PBL engages students in the inquiry process.

Figure 1.1 Relationship between the Inquiry Process and PBL

Inquiry Process	Project-Based Learning
CONNECT	Connects to real-world issues and experiences Relates to student concerns and interests Relates to community concerns and topics Aligns with standards
WONDER	Focuses on essential or overarching questions Relies on additional questions that relate to the essential one Explores the larger topic or issue to gain background knowledge Challenges students to consider impact of the questions on their own lives
INVESTIGATE	Requires a rigorous approach to problem solving Requires a systematic approach to data collection and analysis Encourages use of technology to collect data Involves use of a range of relevant resources including human and online resources
CONSTRUCT/EXPRESS	Requires organization of information Requires constructing meaning from information (i.e., analysis and synthesis of data) Involves creative and appropriate means of communication Encourages use of technology in production Involves communication of finding to real audiences
REFLECT	Requires formative assessment Requires summative evaluation Emphasizes self-assessment and adaptation/modification of projects based upon reflection

Within this context of inquiry, library media specialists partner with teachers to hone students' information literacy skills. They assist students in generating relevant and thoughtful questions, examining data and ideas critically based on information needs, transforming data into knowledge, and developing creative techniques to effectively communicate this knowledge to others.

USING TECHNOLOGY IN PBL

Research indicates that PBL is especially effective when supported by educational technology (Means and Olson 1997). However, there is a caveat. We must be aware that PBL and technology are usually implemented in the context of more comprehensive reform efforts. Therefore, it is not possible to isolate the effects of either intervention on student learning. Nonetheless, the results provide optimistic indications that PBL using technology as a teaching and learning tool is a viable approach (not the only approach) to improve learning.

What we do know with certainty is that there has been a tremendous surge in students' access to computers. Population survey data obtained in 2000 from about 50,000 households revealed that 90% of school-age children had access to a computer (U.S. Census Bureau

2001). In the same year, the National Center for Educational Statistics (Cattagni and Ferris 2001) reported that 98% of the public schools were connected to the Internet. In a 2003 survey conducted by the National Technology Information Agency, 95.9% of young adults between 18 and 24 were using computers (qtd. in Donham 2005, 31).

We also know that technology opens exciting avenues for accessing and producing information. Students use tools such as word processing programs, spreadsheets, and databases to outline ideas, draft reports, analyze numerical data, manage data, and organize information. They use email, online forums, blogs, and chatrooms to communicate and collaborate with contacts around the world. On a more formal level, the Internet provides access to a wealth of resources available in libraries, museums, and geographically remote research sites. Students become "infotectives" who can "ask great questions about data in order to convert the data into information and eventually into insight" (McKenzie 1998, 27). They locate information in online encyclopedias, and in periodical and newspaper databases. Library media specialists help students refine their skills in evaluating all of these resources.

Students can also use an ever-increasing range of software tools to produce creative expressions of their work. Many of them participate in simulations or virtual worlds and work together to accomplish innovative tasks. Internet and digital video technologies promote collaborative activities, even among geographically distant students (Donham 2005). Students can also archive their electronic products for others to review and critique. In addition, technology is used as a tool for assessment and evaluation, e.g., the development of electronic portfolios.

SUMMARY

In this chapter, we described PBL as a viable approach to teaching and learning in the digital information age. We identified important benefits of PBL and pointed out how changes in the roles for students, teachers, library media specialists, and community members might produce a genuine community of learners. We examined how constructivism and inquiry form the backbone of PBL and how information literacy is embedded in the inquiry process. We also explained how technology might be an integral component in PBL.

The appeal of PBL is the potential for students to develop their skills in problem solving and reasoning. Importantly, students create personal connections with their topics as they develop essential questions or lines of inquiry that truly matter to them. It allows them to recognize the knowledge and skill demands of the problem and to develop their own repertoire of strategies, sources, and skills to complete the project. When students work collaboratively, it challenges them to examine possibilities through multiple prisms. By tapping varying expertise within a group, they see "different facets of a complex problem and bring unique needs for completeness and tolerance for ambiguity" (Kelson and Distlehorst 2000, 176). Students begin to move from simplistic notions to more complex meanings of concepts and understandings. If our goal as educators is to inspire engagement and deep learning, PBL has the ingredients for motivating students to participate in this challenge. In the following chapters, we elaborate on how information literacy is critical to student success in PBL and how the library media specialist is strategically positioned to work with both students and teachers.

WORKS CITED

Autodesk Foundation. *Harnessing the Web: Introduction to Networked Project-Based Learning.* 2000. Encinitas: Global SchoolNet Foundation. 30 July 2007. <http://www.gsn.org/web/pbl/whatis.htm>.

Blumenfeld, Phyllis C., Elliot Soloway, Ronald W. Marx, Barry J. Krajcik, Mark Guzdial, and Annemarie Palincsar. "Motivating Project-Based Learning: Sustaining the Doing, Supporting the Learning." *Educational Psychologist* 26.3/4 (1991): 369-98.

Bransford, John D., Ann L. Brown, and Rodney R. Cocking. *How People Learn: Brain, Mind, Experience, and School.* Washington, DC: National Academy Press, 1999.

Brooks, Martin G., and Jacqueline G. Brooks. *In Search of Understanding: The Case for Constructivist Classrooms.* Rev. ed. Alexandria: Association for Supervision and Curriculum Development, 1999.

Buck Institute for Education. *Project Based Learning Handbook.* Novato: Author, 2002. 30 July 2007 <http://www.bie.org/pbl/pblhandbook/intro.php>.

Cattagni, Anne, and Elizabeth Farris. *Internet Access in U.S. Public Schools and Classrooms: 1994-2000.* Washington, DC: National Center for Education Statistics, 2001. 30 July 2007 <http://www.nces.ed.gov/surveys/frss/publications/2001071/>.

Darling-Hammond, Linda. *The Right to Learn: A Blueprint for Creating Schools That Work.* San Francisco: Jossey Bass, 1997.

Donham, Jean. *Enhancing Teaching and Learning: A Leadership Guide for School Library Media Specialists.* 2nd ed. New York: Neal Schuman, 2005.

Exline, Joe. *Inquiry Based Learning.* New York: Educational Broadcasting Corporation, 2004. 30 July 2007 <http://www.thirteen.org/edonline/concept2class/inquiry/index.html>.

Harada, Violet H., and Joan M. Yoshina. "From Rote to Inquiry: Creating Learning that Counts." *Library Media Connection* 23.2 (2004): 22-25.

Kelson, Ann C. Myers, and Linda H. Distlehorst. "Groups in Problem-Based Learning (PBL): Essential Elements in Theory and Practice." *Problem-Based Learning: A Research Perspective on Learning Interactions.* Ed. Dorothy Evenson and Cindy E. Hmelo. Mahwah: Lawrence Erlbaum, 2000. 167-95.

Marzano, Robert. *What Works in Schools: Translating Research into Action.* Alexandria: Association for Supervision and Curriculum Development, 2003.

McDonald, Joseph P. *Redesigning Schools: Lessons for the 21ˢᵗ Century.* San Francisco: Jossey Bass, 1996.

McKenzie, Jamie. "Grazing the Net: Raising a Generation of Free Range Students." *Phi Delta Kappan* 81.1 (1998): 26-31.

Means, Barbara, and K. Olson. *Technology and Education Reform.* Washington, DC: U.S. Government Printing Office, 1997. (ORAD 96-1330). 30 July 2007 <http://www.ed.gov/pubs/EdReformStudies/EdTech/index.html>.

Pappas, Marjorie L., and Ann E. Tepe. *Pathways to Knowledge™ and Inquiry Learning.* Englewood: Libraries Unlimited, 2002.

Perkins, David N. *Smart Schools: Better Thinking and Learning for Every Child.* New York: Free Press, 1992.

Senge, Peter. *Schools That Learn: A Fifth Discipline Fieldbook for Educators, Parents, and Everyone Who Cares about Education.* New York: Doubleday, 2000.

Stites, Regie. "Evaluation of Project-Based Learning: What Does Research Say about Outcomes from Project-Based Learning?" *Project-Based Learning with Multimedia.* San Mateo: San Mateo County Office of Education, 1998. 30 July 2007 <http://pblmm. k12.ca.us/PBLGuide/pblresch.htm>.

Stripling, Barbara K. "Inquiry-Based Learning." *Curriculum Connections through the Library.* Ed. Barbara K. Stripling and Sandra Hughes-Hassell. Westport: Libraries Unlimited 2003. 3-39.

Tomlinson, Carol A., and Jay McTighe. *Integrating Differentiated Instruction and Understanding by Design: Connecting Content and Kids.* Alexandria: Association for Supervision and Curriculum Development, 2006.

United States Census Bureau. "9 in 10 School Age Children Have Computer Access; Internet Use Pervasive Census Bureau Reports." *U.S. Department of Commerce News.* 6 Sept. 2001. 30 July 2007 <http://www.census.gov/Press-Release/www/2001/cb01-147.html>.

The Virtual Schoolhouse. n.d. 30 July 2007 <http://virtualschoolhouse.visionlink.org/pbl. htm>.

2 School Reform and PBL

In the first chapter, we identified the major features of Project-Based Learning (PBL) and the effective implementation of PBL in a school community. We also discussed how PBL results in an inclusive use of technology and critical changes in the roles of students, teachers, library media specialists, and parents. Chapter 2 examines PBL in terms of the bigger school picture.

We hasten to mention that we are not writing a book on school reform here; however, we felt it important to consider PBL in the larger context of school change. We begin by exploring how different stakeholders see the goals of K-12 education for students and then discuss what needs to happen if we wish to achieve these goals. We acknowledge and build upon Tony Wagner's (2002) references to the importance of rigor, relevance, and relationships in school reform and add a fourth R, reflection. These 4 R's become the lenses through which we examine what needs to happen for school improvement. We connect this discussion to the key attributes of PBL and link these attributes to library media specialists and how they might be influential partners in the change process.

INTRODUCTION

In a *Time* article on education and change, Wallis and Steptoe (2006) speculated about how Rip Van Winkle might respond to today's world if he awoke from a hundred-year slumber. The skyscrapers, shopping malls, and fast food chains would disorient Rip. He would be amazed by folks talking on cell phones and teenagers plugged into iPods. Ironically, the one thing that Rip would still recognize would be the schoolroom with seats facing the front, and the blackboard and lectern as standard classroom fixtures. Old Rip would discover that while everything else has changed, schools have not moved very far from an agrarian-industrial model of education. In short, the more things change, the more schools remain the same.

In today's fast-changing world, however, educational inertia is no longer an option. The national spotlight on poor academic achievement and dwindling graduation rates highlight the fact that yesterday's solutions are not working in today's schools. Pressure continues to mount for schools to improve. The voices come from all sectors: the federal and state governments, local school boards, parents, employers, and students. In this chapter, we address the following questions that must drive change regarding how students learn and how we teach:

- What learning prepares students to succeed in today's world?
- How should schools meet this challenge?
- How does PBL help to meet this charge?
- How might the library media specialist be involved?

WHAT MUST STUDENTS LEARN TO SUCCEED IN TODAY'S WORLD?

Tony Wagner (2002) in *Making the Grade* indicates that we need to prepare students in K-12 schools to be global citizens. This requires that students acquire a plethora of skills and dispositions that were not part of traditional schooling in the agrarian or factory societies of an earlier age. According to Wagner, various stakeholders have voiced different ideas about the skills and dispositions that young people need to survive and succeed as global citizens in the twenty-first century.

WHAT THE COMMUNITY SAYS

When members of the public speak out about education reform, they are concerned about human values, work ethic, and life skills. In his countless sessions with community and business leaders, Wagner (2002) found that their biggest concerns centered on work habits, motivation, and curiosity. Granted, they also desired graduates who could read, write, and communicate effectively; however, the community and business leaders placed equal value on workers having good people skills and being able to think outside the box. They recognized that innovative solutions often required diverse teams of people who could leverage their areas of expertise and forge synergistic connections.

The Partnership for 21st Century Skills (2004), a consortia of private and public organizations focused on creating a model of learning for this millennium, identifies the following as key features of twenty-first-century education:

- Broad multidisciplinary themes: global awareness; financial, economic, business and entrepreneurial literacy; civic literacy; and health and wellness awareness
- Learning and thinking skills: information and media literacy, critical thinking and problem solving, communication, and collaboration
- Information and communications technology literacy: using technology to develop content knowledge and skills
- Life skills: ethics, accountability, personal responsibility, people skills, self-direction, and social responsibility
- Assessment beyond standardized testing: measuring learning results in the classroom and using modern technologies to conduct assessment (4-5)

WHAT THE STUDENTS SAY

The Millennials are our newest adult generation with half of them already 18 years old. They are the second largest generation in U.S. history, next to the Baby Boomers. Through focus groups, Sweeney (2005, 167) discovered revealing things about this generation. They:

- Expect more choices
- Learn experientially
- Crave personalization
- Expect instant gratification
- Desire independence and flexibility
- Practice multitasking

- Love gaming
- Demand anytime, anywhere communications

What do these Millennials feel they need in their schooling? Wagner (2002) conducted focus groups with high school graduates in the New England area and asked them what they would have liked to have had in their preparation for college. Their list was consistent with what employers cited: more writing, more emphasis on crucial work habits, more exposure to different strategies that motivate learners and nurture curiosity, and more opportunities to develop team skills. The bottom line was that these young adults wanted learning experiences that were hands-on, open ended, and personalized. They sought options that allowed them to apply information to meaningful problems. Being digital natives, the students also expected technology to be a natural part of their learning.

WHAT EDUCATORS SAY

The literature on curriculum reform echoes the same points raised by the public and by the students. The research also emphasizes the importance of students being challenged with high expectations. In the Consortium on Chicago Schools Research, Johnson and Rudolph (2001) from North Central Regional Educational Laboratory indicated that the students who were challenged, and who were given more opportunities for higher-order thinking and tougher assignments, outperformed less challenged students. They concluded that the teachers and administrators involved in this study placed more emphasis on authentic learning that was meaningful. The active learning environments required collaboration and communication among students. These teachers encouraged more opportunities for analysis, synthesis, and evaluation of information than did their counterparts in traditional classrooms. As a result, students assumed increasing responsibility for their own learning. These findings have also been affirmed in other national reports (e.g., National Governors Association 2002, Peterson 1995).

Educators have also outlined some of the *new basic skills* required (Murnane and Levy 1996). They include solving semi-structured problems where hypotheses must be formed and tested; working in groups with persons of different backgrounds; communicating effectively, both orally and in writing; and using personal computers. Johnson (2006) has drilled deeper to identify the following tiers of sub-skills that he feels are essential for the "knowledge worker of tomorrow" (9-12):

- Basic skills: reading, writing, and solving numeric problems
- Discipline-specific skills: foundational concepts and facts in science, math, history, literature, geography, and other disciplines
- Technology skills: basic operations, social and ethical issues, use of productivity and research tools, and use of tools to solve problems
- Higher-order thinking skills: information problem solving and critical thinking
- Conceptual skills: both left-brain and right-brain thinking

HOW SHOULD SCHOOLS MEET THIS CHALLENGE?

Traditional curriculum programs run counter to the reform expectations expressed in the earlier sections of this chapter. Instead of posing learning in authentic and contextualized settings, conventional schooling is frequently contrived and divorced from real-world concerns (Glatthorn and Jaillal 2000). Instead of integrating concepts across disciplines, teaching often occurs in isolated silos so that learning is fragmented. Rather than focusing on results, the curriculum degenerates into a series of text-related assignments and activities that ignores individual differences.

Reform advocates (e.g., Darling-Hammond and Bransford 2005; Armstrong 2006; Marzano 2003; Murnane and Levy 1996; Newmann, Marks, and Gamoran 1996; Wagner 2002) emphasize the need to re-examine current practices using the prisms of rigor, relevance, relationships, and reflection. In this chapter, we refer to them as the *4 R's of reform*.

RIGOR

Rigor in the educational context refers to learning that stimulates curiosity and discovery. Such learning challenges students to engage in deeper questioning and analysis of topics, issues, and situations. Unfortunately, learning in many schools is often trivial, irrelevant, and meaningless. Newmann, Marks, and Gamoran (1996) stress that standards for *intellectual quality* are critical. They posit the following three criteria for intellectual quality:

- Construction of knowledge: student performances and products reflect understanding at higher levels of thinking and successful application and manipulation of information
- Disciplined inquiry: students not only gather facts but also link them to prior knowledge and questions; they see relationships through interpretation and analysis
- Value beyond school: students see relevance in their achievements because their work has adaptive value in the community and an audience beyond the school

The Bill and Melinda Gates Foundation echoes this same train of thought in identifying the following attributes of effective teaching and learning (qtd. in Wagner 2002, 111):

- Active inquiry: Students are deeply engaged in exploration and research. The activities draw out perceptions and develop understanding. In the process of the investigation, students make decisions about their learning. Importantly, teachers leverage the diverse experiences and talents of students to build these effective learning contexts.
- In-depth learning: Curriculum focuses on substance and not breadth of coverage. While this poses a challenge to teachers, who are attempting to cover numerous standards, focused learning situations provoke students to grapple with complex problems and explore core concepts to develop deeper understanding. The students apply knowledge in real-world contexts.

- Performance assessment: The expectations are clearly defined for students. Students strive to produce quality work products and present to real audiences. Student work shows evidence of understanding rather than simple recall. Assignments reflect higher-order thinking. Wherever possible and appropriate, teachers negotiate the learning goals with students and they monitor progress together.

RELEVANCE

Relevance requires that students see personal connections between their own lives and the assignments in the classroom. They have to see that the content being studied and the skills being learned are applicable to their experiences outside the school. Wagner (2002) identifies the following factors as critical in stimulating and sustaining student motivation:

- Challenge students with engaging, real issues: Instead of mind-numbing exercises that center on regurgitation of facts, focus on questions that students will care about. Ask: how do we know what we know, where is the evidence, whose view is this, how are things connected, what if, and who cares?
- Encourage and respect student voice: Display and celebrate student work. Invite continuous discussion and critiquing.
- Personalize learning: Connect the learning experience to student's life. Appreciate and encourage individual talents and strengths.

RELATIONSHIPS

There are few opportunities for youngsters to interact with adults outside of school.

Csikszentmihalyi and Larson (1984) documented this disturbing trend in their study of what teens do in their waking hours. They discovered that teens spent almost as much time alone, 27% of their week, as they did with friends, which was 29%. Only about 5% of their time was spent with a parent or guardian.

The implication for schools is a critical one: we need to provide more opportunities for young adults to learn with and from adults. This contact can take many forms, e.g., mentors in the community, service learning, family members as resources, and job shadowing. These adult relationships help to connect the school with the rest of the world (Newmann, Marks, and Gamoran 1996).

It is important to note that linking students with members of the larger community is a crucial building block in the creation of knowledge communities (Stefl-Mabry and Lynch 2006). In his work on emotional intelligence, Goleman (1995) indicates that participating in these types of relationships allows young adults to demonstrate empathy and social skills that are crucial to success in a person's work and personal life.

Along with student-adult relationships, it is equally important to encourage student-to-student conversations and peer problem solving. By forming teams to design and execute projects, students learn to harness the power of collective expertise and enjoy the synergy of collaborative discourse. Smaller learning communities emerge from this type of interactive, critical interaction and investigation among students.

Student relationships can also be nurtured through peer mentoring situations. Both the student mentored and the student mentoring gain enormous benefits from such opportunities. Students being mentored by peers frequently mention that this is an effective way to learn because peer mentors can explain things in language they understand. These mentors, in turn, value the experience because they can test their own skills in helping colleagues to understand and master certain concepts and skills.

REFLECTION

Reflection is a necessary component of the learning process. Being able to examine one's own performance and actions are the first steps in self-awareness and self-regulation (Goleman 1995). At the same time, reflection is a difficult skill that requires guidance and patient practice. "Students need to weigh evidence, consider options, and make conscious choices about how to approach problems and issues. Decisions are the result of deliberate thinking and informed problem solving. Metacognition is vital to inquiry learning" (Harada and Yoshina 2004, 16).

As reflection becomes a natural part of the total learning experience, students realize the empowering nature of assessment. They come to recognize that self-assessment provides them with personal insights about improvements for the next phase of their work. This metacognitive knowledge gives them control over their own learning. When students practice this type of thoughtful behavior, they build essential skills and dispositions for self-directed excellence that lead to lifelong self-improvement (Jones 2006).

CONNECTION WITH STANDARDS

In this chapter, we introduced the 4 R's as a valuable framework to examine how schools might prepare students for the twenty-first-century workplace. A critical related issue is how the content and performance standards "fit" with the 4 R's. Actually, they fit quite well. In terms of *rigor,* the standards identify the key concepts and ideas in each of the disciplines. A foundation of thinking permeates the disciplines (Harada 2003a). For example, in social studies, the standards encourage historical analysis. Students formulate questions, obtain data from reliable sources, and evaluate sources for propaganda and distortion. They conduct comparative and causal analyses and construct sound historical arguments. In language arts, the standards require literary analysis and the ability to examine themes from multiple points of view. In science, the standards focus on students being able to formulate testable hypotheses, design and conduct careful investigations, arrive at findings based on examination of data, and defend these findings.

While the standards do not explicitly refer to the issues of *relevance* and *relationships,* projects and units that build on standards can be powerful agents of both. The projects highlighted in this book are examples of such standards-framed initiatives. In Chapter 5, for example, we describe a unit on genetics and the ethical issues surrounding it. The problem is timely and meaningful. Students study it carefully and have heated but reasoned debates on the pros and cons of cloning. They examine the ethical issues from multiple perspectives. Their research includes information from primary resources in print and digital forms and extends to contacts with university and political experts on the topic.

Reflection is a critical component of all standards. The science standards, for example, stress peer critiquing and review as an integral part of the inquiry process. Students review their conclusions and revise them as they discover new evidence. The notion of *assessment as learning* is inherent in the scientific inquiry process; it is central to the generation of increasingly complex questions and the construction of new knowledge.

Studies of high-achieving schools with disadvantaged student populations revealed that integrating learning standards with demanding coursework and high expectations led to a marked improvement in student performance (Johnson and Rudolph 2001). Adelman (1999), following a cohort of students from 1980 to 1993 to determine what contributes to the completion of a bachelor's degree, affirmed that high expectations and a solid academic core were essential for student success.

In short, content and performance standards provide a map of the curriculum that ensures important content is covered. They focus on key concepts and powerful, generative ideas that should be taught in depth, as opposed to a succession of forgettable facts and details (Hill and Crevola 1999). They combine "core knowledge" and "portable skills" (Wallis and Steptoe 2006, 54). Portable skills refer to higher-order thinking skills, making connections between ideas, and knowing how to learn.

Schools striving to build curriculum programs that reflect these standards are also schools that have the potential of helping students develop the knowledge and skills that empower them to succeed. In later sections of this chapter and in the remaining chapters of this book, we elaborate on how these standards can be incorporated into meaningful learning experiences for students.

THE 4 R'S FOR FACULTY

The 4 R's are also critical lenses to apply in examining what we do as adults, who work with students. This includes all school professionals, i.e., teachers, library media specialists, technology coordinators, and other resource specialists who participate in instructional planning and delivery. To elaborate:

- **Rigor:** The curriculum teams start with a clear agreement on the learning targets or goals and the assessment criteria to determine whether or not the goals have been achieved. The performance tasks reflect a carefully scaffolded structure that helps students achieve these targeted learning goals. Wiggins and McTighe (1998) detail this "backward design" in their text, *Understanding by Design* (146). Teams also become familiar with current research in education and the sciences to inform their work.
- **Relevance:** Professional development occurs on site with team members examining their instruction as the basis for improvement. Rather than one-shot workshops with experts, this practice-based approach focuses on engagement in authentic experiences involving an analysis of the team's own teaching. Their daily work becomes the object of study rather than an abstract case study from a textbook (Darling-Hammond and Bransford 2005). In such practice-focused training, instructors might collaboratively design interdisciplinary projects that encompass connections within and beyond the school.
- **Relationships:** The development of relationships is paramount when the planning and implementation of curriculum brings professionals together in meaningful dialogue about their work with students. They discover

that the conversations are synergistic. They come to realize that more heads are better than one. Importantly, teams feel empowered to take risks when they recognize that they are not struggling alone. Frequently, they establish informal study groups or form peer-coaching partnerships. Teams also reach out to people outside the school as mentors and valuable resources, who expand the learning opportunities for both educators and students.

They also develop richer relationships with their students as they attempt to differentiate and personalize instruction. By discussing the selection of topics and issues to study and by conferring on progress being made, both instructors and students strengthen their bonds. Learning becomes increasingly student-focused as instructors develop a deeper appreciation and understanding of students' learning styles and their strengths and weaknesses.

- **Reflection:** As much as reflection is a crucial part of the learning process for students, it is equally critical for the members of the teaching teams. As they examine their instructional practices, they ask deeper questions about the validity of what they teach and how they teach. They refine their skills in designing assessment techniques and using the data and student feedback gathered to analyze results and drive improvement.

HOW DOES PBL HELP TO MEET THIS CHARGE?

PBL is an approach to learning that embodies the 4 R's. The following observations are supported by reports from the North Central Regional Educational Laboratory (Johnson and Rudolph 2001) and the National Association of Secondary School Principals (2004). Leading researchers in education (e.g., Marzano 2003, Blumenfeld et al. 1991) also substantiate these findings.

- **Rigor:** PBL introduces opportunities for cognitively complex tasks to solve real problems rather than low-level, fact-gathering tasks that contribute to shallow performances. The students start with a driving question. They use multiple sources of information and learn in a social context. They are motivated to persist when teachers scaffold instruction by breaking down tasks, and use modeling, prompting, facilitation, and coaching. Students construct artifacts and performances that are representations of their findings and solutions.
- **Relevance:** PBL focuses on meaningful learning that connects to the real world. It's possible to individualize learning paths within projects and allow for options to meet the needs of a diverse student population. Students have degrees of choice and control regarding what to work on, how to work, and what products to generate.
- **Relationships:** PBL encourages collaboration among students, dialogue between students and instructors, and communication between students and people in the community. Youngsters often extend their connections by establishing links to a global network of resources.

- **Reflection:** PBL requires continuous self-assessment (Harada and Yoshina 2005). This allows instructional teams to provide early intervention and individualized assistance. Importantly, students examine their own progress and identify strengths and weaknesses in their work that eventually lead to improvement.

Figure 2.1 provides examples of strategies in PBL that contribute to the 4 R's.

Figure 2.1 Building the 4 R's through PBL

4 R's	Examples of Strategies in PBL
RIGOR	Have clear and high expectations Address big ideas and concepts reflected in standards Focus on essential questions and inquiry Emphasize higher-order thinking Require demonstration of performance
RELEVANCE	Focus on current issues and problems Connect to school, community, and global concerns Apply knowledge to real-world scenarios Encourage hands-on experiences Incorporate field work Integrate technology
RELATIONSHIPS	Work in interdisciplinary teams as instructors Design projects that require collaborative teamwork Build in time for dialogue between students and instructors Encourage peer and buddy tutoring Foster formal and informal mentoring Develop understanding of students' strengths, weaknesses, talents, and interests
REFLECTION	Promote self-assessment Allow for instructor's analysis of student assessment Provide checkpoints for student feedback Encourage peer critiquing Create portfolios Participate in learning communities

HOW MIGHT THE LIBRARY MEDIA SPECIALIST GET INVOLVED?

General reform literature has not recognized the role of school libraries in relation to student achievement. Yet the evidence of the relationship between high-performing schools and successful library programs has grown over the last several decades. For example, Keith Curry Lance and his associates have conducted studies of school library programs in numerous states that indicate a positive correlation between student achievement and a high-quality school library media program staffed with a certified full-time library media specialist (Lance and Loertscher 2005). Baughman (2000) has reported similar findings in Massachusetts.

As information professionals, library media specialists possess valuable expertise to "sift, sort, select, evaluate, and communicate information resources" in a digital age

(Stefl-Mabry and Lynch 2006, 68). They not only help students and faculty locate and access information in a bewildering Web-driven world, but they also teach them to navigate and develop skills as wiser consumers of information. In PBL, they help students manage, interpret, validate, and use information.

As members of instructional teams, library media specialists find resources and develop lessons that help to individualize learning for students. Because they are aware of the multiple literacies needed to build fluency in information evaluation and use, they provide access to sources in diverse forms. They harness the power of digital and multimedia tools to motivate learning. They are critical members of any team because they serve as the community collaborators, establishing connections to the outside world (Harada 2003b). As co-teachers, the library media specialists are responsible for the assessment of performance tasks originating in the library. They also collaborate on instruments to assess culminating products (Harada and Yoshina 2005).

SUMMARY

Education reform places students at the center. This type of reform is about creating a culture safe for experimentation. It capitalizes on and celebrates the talents and achievements of all stakeholders in the school community. It demands continuous analysis and refinement of thinking through questioning (National Association for Secondary School Principals 2004).

The real conversation that is needed to effect change is whether "an entire generation of kids will fail to make the grade in the global economy because they can't think their way through abstract problems, work in teams, distinguish good information from bad" (Wagner 2002, 52).

In this chapter we presented PBL as an approach to teaching and learning that brings curriculum in line with the way the world really works. PBL challenges students to wrestle with issues and problems in the community and to work collaboratively in understanding them and moving toward thoughtful solutions. It promotes core knowledge and portable skills. Library media specialists can be key project-shapers in helping teams to integrate important concepts and connect current issues and events with their historical threads. By participating in reform efforts that emphasize the importance of rigor, relevance, relationships, and reflection, they work with their professional colleagues to position students for success, not failure.

WORKS CITED

Adelman, Clifford. *Answers in the Toolbox: Academic Intensity, Attendance Patterns, and Bachelor's Degree Attainment.* Washington, DC: U.S. Department of Education Office of Educational Research and Improvement, 1999. (ERIC Reproduction Service Document No. ED431363).

Armstrong, Thomas. *The Best Schools.* Alexandria: Association for Supervision and Curriculum Development, 2006.

Baughman, James C. *School Libraries and MCAS Scores.* Paper presented at symposium, Graduate School of Library and Information Science, Boston College, October 26, 2000.

Blumenfeld, Phyllis C., Elliot Soloway, Ronald W. Marx, Joseph S. Krajcik, Mark Guzdial, and Annemarie Palincsar. "Motivating Project-Based Learning: Sustaining the Doing, Supporting the Learning." *Educational Psychologist* 26.3/4 (1991): 369-99.

Csikszentmihalyi, Mihaly, and Reed Larson. *Being Adolescent: Conflict and Growth in the Teenage Years.* New York: Basic Books, 1984.

Darling-Hammond, Linda, and John Bransford (Eds.). *Preparing Teachers for a Changing World: What Teachers Should Learn and Be Able to Do.* San Francisco, Jossey-Bass, 2005.

Glatthorn, Allan A., and Jerry Jailall. "Curriculum for the New Millennium." *Education in a New Era.* Ed. Ronald S. Brandt. Alexandria: Association for Supervision and Curriculum Development, 2000. 97-121.

Goleman, Daniel. *Emotional Intelligence.* New York: Bantam, 1995.

Harada, Violet H. "Empowered Learning: Fostering Thinking across the Curriculum." *Curriculum Connections through the Library: Principles and Practice.* Ed. Barbara K. Stripling and Sandra Hughes-Hassell. Westport: Libraries Unlimited, 2003a. 41-66.

Harada, Violet H. "Taking the Lead in Developing Learning Communities." *Knowledge Quest* 31.2 (2003b): 12-16.

Harada, Violet H., and Joan M. Yoshina. *Assessing Learning: Librarians and Teachers as Partners.* Westport: Libraries Unlimited, 2005.

Harada, Violet H., and Joan M. Yoshina. *Inquiry Learning through Librarian-Teacher Partnerships.* Worthington: Linworth Publishing, Inc., 2004.

Hill, Peter W., and Carmel A. Crevola. "The Role of Standards in Educational Reform for the 21st Century." *Preparing Our Schools for the 21st Century.* Ed. David D. Marsh. Alexandria: Association for Supervision and Curriculum Development, 1999. 117-42.

Johnson, Debra, and Angela Rudolph. *Critical Issue: Beyond Social Promotion and Retention—Five Strategies to Help Students Succeed.* Washington, DC: Learning Point Associates/North Central Regional Educational Laboratory, 2001. 30 July 2007 <http://www.ncrel.org/sdrs/areas/issues/educatrs/leadrshp/le400.htm>.

Johnson, Doug. "Skills for the Knowledge Worker." *Teacher Librarian* 34.1 (2006): 8-13.

Jones, Jami Biles. "The Numbers Are Astounding: The Role of the Media Specialist in Dropout Prevention." *Library Media Connection* 25.2 (2006): 10-13.

Lance, Keith Curry, and David V. Loertscher. *Powering Achievement: School Library Media Programs Make a Difference.* 3rd ed. Salt Lake City: Hi Willow Research & Publishing, 2005.

Marzano, Robert J. *What Works in Schools: Translating Research into Action.* Alexandria: Association for Supervision and Curriculum Development, 2003.

Murnane, Richard J., and Frank Levy. *Teaching the New Basic Skills: Principles for Educating Children to Thrive in a Changing Economy.* New York: Free Press, 1996.

National Association of Secondary School Principals. *Breaking Ranks II™: Strategies for Leading High School Reform.* Reston: Author, 2004.

National Governors Association. *A Governor's Guide to Creating a 21st Century Workforce.* Washington, DC: Author, 2002. 30 July 2007 <www.nga.org>.

Newmann, Fred M., Helen M. Marks, and Adam Gamoran. "Authentic Pedagogy and Student Performance." *American Journal of Education* 104.4 (1996): 280-313.

Partnership for 21st Century Skills. *Framework for 21st Century Learning.* Tucson: Author, 2004.

Peterson, Kent. "Creating High-Achieving Learning Environments." *Pathways to School Improvement.* Chicago: North Central Regional Educational Laboratory, 1995. 30 July 2007 <http://www.ncrel.org/sdrs/areas/issues/educatrs/leadrshp/le400.htm>.

Stefl-Mabry, Joette, and Barbara L. Lynch. *Knowledge Communities: Bringing the Village into the Classroom.* Lanham: Scarecrow Press, 2006.

Sweeney, Richard T. "Reinventing Library Buildings and Services for the Millennial Generation." *Library Administration & Management* 19.4 (2005): 165-76.

Wagner, Tony. *Making the Grade: Reinventing America's Schools.* New York: Routledge/ Falmer, 2002.

Wallis, Claudia, and Sonja Steptoe. "How to Bring Our Schools Out of the 20th Century." *Time* 168.25 (2006): 50-56.

Wiggins, Grant, and Jay McTighe. *Understanding by Design.* Alexandria: Association for Supervision and Curriculum Development, 1998.

3 The Role of the Library Media Specialist in PBL

This chapter examines the potential role of the library media specialist in Project-Based Learning (PBL). It begins with the connection between information literacy and PBL and delves into the roles of the library media specialist as a connector, an integrator, and ultimately, an instructional leader.

Educators, who really want to make a difference in the lives of students, need to become skilled change agents that support and encourage others to adopt innovation and to pursue improvements (Fullan 1993; Hord, Rutherford, Hulling-Austin, and Hall 2006). They act as facilitators, enablers, and negotiators (Hughes-Hassell and Harada 2007). Library media specialists are in a strategic position to perform as change agents. In this chapter, we explain how library media specialists can become critical curriculum leaders through their productive and proactive partnerships in PBL with classroom teachers.

CONNECTION BETWEEN INFORMATION LITERACY AND PBL

PBL actively engages students in deeper levels of comprehension and interpretation about what they study and how they study. Stripling (2007) indicates that the acquisition of knowledge "must be an active process that is an amalgam of the 'world' to be understood and the mental processes and dispositions that enable understanding" (40). In short, we cannot view learning as a polarized issue of process versus content (Case 2005, Wiggins and McTighe 2005). Library media specialists fully agree with this stance. In their instruction, they have always strongly advocated for teaching information skills in the context of relevant classroom content. Collaborating with teachers on PBL, therefore, provides library media specialists with a unique opportunity to assist students in not only grasping content, but also effectively mastering *how* they develop disciplinary knowledge and *how* they design and implement meaningful projects.

Although teachers might work on projects without soliciting assistance from support faculty in a school, the power of collaborative planning and implementation is undeniable. While the classroom teacher has the disciplinary knowledge, the library media specialist can assist the teacher with the process or thinking skills necessary for students to create meaning for themselves. The synergy of working together produces a seamless blend of holistic learning.

Based on the premise that critical thinking permeates PBL, library media specialists are major partners in identifying the relationships existing between thinking skills and the ways of knowing embedded in various disciplines. They introduce the notion of information literacy as the foundation for deeper understanding. Information literacy alludes to the skills and habits of mind (Costa 1991) that learners develop when they interpret, evaluate, and apply information and knowledge to a new context. As part of this process, students challenge as well as interpret information and extend their knowledge to different situations.

Educators and researchers (e.g., Case 2005, Harada 2003, Harada and Yoshina 2005, Beyer 1992, Ennis 1992) have delineated some of the specific thinking behaviors that learners demonstrate at critical phases of information seeking and use. They include the following:

- Perception and recognition of a problem or issue: The learner recognizes a problem, recalls prior related experience, identifies the learning goal, defines terms important for the context studied, generates appropriate questions, analyzes alternatives, and devises a plan of action.
- Storage and retrieval of data: The learner determines sources for relevant data, devises strategies to locate data, defines key terms and elements for search, and judges the authority of sources.
- Organization and transformation of data: The learner organizes data in multiple formats, interprets data, distinguishes between fact and opinion, distinguishes relevant from irrelevant information, determines accuracy and credibility, detects bias and distortion, recognizes multiple perspectives, and identifies conclusions.
- Reasoning and use of information: The learner reasons inductively and deductively; recognizes logical inconsistencies; develops and defends a position on an issue; and synthesizes, evaluates, and communicates information in a variety of formats.
- Metacognition: The learner validates concepts learned in terms of results and solutions, reflects on the research process used in terms of efficiency and effectiveness, and assesses self-efficacy in terms of personal feelings and attitudes.

The Information Literacy Standards (AASL and AECT 1998, 9-43) embody these thinking skills. Figure 3.1 shows the connection between examples of thinking skills required in PBL and the Information Literacy Standards.

Figure 3.1 Sampling of Thinking Skills and Information Literacy Standards

Thinking Skills	Information Literacy Standards
Recognition of a problem or issue • Taps prior knowledge • Defines learning goal • Identifies important terms • Generates meaningful questions • Analyzes alternatives • Devises a plan of action	Standard 1: Accesses information efficiently and effectively • Recognizes the need for information • Formulates questions based on information needs Standard 9: Participates effectively in groups to pursue and generate information • Collaborates with others, both in person and through technologies, to identify information problems and to seek their solutions

continued

Thinking Skills	Information Literacy Standards
Storage and retrieval of data • Identifies appropriate sources • Devises strategies to locate information • Defines key terms for search • Plans for study • Evaluates data sources	Standard 1: Accesses information efficiently and effectively • Identifies a variety of potential sources of information • Develops and uses successful strategies for locating information Standard 2: Evaluates information critically and competently • Determines accuracy, relevance, and comprehensiveness Standard 7: Recognizes the importance of information to a democratic society • Seeks information from diverse sources, contexts, disciplines, and cultures Standard 8: Practices ethical behavior in regard to information and information technology • Respects intellectual property rights • Uses information technology responsibly
Organization and transformation of data • Organizes and interprets data • Distinguishes fact from opinion • Delineates relevant from irrelevant information • Detects bias • Recognizes multiple perspectives • Identifies conclusions	Standard 1: Access information efficiently and effectively • Recognizes that accurate and comprehensive information is the basis for intelligent decision making Standard 2: Evaluates information critically and competently • Distinguishes among fact, point of view, and opinion • Identifies inaccurate and misleading information • Selects information appropriate to the problem or question at hand Standard 5: Appreciates literature and other creative expressions of information • Derives meaning from information presented creatively in a variety of formats
Reasoning and use of information • Reasons inductively and deductively • Develops a position • Analyzes and synthesizes information • Applies information • Communicates findings	Standard 3: Uses information accurately and creatively • Organizes information for practical application • Integrates new information into one's own knowledge • Applies information in critical thinking and problem solving • Produces and communicates information and ideas in appropriate formats Standard 5: Appreciates literature and other creative expressions of information • Develops creative products in a variety of formats Standard 9: Participates effectively in groups to pursue and generate information • Shares knowledge and information with others • Respects others' ideas and backgrounds and acknowledges their contributions • Collaborates with others, in person and through technologies, to design, develop, and evaluate information products and solutions
Metacognition • Validates conclusions • Assesses solutions • Reflects on personal work	Standard 6: Strives for excellence in information seeking and knowledge generation • Assesses the quality of the process and products of personal information seeking • Devises strategies for revising, improving, and updating self-generated knowledge Standard 9: Participates effectively in groups to pursue and generate information • Collaborates with others, both in person and through technologies, to design, develop, and evaluate information products and solutions

LIBRARIAN AS A CONNECTOR

Library media specialists, working with entire school populations, have a "big picture view" of school needs and priorities (McGregor 2003, 210). Having this holistic view of the school enables library media specialists to facilitate discussions with faculty about integrating and merging priorities across content areas. While teachers will necessarily focus on their specific teaching areas, library media specialists are in a strategic position to look for conceptual coherence (Stripling 2007), i.e., how ideas are held together by overarching themes, perspectives, and patterns. This curricular view is vital for successful PBL initiatives that link disciplines.

Because PBL leverages themes and perspectives that cut across content areas, textbooks are not sufficient for the information needs of the learners. It requires a wide range of resources for a diverse community of students with different styles of learning. Library media specialists must not only provide strong print collections to meet these needs, they must also make digital sources accessible to everyone (e.g., subscribing to databases and flagging sites that are relevant for specific projects). In addition, human resources are critical. Library media specialists are valuable liaisons linking students and teachers with experts in the larger community.

As an instructional partner, the library media specialist can be a major player in developing and teaching the effective and efficient use of technology, i.e., "the person who assists teachers and students to become technology literate" (Kearney 2000, 103). To serve as linkers to the digital information world, library media specialists must acquire "skills in computer networking, collection development, database maintenance, information input, and searching catalogs and databases, as well as have experience with a broad range of online systems" (Blake, 1996, 13). Through their expertise in using the Internet, library media specialists enable students and teachers to efficiently locate the information needed to develop projects. By doing this, they reduce the amount of time that students spend hunting for resources and more time actually evaluating and using the information (Berger 1998).

Figure 3.2 provides an example of what a library media specialist might do as a connector.

Figure 3.2 Snapshot of Librarian as a Connector

Cindy, the library media specialist at Oceanside High School, has worked individually with the social studies and language arts departments in the past. As a result of a series of workshops on PBL at their school, the 11th grade teachers in the two departments have expressed an interest in working more closely together. Because Cindy has been involved in prior research projects with these teachers they have invited her to work with them.

One of the first things that Cindy does is to look over the content standards in both disciplines to see if there are themes or concepts that might connect the two content areas and provide a focus for the collaborative project. She accesses the state's content standards online and discovers that a possible theme from the social studies standards might be *global interdependence*. More specifically, the standard has a benchmark: explain the effects of global exchanges in the Americas, Europe, Asia, and Africa. This might include the spread of food crops and diseases, the exchange of trade goods, and migrations of people. She also notes that there is a language arts standard on locating sources and gathering information. A specific benchmark for this standard is: use primary and secondary sources to develop and modify a research plan in response to problems and opportunities encountered in accessing print and online resources to support a thesis.

She shares this information on the two standards with the teachers when they meet. Several teachers indicate that they have also been considering this possible match and they welcome Cindy's confirmation. After some discussion, the entire group decides that these specific standards will be the joint focal points of the project. Cindy indicates that she will be happy to start searching for primary and secondary sources for this initiative. She volunteers to create a pathfinder for the students and identify online professional resources for the teachers. In addition, she informs the teachers that she will bookmark useful Web sites and link them to the library's Web site as well as check for community experts that might provide valuable information. The teachers are delighted about receiving this type of library support.

LIBRARIAN AS AN INTEGRATOR

Teaching in a PBL context requires that instructional teams move from operating in isolated classroom silos with lecture-driven, fact-based lessons to collaborative instruction that emphasizes constructivist, concept-focused learning (Stripling 2007). This requires that instructors not only have secure and competent knowledge of the discrete disciplines but the ability to identify integrative concepts that bring together several disciplines. In this context, team members must also explore strategies to execute projects that merge tasks and skills from several disciplines.

Kearney (2000) identifies some of the challenges of attempting integration. For one, an interdisciplinary unit might include a superficial sampling of information from each subject area. In addition there might be a lack of clarity in curriculum design resulting in teachers feeling that their own curriculum is being diluted and compromised. To address these issues, Kearney (2000) recommends that a "scope and sequence" be introduced for a project and that "a research process promoting critical thinking and problem solving as well as a carefully designed assessment model" be developed (111).

Library media specialists, who promote the connections across the disciplines and negotiate the links with the necessary information resources, are team members that can facilitate the integration process. Kearny (2000) maintains that the library media center can be the hub for interdisciplinary learning because it is frequently the physical place where information resources and equipment are located. She states: "It is often in the library media center where the interdisciplinary team can find the focus for the unit, decide what they want students to be able to do at the end of the unit, determine a variety of acceptable assessments, and plan the learning activities as well as the instruction" (111).

As part of the integrative process, library media specialists also suggest ways to incorporate the information literacy skills at various points in the projects. Although all the content standards include information-related skills, the connection with the library media program is implied rather than stated. Library media specialists must proactively review the content standards of their respective states and identify those standards that have library media applications to ensure that information literacy standards are integrated into the various content areas (Kearney 2000).

Figure 3.3 on page 28 describes what a librarian might do as an integrator. We expand on the example described in Figure 3.2 where Cindy, the library media specialist, is working with 11th grade teachers in social studies and language arts on global interdependence.

Figure 3.3 Snapshot of Librarian as an Integrator

Cindy and the social studies and language arts teachers decide on essential questions to frame the unit on global interdependence. They come up with the following:

- What does global interdependence mean?
- How does it happen?
- How does it change things?
- To what extent does global interdependence affect my personal life? My community?

They also brainstorm criteria for assessing student performance. In social studies, the teachers decide that a major criterion is being able to explain, with clear and precise details, the impact of a specific global exchange (e.g., a food crop, a disease, a trade good, a migration) on different parts of the world. In language arts and in the library, the teachers and Cindy agree that the important assessment criteria will be students evaluating primary and secondary sources and using relevant sources to develop their specific projects.

The instructional team wants to allow students the freedom to select different formats for their final products. All student work will be shared at "History Alive!", a culminating event staged in the library media center. Cindy takes the initiative to conduct Web site searches on possible products and shares these creative examples with the teachers. For instance, a student group researching the history of small pox might devise a giant timeline with a three-dimensional world map tracing the spread of this deadly disease. A second group studying the origin and spread of rice crops might stage a cooking demonstration of rice dishes from around the world. A third group might enact a "living history account" of a Chinese immigrant arriving at Angel Island in California in the 1800s. A fourth group might devise an online game that challenges peers to determine how specific trade goods impacted lifestyles through history.

These examples excite the teachers and they launch into planning the assignments and tasks to guide students through their projects. To frame their plans, Cindy suggests that they use a research model based on the Big 6 (Eisenberg and Berkowitz 1990) since teachers in both departments have used this model with past assignments. Importantly, this gives Cindy the opportunity to integrate the information literacy skills and suggest places where she can take the lead in helping the students. She also serves as the "neutral" member of the team helping the two departments negotiate how the social studies teachers can introduce content knowledge and how the language arts teachers and the library media specialist can integrate process skills with content teaching. Knowing how busy the teachers are, Cindy also volunteers to summarize these plans and disseminate them to the team via the school's email system.

LIBRARIAN AS AN INSTRUCTIONAL LEADER

At the beginning of this chapter, we posited that the library media specialist might serve as a change agent in curriculum and instruction. Leadership is a "quality of influencing others through a sharing of vision, a respect for individual goals, an ability to build consensus, and collaborative work toward mutual purposes" (Wilson and Lyders 2001, 3). One does not have to be the principal of a school to be considered a leader. Rather the notion of *teacher leadership* has emerged from current school reform initiatives (Gabriel 2005, Glanz 2002). This form of leadership flows throughout a school community and is not dependent on the official hierarchical organization of the school.

Educators also refer to this as "leading from the middle" (Kearney 2000, 7) indicating that an individual steps forward and takes the initiative as the situation merits this action. Donham (2005) states that this person "leads more often through influence; the position he or she holds, is collegial, not superior to the rest of the faculty" (299). She elaborates that having influence "requires establishing one's expertise, working collegially with others, articulating one's ideas clearly, maintaining a good 'say-do' ratio … and establishing processes for continuous reflection and assessment" (300). The critical message is that leading from the middle can influence improvements and change.

Library media specialists can be such leaders. They possess special skills and tools to help both teachers and students in the accomplishment of their instructional and learning goals. Various educators (e.g., Lankford 2006, Donham 2005, Gabriel 2005, Glanz 2002, Bennis 1989, Hughes-Hassell and Harada 2007) have cited the following as essential leadership qualities:

- Trustworthiness: getting things done, following through on promises, and maintaining confidentiality
- Organization: having a system in place to stay focused and on track that enables the person to juggle a multitude of jobs and responsibilities
- Perceptiveness and empathy: listening carefully to what others are saying; being sensitive to facial expressions, gestures and other nonverbal clues; sensing what people need and when they need it; and understanding what others are going through
- Accessibility: having an open-door policy within reasonable limits
- Humility: empowering others and giving them the credit, being willing to own up to mistakes, and highlighting the accomplishments of others
- Forward thinking: anticipating and planning for what may be coming next
- Global visioning: seeing the bigger picture and facilitating problem solving in this larger context
- Resilience: managing ambiguity to effectively implement change, using all available resources to leverage support for change, and looking for the opportunities associated with change rather than focusing on the negative (i.e., looking at things from the stance of "what I can do about this" rather than "I can't do anything about this")

Figure 3.4 on page 30 provides a checklist to assess one's leadership readiness. It capitalizes on prior work relating to leadership conducted by Donham (2005), Glanz (2002), Kearney (2000), and Bennis (1989).

Figure 3.4 Checklist to Gauge Your Leadership Readiness

Leadership Characteristics	Self-Rating		
	Strong	Adequate	Weak
Character			
I maintain people's trust and confidentiality.			
I am resilient and flexible.			
I am willing to take risks.			
I am approachable.			
Organization and Management			
I have a vision and goals for the library media center.			
I have a strategic plan of action to achieve my goals.			
I maintain clear and continuous avenues for communication with the rest of the school community.			
I get things done in a timely manner.			
I anticipate and plan for what may be coming next.			
I follow through on promises made.			
I can juggle a multitude of jobs and responsibilities.			
Interpersonal			
I listen carefully to what is being said.			
I suspend judgment.			
I encourage others to express their ideas and feelings.			
I strive to confirm and clarify information received.			
I am sensitive to facial expressions and other nonverbal cues.			
I acknowledge the accomplishments of others and give them credit.			
Conceptual and Technical			
I see the bigger picture and facilitate problem solving in this larger context.			
I seek connections between the school's mission and goals and those of the library media center.			
I keep abreast of current issues and research in school reform as well as my profession.			
I am knowledgeable about learning theories and research that inform my teaching.			
I keep abreast of the latest trends and research in the applications of technology for teaching and learning.			
I regularly reflect on what I am doing to improve my professional practices.			

SUMMARY

Gabriel (2005) says that instructional leaders are people viewed as a "treasure chest of ideas" (125). They are the point people that others seek out for advice and resources. Ideally, they have taught a range of grades and ability levels so that they can relate to various teaching situations.

Library media specialists can position themselves to be such leaders and partners in PBL. They are the connectors and integrators between the subject material and students' lives. They work side by side with teachers to create learning experiences that "affect student learning, contribute to school improvement, inspire excellence in practice, and empower stakeholders to participate in educational improvement" (Childs-Bowen and Moller 2000, 28). In short, they can facilitate and lead change that results in a win-win situation for everyone.

WORKS CITED

American Association of School Librarians, and the Association for Educational Communications and Technology. *Information Power: Building Partnership for Learning*. Chicago: American Library Association, 1998.

Bennis, Warren G. *On Becoming a Leader*. Reading: Addison-Wesley, 1989.

Berger, Pam. *Internet for Active Learners: Curriculum-Based Strategies for K-12*. Chicago: American Library Association, 1998.

Beyer, Barry K. "Teaching Thinking: An Integrated Approach." *Teaching for Thinking*. Ed. James W. Keefe and Herbert J. Walberg. Reston: National Association of Secondary Principals, 1992. 93-110.

Blake, Virgil L. P. "The Virtual Library Impacts the School Library Media Center: A Bibliographic Essay." *The Virtual School Library: Gateway to the Information Superhighway*. Ed. Carol C. Kuhlthau. Englewood: Libraries Unlimited, 1996. 3-19.

Case, Roland. "Bringing Critical Thinking to the Main Stage." *Education Canada* 45.2 (2005): 45-49.

Childs-Bowen, Deborah, and Gayle Moller. "Principals: Leaders of Leaders." *NASSP Bulletin* 84.616 (2000): 27-34.

Costa, Arthur L. *Developing Minds*. Rev. ed. Alexandria: Association for Supervision and Curriculum Development, 1991.

Donham, Jean. *Enhancing Teaching and Learning: A Leadership Guide for School Library Media Specialists*. 2nd ed. New York: Neal Schuman, 2005.

Eisenberg, Michael B., and Robert E. Berkowitz. *Information Problem-Solving: The Big Six Skills Approach to Library & Information Skills Instruction*. Norwood: Ablex, 1990.

Ennis, Robert H. "Assessing Higher-Order Thinking for Accountability." *Teaching for Thinking*. Ed. James W. Keefe and Herbert J. Walberg. Reston: National Association of Secondary Principals, 1992. 73-92.

Fullan, Michael. *Change Forces: Probing the Depths of Educational Change*. Bristol: Falmer Press, 1993.

Gabriel, John G. *How to Thrive as a Teacher Leader*. Alexandria: Association for Supervision and Curriculum Development, 2005.

Glanz, Jeffrey. *Finding Your Leadership Style: A Guide for Educators*. Alexandria: Association for Supervision and Curriculum Development, 2002.

Harada, Violet H. "Empowered Learning: Fostering Thinking across the Curriculum." *Curriculum Connections through the Library: Principles and Practice.* Ed. Barbara K. Stripling and Sandra Hughes-Hassell. Westport: Libraries Unlimited, 2003. 41-66.

Harada, Violet H., and Joan M. Yoshina. *Assessing Learning: Librarians and Teachers as Partners.* Westport: Libraries Unlimited, 2005.

Hord, Susan W., William L. Rutherford, Leslie Hulling-Austin, and Gene Hall. *Taking Charge of Change.* Rev. ed. Austin: Southwest Educational Development Laboratory, 2006.

Hughes-Hassell, Sandra, and Violet H. Harada. "Change Agentry: An Essential Role for Library Media Specialists." *School Reform and the School Library Media Specialist.* Ed. Sandra Hughes-Hassell and Violet H. Harada. Westport: Libraries Unlimited, 2007. 1-16.

Kearney, Carol A. *Curriculum Partner: Redefining the Role of the Library Media Specialist.* Westport: Libraries Unlimited, 2000.

Lankford, Mary D. "Critical Attributes of Library Leaders." *Leadership and the School Librarians: Essays from Leaders in the Field.* Ed. Mary D. Lankford. Worthington: Linworth Publishing, Inc., 2006. 23-28.

McGregor, Joy. "Collaboration and Leadership." *Curriculum Connections through the Library: Principles and Practice.* Ed. Barbara K. Stripling and Sandra Hughes-Hassell. Westport: Libraries Unlimited, 2003. 199-219.

Stripling, Barbara K. "Teaching for Understanding." *School Reform and the School Library Media Specialist.* Ed. Sandra Hughes-Hassell and Violet H. Harada. Westport: Libraries Unlimited, 2007. 37-56.

Wiggins, Grant, and Jay McTighe. *Understanding by Design.* Expanded 2nd ed. Alexandra: Association for Supervision and Curriculum Development, 2005.

Wilson, Patricia P., and Rosette A. Lyders. *Leadership for Today's School Library: A Handbook for the Library Media Specialist and the School Principal.* Westport: Libraries Unlimited, 2001.

4 Planning for PBL

This chapter details the following important considerations in launching and implementing Project-Based Learning (PBL) in a school: readiness for PBL, steps in planning for PBL, and practical tips and caveats for school teams in developing projects. In addition, a checklist to assess a project is provided at the end of the chapter.

CONSIDERING YOUR READINESS FOR PBL

There is no one "best way" to implement PBL; it doesn't work with a cookie cutter approach. However, starting early and developing a plan are crucial requirements. Before you actually start, step back for a moment and think about the following questions. Your responses will provide a gauge as to your team's readiness to embark in PBL.

ARE YOUR STUDENTS READY FOR PBL?

PBL focuses on student motivation and leadership in the design and execution of the projects. Students can be involved in the creation of the overarching or essential questions that frame the project as well as the activities leading to the final product. Giving students the freedom to decide on the artifacts they want to create opens the door to original and innovative expression. Realistically speaking, however, the degree of student involvement will depend on students' experience and proficiency in several crucial areas: problem solving, communication, and self-management (Buck Institute for Education 2002).

Figure 4.1 identifies important questions to consider about what students already know and can do as you plan for their effective participation in PBL. Your responses will determine where to start and help you set realistic expectations. These questions have been adapted from works by Herman, Aschbacher, and Winters (1992) and the Northwest Regional Educational Laboratory (Railsbeck 2002).

Figure 4.1 Student Readiness for PBL

1. Which concepts and principles have the students already covered and reasonably mastered? (This links to standards)
2. What social and affective skills have they already demonstrated? (This involves working effectively in pairs and small groups on cooperative and collaborative tasks)
3. What metacognitive skills do they already practice? (This involves assessing their progress and reflecting on completed products)
4. What types of resources have they already used?
5. What information literacy skills have they already developed? (This involves retrieving, evaluating, and using information)

The challenging nature of PBL requires thinking about how best to introduce student participation in stages. For example, if students don't have the necessary confidence and competence in selecting a project topic, the teacher and library media specialist must mentor students in doing this. Most students also need to develop their skills in collaboration, research, project management, and delivery of presentations. Counseling individual students and groups provide the teaching team with critical opportunities to differentiate instruction and to scaffold the learning experiences (Tomlinson and McTighe 2006).

ARE YOU READY FOR PBL?

Along with reflecting on what your students know and can do, you must also examine your own teaching styles and skills. In the preceding chapters, we have identified some of the major attributes of PBL. These attributes have implications for the teaching approaches that foster learning in PBL environments. Some important teaching characteristics are identified in Figure 4.2.

Table 4.2 Teaching Skills That Nurture PBL

Teaching skills	Sample teaching behaviors in PBL
Counseling and coaching	Practices active listening Responds to students' questions Restates comments to get them clarified Invites thoughtful questions Asks questions that help students expand and revise their original thoughts Provides constructive suggestions Gives positive support Provides models Allows for one-on-one dialogue to assist with individualized pursuits Nurtures complex thinking and rigorous investigations
Facilitation	Encourages student initiative Designs activities so that guided practice and feedback are essential components Encourages student-led discussions and serves as a guide on the side Nurtures group work to complete tasks Creates an environment supporting learning through experimentation, investigation, and research Encourages questioning and discovery Keeps students on track and on deadline Coordinates outside of school/classroom resources (i.e., internships) Encourages active participation and interest in learning and assessment practices
Co-learning	Respects and appreciates the opinions of students Encourages new ideas Invites learning from and with students Honestly reflects on personal strengths and weaknesses Acknowledges that answers can be derived from multiple sources and strategies Realizes that there is no single correct answer to an essential question

continued

Teaching skills	Sample teaching behaviors in PBL
Teaming with colleagues	Practices respectful listening Welcomes multiple perspectives and differing opinions on topics and issues Suspends judgment Offers specific, constructive feedback Shares expertise Accepts and follows through on responsibilities Assumes leadership when it is appropriate Facilitates representation of different subject content/standards in integrated team projects Acknowledges that team members will be at different comfort levels regarding integrative projects

WHAT'S ALREADY HAPPENING AT YOUR SCHOOL THAT SUPPORTS PBL?

PBL works better in schools that have extended blocks of time instead of 50-minute class periods (Buck Institute for Education 2002). This allows for longer sessions, which students often need to complete their investigations. It also gives instructors valuable time to confer and counsel with individuals and groups.

Another important consideration is whether schools are organized around small learning communities such as academies or houses. When these types of structures are in place, the instructors are usually more willing to collaborate and develop multidisciplinary projects. Because the student populations are smaller, students receive more personalized attention and develop a sense of connection that makes for a closer identification with their colleagues and faculty. We hasten to add that extended blocks of time and small learning communities are not requirements for PBL; however, we flag them as elements of the school infrastructure that nurture this approach.

STEPS IN PLANNING

Effective instructional planning starts with an idea of what students must be able to do *at the end of the learning experience*. Wiggins and McTighe (1998) popularized the term *backward design* to describe this concept in curriculum planning. However, this planning approach is not really new. Other educators (Perkins 1992, Wiske 1994, Mitchell et al. 1995, Luongo-Orlando 2003) have also advocated similar approaches to instructional design. This notion of planning with the end in mind is crucial for PBL.

In designing for PBL, start with the project concept: consider the dispositions you want students to develop and the concepts and understandings students will need to master (Newell 2003, Brewster and Fager 1998, Railsbeck 2002).

The instructional plan that is based on the project concept should include:

- The situation or problem that the project addresses (what students will be studying)
- The project description and purpose (what students will be doing)
- The performance specifications (how you will know the students have achieved the project's targets)

- The guidelines for working on the project (how the project will be conducted or implemented; the timeline for performing the tasks)
- A list of participants (faculty, community, families who will be involved)
- Assessment results (demonstrable evidence of what students have actually learned)

A possible sequence in planning might include the following:

- Identify key student outcomes and content standards to be addressed.
- Brainstorm project ideas and select a project that targets the outcomes and standards identified.
- Identify requisite skills that students must already know before undertaking the project.
- Develop the essential or overarching question for the project.
- Determine criteria to assess the final project/performance.
- Determine criteria to assess key benchmarks in the process.
- Develop tools to perform the assessments.
- Outline the instructional plan that identifies where different standards are taught; include a timeline.
- Identify and agree upon the instructional team's roles and responsibilities in the project.

In this process it is important to make expectations and criteria for achieving them as explicit as possible. Ask yourself: Are the guidelines clear to everyone? Do students know how their work will be assessed? Better still, will students be involved in the establishment of the criteria for assessment? At the same time, these expectations and criteria should also be communicated to parents. They are key partners in the success of PBL since tasks and assignments frequently extend beyond the school day and often involve contacting and working with community members. They need to know how the projects will be assessed and how grades will be assigned. Parents must support the relevance of the projects.

Since assessment is a critical part of PBL, learners need to examine samples of student work. This requires that time be allocated for reflection and coaching as well as peer critiquing and self-assessment.

Establishing benchmarks and milestones are crucial in PBL. Students can lose interest and get mired in projects that extend over a long period of time. By chunking the assignments and tasks, teachers make the project easier for students. The students also experience a sense of progress and achievement if they receive feedback at checkpoints in the process. Chunking the work also makes assessment and scoring more manageable for the instructors.

PRACTICAL TIPS AND CAVEATS

Teams that have worked on projects offer the following pragmatic advice based on their own successes and challenges (Railsbeck 2002, Kraft 2005).

- Start early. PBL takes extensive planning. Dialogue and negotiation are necessary for all roles to be understood and accepted. Careful planning upfront yields an orderly administration of the project. It is critical for library media specialists to be involved from the beginning stages. They help teachers see connections across disciplines and flag potentially useful resources for both teachers and students. They also identify places in the project where they can incorporate information literacy skills.

- The implementation of PBL frequently takes longer than expected. Students must gather and interpret the data to create projects that demonstrate their mastery of learning. A substantial length of time is also needed for students to prepare quality projects and presentations.

- The process for teachers, library media specialists, and students is nonlinear; it is also spiraling. At many points within PBL, segments may need to be repeated for more complete understanding of concepts. Working with the teacher and the library media specialist, students frequently go back and forth as they realize that they need to clarify, elaborate, or actually alter previous work. Spiraling results as reflection and experimentation allow students to gain proficiency in certain areas and move on to more rigorous learning challenges.

- There is often a tension between too much teacher direction and too much student independence. This will be a continual challenge for both students and instructors. At times, instructors must do more direct teaching and modeling because the concepts or tasks are new ones for the students. At other points in the process, however, they may be pleasantly surprised to see how students are able to initiate suggestions for their work and demonstrate their independence. The search for balance drives PBL.

- There will also be a tension between handling content *breadth* and *depth*. This is one of the biggest hurdles for teachers to overcome. Giving up content for the sake of in-depth knowledge is not easy when the teachers are faced with curriculum guidelines that mandate certain content be covered within the year. PBL requires give-and-take in the curriculum to accommodate for this.

- Assessment must be a continuous activity. Because of the length of many projects and the diversity of learners, there must be checkpoints to assess student progress. The assessment data determine the modifications needed to adjust the learning pace and facilitate the progress of students within the class. For teachers, who are accustomed to traditional modes of assessment (i.e., quizzes and tests), the development of alternate assessment strategies that are performance based will be a new learning experience (Luongo-Orlando 2003). Library media specialists must also examine their own instruction and figure ways to assess for learning that occurs in the library setting (Harada and Yoshina 2005).

- Motivation is also a challenge. The areas that students select to investigate must be personally relevant. The project itself must be one that students find intrinsically rewarding because much of it will rely on students' self-direction. Chunking the activities and tasks so that students receive frequent feedback and encouragement from teachers, library media specialists, and peers help them to experience small successes. Similarly, the instructional team is also encouraged and motivated by these successes.

- It's important to allow time to learn new technical skills or technologies. If students are not familiar with the technologies they plan to use, they need training and assistance to master the necessary skills. Because the use of technology is tremendously appealing to students, they are often willing to invest extra time outside the classroom to perfect their skills. This is an area where classmates frequently serve as mentors.

CHECKLIST TO ASSESS A PROJECT DESIGN

Figure 4.3 provides a checklist for planning a project. The authors used it to assess the projects that are outlined in the remaining chapters of this book.

Figure 4.3 Checklist to Assess a Project Design

Tasks	Clearly evident	Needs minor revision	Requires major work
1. We state the student outcomes expected: what students are expected to learn.			
2. We describe the product or performance that will demonstrate the expected student learning outcomes.			
3. We align learning outcomes with the content standards.			
4. We identify the overarching questions that frame the project.			
5. We establish criteria to assess key benchmarks in the process and the final product or performance.			
6. We establish a timeline that outlines the sequence of inquiry tasks and activities throughout the project.			
7. We define who takes the lead at different points in the project.			
8. We identify checkpoints in the project to assess student work.			
9. We design tools to assess student work at different points in the process.			
10. We include the key resources we plan to use at different points in the project including community resources.			
11. We provide samples of student work.			
12. We reflect on our work to improve our teaching.			

SUMMARY

Planning for PBL must take into account what is realistically possible in different classrooms and library media centers. In this chapter we introduced important considerations to ponder before launching into PBL. We suggested an outcome-based approach to planning and a possible sequence for planning. We offered tips and caveats and a checklist for designing a project.

In its PBL guide, the Buck Institute for Education (2002) states: "It is important not to think of PBL as taking time away from the regular curriculum. Instead, consider a standards-focused project as a central method of teaching and learning that replaces conventional instruction for a portion of your course" (online). There is a sizeable investment of time and energy in planning for PBL; however, effectively implemented projects reap tremendous rewards for both students and adults involved in this enterprise. As an integral member of the teaching team, the library media specialist contributes invaluable expertise and resources to the initiative.

WORKS CITED

Brewster, Cori, and Jennifer Fager. "Connecting the Curriculum to Real Life." *Breaking Ranks: Making It Happen.* Reston: National Association of Secondary School Principals, 2000. (ERIC Reproduction Service Document No. ED434413).

Buck Institute for Education. *Project Based Learning Handbook.* Novato: Author, 2002. 30 July 2007 <http://www.bie.org/pbl/pblhandbook/intro.php>.

Harada, Violet H., and Joan M. Yoshina. *Assessing Learning: Librarians and Teachers as Partners.* Westport: Libraries Unlimited, 2005.

Herman, Joan L., Pamela R. Aschbacher, and Lynn Winters. *A Practical Guide to Alternative Assessment.* Alexandria: Association for Supervision and Curriculum Development, 1992.

Kraft, Nancy. *Criteria for Authentic Project-Based Learning.* Denver: RMC Research Corporation, 2005. 30 July 2007 <http://www.rmcdenver.com/useguide/pbl.htm>.

Luongo-Orlando, Katherine. *Authentic Assessment: Designing Performance Based Tasks.* Ontario: Pembroke Publishers Limited, 2003.

Mitchell, Ruth, Marilyn Willis, and The Chicago Teachers Union Quest Center. *Learning in Overdrive: Designing Curriculum, Instruction, and Assessment from Standards.* Golden: North American Press, 1995.

Newell, Ronald J. *Passion for Learning: How Project-Based Learning Meets the Needs of 21st Century Students.* Lanham: Scarecrow Press, 2003.

Perkins, David N. *Smart Schools: Better Thinking and Learning for Every Child.* New York: Free Press, 1992.

Railsbeck, Jennifer. *Project-Based Instruction: Creating Excitement for Learning.* Portland: Northwest Regional Educational Laboratory, 2002. 30 July 2007 <http://www.nwrel.org/request/2002aug/>.

Tomlinson, Carol A., and Jay McTighe. *Integrating Differentiated Instruction and Understanding by Design: Connecting Content and Kids.* Alexandria: Association for Supervision and Curriculum Development, 2006.

Wiggins, Grant, and Jay McTighe. *Understanding by Design.* Alexandria: Association for Supervision and Curriculum Development, 1998.

Wiske, Martha S. "How Teaching for Understanding Changes the Rules in the Classroom." *Educational Leadership* 51.5 (1994): 19-21.

5 Are You My Clone? The Controversy over Genetics

<table>
<tr><td>

COURSE: Biology/Human Physiology, American Problems
GRADES: 11-12
DURATION OF PROJECT: One quarter
STUDENT OUTCOMES
   CONTENT GOALS:
      Students will demonstrate an understanding of genetics, the related
      ethical issues and their impact on society through:

        • Identifying, defining, and analyzing genetic issues.
        • Presenting data on the societal and controversial impacts
          of genetics.
        • Debating issues and effectively communicating individual
          points of view.
        • Performing decision-making skills and the practice of
          developing official policies and guidelines.

   PROCESS GOALS:
      Students will develop information literacy skills needed to foster
      complex and higher-order thinking.

</td></tr>
</table>

DESCRIPTION OF PRODUCT OR PERFORMANCE

Constant medical and technical advances in genetics have resulted in the need for global regulations to govern its research, patent, and practice. Students will participate in a statewide Bioethical Genetic Summit to present summaries of various genetic discoveries and their positive and negative impacts on society. At the summit, students prepare a debate to share various points of view on each topic. Students also collaboratively develop guidelines to regulate policies and practice related to genetics at the culmination of the summit. They ultimately present their recommendations to a panel of scientists, legislators, and other public policy makers. Students will be responsible for:

    • Gathering and analyzing information on scientific research relating to the
      cloning issue.

- Identifying the positive and negative impacts of these discoveries on society.
- Communicating their findings to summit participants.
- Debating these discoveries by examining the research from various points of view.
- Using a decision-making process to reach consensus on global genetic regulations or policies.
- Presenting their final recommendations to a committee of experts (e.g., geneticists, scientists, politicians).
- Reflecting on the learning process by completing evaluations and journal logs and compiling an evidence portfolio.

CONNECTION WITH STANDARDS

Standards from Language Arts, Social Studies, Science, Technology, and Information Literacy are integrated in this project.

LANGUAGE ARTS

Standards addressed in this unit deal with using language to communicate with various audiences, employing a range of writing strategies, applying language conventions, and conducting research that requires a variety of informational and technological resources. For more detailed information on the standards refer to <http//:www.ncte.org/about/over/standards/110846.htm>.

SOCIAL STUDIES

Standards addressed in this unit focus on specific skills within broad thematic standards that deal with time, continuity, and change; science, technology, and society; and global connections. For more detailed information on the standards refer to <http://www.socialstudies.org/standards/>.

SCIENCE

Standards addressed in this unit deal with the broad domains of science as inquiry, science and technology, and the history and nature of science. For more detailed information on the standards refer to <http://books.nap.edu/html/nses/html/6e.html#ps>.

TECHNOLOGY

Standards addressed in this unit deal with basic operations and concepts; social, ethical, and human issues; technology productivity tools; and technology tools for communication and research. For more detailed information on the standards refer to <http://cnets.iste.org/students/s_stands.html>.

INFORMATION LITERACY

Standards addressed in this unit focus on the access, evaluation, and use of information; appreciation for all forms of creative expression; development of self-reflection skills in knowledge acquisition; and social responsibility in working with information. For more detailed information on the standards refer to <http://www.ala.org/ala/aasl/aaslproftools/informationpower/InformationLiteracyStandards_final.pdf>.

OVERARCHING PROJECT QUESTIONS

- What is happening in genetics research today?
- Why should we care about this research? How does it affect our lives?
- What are the consequences of unethical genetic practices?
- How do different stakeholders in our community view this research?
- How do we explain the pros and cons of this research to the general public so that they can make informed decisions?
- Why is it important to develop worldwide genetic regulations and policies?

TIMELINE FOR PROJECT

Figure 5.1 Project Timeline

Time	Instructor's Tasks (LMS/T)	Student's Performance Tasks
Day 1	**CONNECT** • Utilize articles/newscasts to introduce genetic issues and ethical concerns. (T)	**CONNECT** • Examine articles/newscasts and discuss genetics' positive and negative impact on society. • Conduct this activity in small groups. • Share findings with the class.
Days 1-2	**WONDER** • Discuss medical advancements being made in organ transplants. (T)	**WONDER** • Discuss society's views of transplants as it changed from its beginnings to the present. • Compile results into *Organ Transplants Compare and Contrast Chart.* (See Figure 5.3) • Discuss the results and determine causes for the shift in view. • Apply theories to formulate a response for the following essential question (based upon results of the discussion). — How can we explain the research on genetic engineering so that the general public can make informed decisions?
Day 3	**CONNECT** • Have the students decide on the most appropriate presentation formats to use based on the information in their journal entries. (T) • Inform students that they will present their issues at an educational summit in which global regulations and policies will be created to govern advancements and implementation in the field. (T)	**CONNECT** • Decide on topic and presentation format for the summit.

continued

Time	Instructor's Tasks (LMS/T)	Student's Performance Tasks
Days 3-4	**INVESTIGATE** • Conduct a WebQuest with the class to gather information on different genetic topics and issues. (LMS) • Provide access to and instruction on the library's online databases and encyclopedias. (LMS)	**INVESTIGATE** • Perform a WebQuest. • Complete a *Genetic Issues Impact Organizer* (See Figure 5.5)
Days 5-25	**CONSTRUCT/EXPRESS** • Have students synthesize information. (T) • Model how to draft background information on the topic and the issues surrounding it. (T) • Encourage more questions to fill information gaps. (T)	**CONSTRUCT/EXPRESS** • Analyze information and select pertinent background information to be used for the project. • Construct an introduction for the presentation. • Pursue higher-order and more challenging driving questions utilizing data collected through research.

	INVESTIGATE
	• Introduce research skills and new resources to assist students in furthering their inquiry. (LMS)
	• Utilize driving questions along with student-generated inquiries to foster deeper research. Questions include:
	  – What are the consequences of unethical genetic practices?
	  – Why is it important to develop worldwide genetic regulations and policies? (T)
		INVESTIGATE
		• Continue with the research process and utilize new resources to retrieve additional data.
		• Organize information using the *Genetics Debate Persuasion Map*. (See Figure 5.7)

	CONSTRUCT/EXPRESS • Allot time for students to analyze data and prepare the presentation. (T/LMS) • Introduce possible multimedia formats including Web page development, video editing and streaming video (i.e., Podcasting or QuickTime videos). (LMS)	**CONSTRUCT/EXPRESS** • Receive instruction and training on use of various multimedia formats. • Draft and critique presentations for the summit. • Refine presentations.
	REFLECT • Conduct ongoing assessment to evaluate each student's progress. (T/LMS) • Provide coaching sessions, and individual assistance and guidance as projects develop. (T/LMS)	**REFLECT** • Identify areas for improvement through ongoing conferencing, self-reflection, and peer review sessions. • Repeat prior steps in the PBL process as needed.
Days 26-27	**CONSTRUCT/EXPRESS** • Stage presentations at the educational summit. (T/LMS) • Invite guests to participate as conference attendees. (T/LMS) • Organize a formal debate regarding each of the genetic issues. (T/LMS)	**CONSTRUCT/EXPRESS** • Share presentations at the summit to educate the conference attendees on genetic issues. • Participate in a genetic issue debate and share individual views on each topic. • Reach consensus on worldwide genetic regulations and policies based upon the conclusion of the debates.
	REFLECT • Evaluate each student's product and presentation. (T/LMS) • Provide coaching sessions to collect individual feedback and points for improvement. (T/LMS)	**REFLECT** • Conduct self-reflection and peer reviews to provide feedback.

ASSESSMENT CHECKPOINTS

Figure 5.2 Project Assessment Plan

Checkpoints in the process	What is assessed	Who assesses	Assessment tool
Connect	Student participation and content understanding	Teacher Student	Observation
Wonder	Higher-order thinking and ability to compare and contrast data	Teacher Student	Journal entry *Organ Transplants Compare and Contrast Chart* (See Figure 5.3)
Investigate	Information retrieval and the efficient and effective use of resources	Library media specialist Student	*Genetic Issues Impact Organizer* (See Figure 5.5) Observation Consultation
Construct/Express	Evaluation, synthesis, and presentation of data in a clear and convincing manner	Teacher Library media specialist Student	*Genetics Debate Persuasion Map* (See Figure 5.7) *Genetic Presentation Rubric* (See Figure 5.9) Observation
Reflect	Assessment and evaluation of personal progress, making modifications for continued improvement	Teacher Library media specialist Student	Journal entry Project portfolio Self-reflection Peer review

RESOURCES USED IN THE PROJECT

Australian Broadcasting Corporation. *Waiter There's a Gene in My Food.* Australian Broadcasting Corporation, 1999. 9 Aug. 2007 <http://www.abc.net.au/science/slab/consconf/default.htm>.

Biotechnology in Food and Agriculture. New York: Food and Agriculture Organization of the United Nations, 2006. 9 Aug. 2007 <http://www.fao.org/biotech/country.asp?lang=en>.

Biotechs. World News Network. 9 Aug. 2007 <http://www.wn.com/biotechs>.

Bren, Linda. "Genetic Engineering: The Future of Foods." *FDA Consumer Magazine.* Nov.-Dec. 2003. U.S. Food and Drug Administration. 9 Aug. 2007 <http://www.fda.gov/fdac/features/2003/603_food.html>.

Devitt, Terry (Ed.). "Field of Genes." *The Why Files.* Apr. 1998. 9 Aug. 2007 <http://www.whyfiles.org/062ag_gene_eng/index.html>.

Jefferson, Valeria. "The Ethical Dilemma of Genetically Modified Food." *Journal of Environmental Health* 69.1 (2006): 33-34.

Juma, Calestous. "Biotechnology in a Globalizing World: The Coevolution of Technology and Social Institutions." *BioScience* 55.3 (2005): 265-72.

Molitor, Graham T. T. "Food and Agriculture in the 21st Century: Rethinking Our Paradigms." *The Futurist* 37.5 (2003): 40-47.

The President's Council on Bioethics. *Advising the President on Ethical Issues Related to Advances in Biomedical Science and Technology.* Washington, DC: National Bioethics Advisory Commission, n.d. 9 Aug. 2007 <http://www.bioethics.gov/>.

Schlundt, Jorgen, Wim Van Eck, and Mary Vallanjon. "WHO and FAO Have a Recipe for Safer Food." *Bulletin of the World Health Organization* 81.5 (2003): 315. 9 Aug. 2007 <http://www.who.int/bulletin/volumes/81/5/Schlundt0503.pdf>.

"Taking Stock." *Ecologist* 7 (2003): 32-34. 9 Aug. 2007 <http://www.theecologist.org/archive_detail.asp?content_id=210>.

Viale delle Terme di Caracalla. CODEX Alimentarius. 2006. 9 Aug. 2007 <http://http://www.codexalimentarius.net/web/index_en.jsp>.

STANDARDS CITED

American Association of School Librarians, and the Association for Educational Communications and Technology. *Information Literacy Standards for Student Learning.* Chicago: American Library Association, 1998. 2 Aug. 2007 <http://www.ala.org/ala/aasl/aaslproftools/informationpower/InformationLiteracyStandards_final.pdf>.

International Society for Technology in Education. *National Educational Technology Standards: The Next Generation. National Educational Technology Standards for Students.* Washington, DC: Author, 2007. 2 Aug. 2007. <http://cnets.iste.org/students/s_stands.html>.

National Committee on Science Education Standards and Assessment, National Research Council. *National Science Education Standards.* Washington, DC: National Academies, 1996. 2 Aug. 2007 <http://books.nap.edu/html/nses/html/6e.html#ps>.

National Council of Teachers of English, and International Reading Association. *Standards for the English Language Arts.* Urbana: International Reading Association, 1996. 2 Aug. 2007 <http://www.ncte.org/about/over/standards/110846.htm>.

Task Force of the National Council for the Social Studies. *The Curriculum Standards for Social Studies.* Silver Spring: National Council for the Social Studies, 1994. 2 Aug. 2007 <http://www.socialstudies.org/standards/>.

SAMPLES OF STUDENT WORK

FIGURE 5.4: ORGAN TRANSPLANTS COMPARE AND CONTRAST CHART (STUDENT EXAMPLE)

Criteria for evaluation of student work:

- Gathers accurate and relevant information from class discussions on the topic.
- Collects accurate and relevant data from other credible resources.
- Addresses all questions in the organizer.

FIGURE 5.6: GENETIC ISSUES IMPACT ORGANIZER (STUDENT EXAMPLE)

Criteria for evaluation of student work:

- Collects accurate and relevant data from a range of credible resources.
- Addresses all questions in the organizer.

FIGURE 5.8: GENETICS DEBATE PERSUASION MAP (STUDENT EXAMPLE)

Criteria for evaluation of student work:

- Clearly states a personal position.
- Effectively uses data from research to support the position.
- Addresses all components of the organizer to form a sound argument for debate at the Bioethical Genetic Summit.

REFLECTION OF THE INSTRUCTORS

Developing an interdisciplinary project-based (PBL) unit is challenging! Given the demands of covering numerous content standards, our team was hard pressed to find a way to incorporate all the material they needed to cover while sharing the time required to develop and execute a project of this magnitude. Nonetheless, the team felt the effort was worthwhile.

The resulting unit focused on the standards in depth (not breadth). We felt that the students came away from the project with a deeper understanding of the latest breakthroughs in science and the impact that genetic issues have had in their communities and in the global society. Students also gained new knowledge about how national and international policies, laws, and guidelines are developed and implemented. In short, the students gained a greater appreciation of the content being studied and its relevance to their world.

As library media specialists, we were challenged to facilitate assessment-driven curriculum. Mastery of skills required additional periods of application and practice. As we conducted periodic assessments, we addressed student weaknesses through additional mini-lessons and individual coaching sessions. We developed and used different assessment tools, gathered and interpreted data, and adjusted the curriculum based on what we found.

Our recommendation: because of the complex thinking skills required for the completion of this project, we suggest that the project be implemented during the second half of the school year. By doing this, instructors can introduce some of the requisite skills during the first semester and better prepare students for this assignment.

TEMPLATES AND RUBRICS FOR VARIOUS TASKS

Figure 5.3 Organ Transplants Compare and Contrast Chart

The first successful organ transplant procedure occurred in 1954. Since that time this scientific breakthrough has become a commonly accepted course of medical treatment due to changing societal views on the issue of bioethics. As we discuss transplant history, compile concerns/benefits that have been raised as well as the significant milestones in history that have made an impact on the acceptance of this practice.

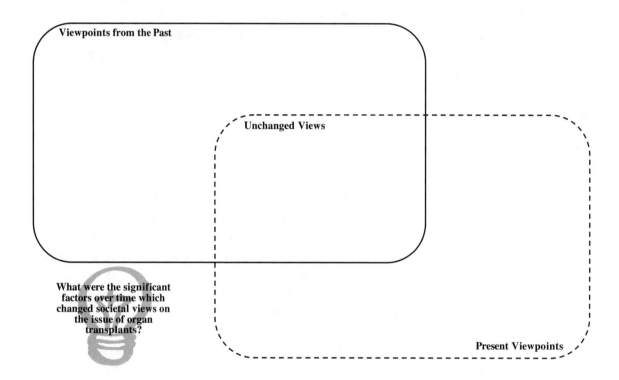

Viewpoints from the Past

Unchanged Views

What were the significant factors over time which changed societal views on the issue of organ transplants?

Present Viewpoints

Figure 5.4 Organ Transplants Compare and Contrast Chart (Student Example)

Evaluation of student work: This piece met all of the requirements for this assignment. The information gathered from the class discussion and research is accurate. The organizer is complete and all questions posed within the graphic organizer have been addressed. Furthermore, as this student discussed the data gathered, his clear understanding of the topic was evident. He expressed thoughtful opinions about plausible theories to answer the driving questions and demonstrated command of critical-thinking skills.

View Points from the Past

- Doctors accused of harvesting organs, donors not given a fighting chance to live.
- Transplant patients' odds of survival and organ rejection poor.
- Unethical to use the organs of the deceased.
- Complications that follow the procedure include pain and a decreased quality of life for the patient.

Unchanged Views

- An organ transplant is a risky procedure and should be considered only as a last resort.
- Procedure violates religious beliefs and practiced cultural observances.
- Unethical to use animals in testing and as organ donors for humans.

What were the significant factors over time which changed societal views on the issue of organ transplants?

- Organ transplant surgery has had higher success rates (less organ rejection).
- Transplant patients are living longer.
- More patients are placing themselves on the donor list due to their doctors' recommendations.
- Doctors are looking at transplants as a viable option for many diseases.

Present View Points

Figure 5.5 Genetic Issues Impact Organizer

As you perform your WebQuest, organize your information by categorizing it within the sections below. Focus on retrieving data that especially supports your topic's who, what, when, where, why, and how. The information will assist you in formulating a personal position and persuasive argument for your issue. Throughout the process, be sure to evaluate your resources for validity, currency, accuracy, and bias.

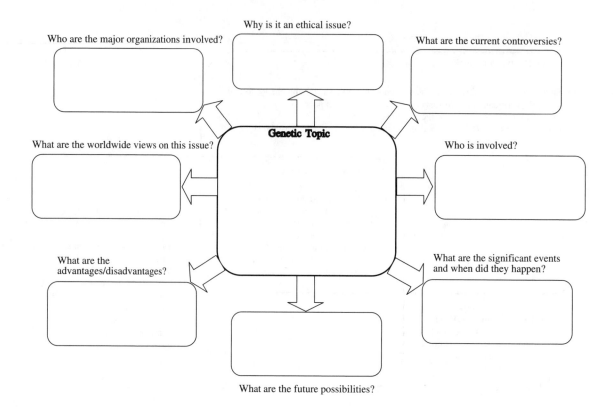

Figure 5.6 Genetic Issues Impact Organizer (Student Example)

Evaluation of student work: Sample exceeded the assignment criteria. All question prompts were answered and supported with accurate data. Throughout the activity, the student demonstrated the ability to discern fact from opinion, bias, commercialism, and slant.

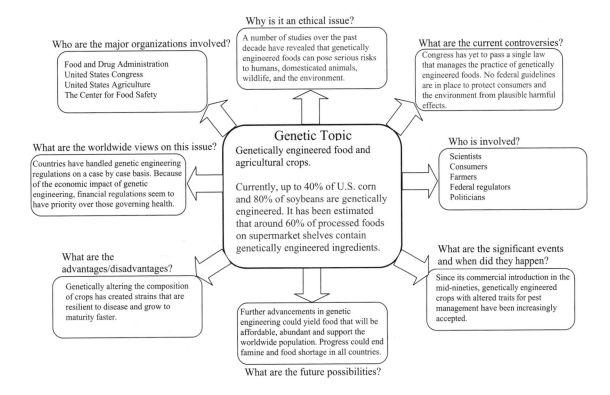

Why is it an ethical issue?
A number of studies over the past decade have revealed that genetically engineered foods can pose serious risks to humans, domesticated animals, wildlife, and the environment.

Who are the major organizations involved?
Food and Drug Administration
United States Congress
United States Agriculture
The Center for Food Safety

What are the current controversies?
Congress has yet to pass a single law that manages the practice of genetically engineered foods. No federal guidelines are in place to protect consumers and the environment from plausible harmful effects.

Genetic Topic
Genetically engineered food and agricultural crops.

Currently, up to 40% of U.S. corn and 80% of soybeans are genetically engineered. It has been estimated that around 60% of processed foods on supermarket shelves contain genetically engineered ingredients.

What are the worldwide views on this issue?
Countries have handled genetic engineering regulations on a case by case basis. Because of the economic impact of genetic engineering, financial regulations seem to have priority over those governing health.

Who is involved?
Scientists
Consumers
Farmers
Federal regulators
Politicians

What are the advantages/disadvantages?
Genetically altering the composition of crops has created strains that are resilient to disease and grow to maturity faster.

What are the significant events and when did they happen?
Since its commercial introduction in the mid-nineties, genetically engineered crops with altered traits for pest management have been increasingly accepted.

Further advancements in genetic engineering could yield food that will be affordable, abundant and support the worldwide population. Progress could end famine and food shortage in all countries.

What are the future possibilities?

Figure 5.7 Genetics Debate Persuasion Map

Using the information that you have collected, develop a personal position on your topic. To support your opinion, list three main points and their supporting evidence. Once completed, this will serve as a guide to prepare you for your participation in the upcoming Bioethical Genetic Summit.

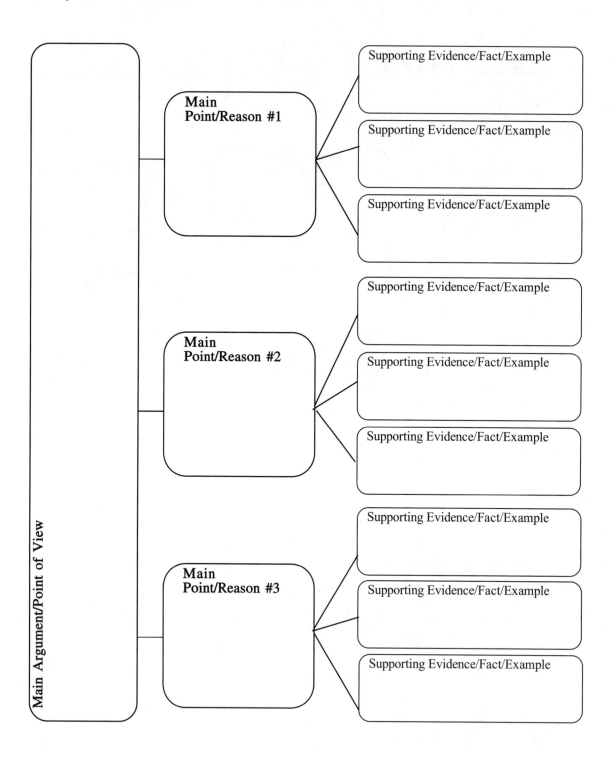

Figure 5.8 Genetics Debate Persuasion Map (Student Example)

Evaluation of student work: Overall, this sample showcases the student's synthesis of information and his deep understanding of his selected topic. It exhibits a well-formulated personal position that is supported with accurate data. The student was also able to connect his main points. As a participant in the genetic summit, the student used this information to express his arguments and gain support from members of the assembly.

Main Argument/Point of View

The current practice of genetically engineered crops is unethical. Without regulations in place, implementation should cease until a proper study of health and environmental impact concerns can be conducted.

Main Point/Reason #1

Scientific advancements in the genetic engineering of crops are progressing at an alarming rate. Without regulation the impact may produce serious health and environmental risks.

Supporting Evidence/Fact/Example
A number of studies over the past decade have revealed that genetically engineered foods can pose serious risks to humans, domesticated animals, wildlife, and the environment.

Supporting Evidence/Fact/Example
Human health effects can include higher risks of toxicity, allergic reactions, antibiotic resistance, immune-suppression, and cancer.

Supporting Evidence/Fact/Example
In agriculture, this leads to more pollution, threatening microbial, plant and animal species, contaminating non-genetically engineered life forms with genetic material.

Main Point/Reason #2

The federal government needs to revisit and update current laws and legislation to address present and future concerns raised by the genetic engineering of crops.

Supporting Evidence/Fact/Example
Congress has yet to pass a single law intended to address the human health/environmental impacts and manage the practice of genetically engineered food.

Supporting Evidence/Fact/Example
Eight federal agencies currently regulate biotechnology using 12 different statutes or laws that were written before food and animals were genetically engineered.

Supporting Evidence/Fact/Example
Where any regulation exists, existing laws are manipulated to manage threats they were never intended to regulate.

Main Point/Reason #3

Without worldwide regulation in place, countries looking to profit from the technology will practice genetic engineering concepts without regard for negative future implications.

Supporting Evidence/Fact/Example
Further advancements in genetic engineering could yield food that will be affordable and support the world population. Progress could end famine and food shortage in all countries.

Supporting Evidence/Fact/Example
Countries handle regulations on a case by case basis. Often, they favor economic rather than health factors.

Supporting Evidence/Fact/Example
Since its commercial introduction in the mid-nineties, genetically engineered crops with altered traits for pest management have been increasingly accepted.

Figure 5.9 Genetic Presentation Rubric

Criteria	Exceeds (3)	Meets (2)	Approaches (1)	Score
Coverage	Answers the basic questions of who, what where, when, why, how with ample supporting information.	Answers the basic questions with limited supporting information.	Attempts to answer the basic questions but much of the information has no supporting details.	
Organization	Presents information in a clear, non-biased format.	Presents most of the information in non-biased format, however, points are not always clearly organized.	Presents information that is frequently unorganized. Bias is also noted.	
Content	Provides thorough information that gives the reader essential knowledge of the topic.	Provides information that gives the reader basic knowledge on most aspects of the topic.	Provides minimum coverage of the topic.	
Clarity	Provides all information in a compelling and clear style.	Provides most information in a clear style.	Provides a lot of information that is unclear and unrelated.	
Sources	Uses a variety of print and online resources. All references are correctly cited.	Uses a limited number of resources. Most references are correctly cited.	Uses only 1 or 2 resources. References are not correctly cited.	
Grammar, usage and mechanics	No errors noted.	Minimal errors noted.	Numerous errors noted.	
			Total	

Rubric Scoring Guide:

Exceeded the standards	16 to 18 points
Met the standards	12 to 15 points
Approaching the standards	6 to 11 points
Not met	5 points and below

6 A Taste of Culture

COURSE: Foreign Languages, Social Studies (Geography)
GRADES: 9-12
DURATION OF PROJECT: One quarter
STUDENT OUTCOMES
    CONTENT GOALS:
    Students will demonstrate understanding of the interrelationships
    inherent in a country's geography, history, and culture by:

- Researching the foods and food-related traditions
  of a country.
- Interviewing a representative from an ethnic group about
  their food-related traditions.
- Analyzing how food is reflective of geography, history,
  and culture.
- Presenting findings through an oral presentation,
  multimedia project, or display.

    PROCESS GOALS:
    Students will develop information literacy skills needed to foster
    complex and higher-order thinking.

DESCRIPTION OF PRODUCT OR PERFORMANCE

Food is only one aspect of culture, yet it is one of the most enduring. What we consume, how we prepare what we eat, and even when we eat it may be directly influenced by a country's geography, history, and culture. Students will participate in a cultural fair where they share their research through multimedia or display presentations. Students will investigate the preparation, ingredients, and significance of a traditional dish. Students will be responsible for:

- Identifying a specific culture and its distinguishing features.
- Gathering information on the origin, preparation, ingredients, use, and significance of a cultural dish.

- Creating an essay that analyzes how a food is reflective of a country's culture, geography, and history.
- Augmenting the essay with an oral, visual, or multimedia presentation for audiences attending the cultural fair.

CONNECTION WITH STANDARDS

Standards from Social Studies, Foreign Languages, Language Arts, Technology, and Information Literacy are integrated in this project.

SOCIAL STUDIES

Standards addressed in this unit focus on specific skills within broad thematic standards that deal with culture; people, places and environments; and individual development and identity. For more detailed information on the standards refer to <http:www.socialstudies.org/standards>.

FOREIGN LANGUAGES

Standards addressed in this unit target specific skills under broader topics that deal with communication, and increased knowledge and understanding of other cultures. For more detailed information on the standards refer to <http://www.actfl.org/i4a/pages/index.cfm?pageid=3392>.

LANGUAGE ARTS

Standards addressed in this unit deal with reading a wide range of print and nonprint texts, and utilizing a range of writing strategies. For more detailed information on the standards refer to <http//:www.ncte.org/about/over/standards/110846.htm>.

TECHNOLOGY

Standards addressed in this unit deal with basic operations and concepts; social, ethical, and human issues; technology communication tools; and technology research tools. For more detailed information on the standards refer to <http://cnets.iste.org/students/s_stands.html>.

INFORMATION LITERACY

Standards addressed in this unit focus on the access, evaluation, and use of information; development of self-reflection skills in knowledge acquisition; and ethical and socially responsible behavior in working with others on information-related tasks. For more detailed information on the standards refer to <http://www.ala.org/ala/aasl/aaslproftools/informationpower/InformationLiteracyStandards_final.pdf>.

OVERARCHING PROJECT QUESTIONS

- What defines a culture?
- What can a country's foods tell us about its:
  - Social customs?

– Religion and beliefs?

– Geography?

– Festivals and special observances?

– History?

– Lifestyle?

- Why and how is food an important aspect of culture?
- How can food contribute to one's cultural awareness and appreciation?

TIMELINE FOR PROJECT

Figure 6.1 Project Timeline

Time	Instructor's Tasks (LMS/T)	Student's Performance Tasks
Day 1	**CONNECT** • Explain to students they will participate in a cultural exchange program using food as the focus of study. (T) • Share a cultural dish with the class to engage thinking about food and culture. Introduce focus questions for student discussion. (T)	**CONNECT** • Examine a dish and respond to question prompts regarding it in small groups. – Where does this dish originate? – What ingredients were used to create it? – How was it prepared? – When is it eaten? – Who eats it? – What cultural significance does it have? – What can it tell us about the culture and country of origin? • Share answers with class.
Days 1-2	**WONDER** • Lead discussion regarding what food can tell us about a country and its culture. Organize student responses in a concept web that includes: – Social customs – Religion and beliefs – Geography – Festivals and special occasions – History – Lifestyle (T) • Introduce project and requirements. Form student groups. Groups should divide responsibilities for the country and dish being investigated. (T)	**WONDER** • Discuss what culture is and what can be learned about a country and its culture by looking at their foods. Create concept web based on answers. Use the *Culture Concept Web*. (See Figure 6.3) • Listen to project requirements and select three possible ethnic dishes to research. Refer to the *Student Project Requirements*. (See Figure 6.5)

continued

Time	Instructor's Tasks (LMS/T)	Student's Performance Tasks

Days 3-18	**INVESTIGATE**
	• Review project and requirements. (T)
	• Utilize the pre-search worksheet to have students explore possible resources for three dishes of interest. Provide various resources including ethnic cookbooks for students to browse for possible topic selection. Have students evaluate information to select final topic. (LMS)
	• Have students create questions to guide research. Encourage critical questions for deeper insight into the food-culture connection. (T)
	• Conduct instruction on access and annotated citation of library's print and online resources. Review criteria for good notes, e.g., relevance, accuracy. (LMS)
	• Describe the purpose of interviews for this project. Conduct instruction on interview process. (LMS)
	• Provide individual assistance and guidance as students progress with interviews. (T/LMS)
	• Conduct ongoing assessment to evaluate each student's progress and provide individual and group assistance and guidance as project develops. (T/LMS)
		INVESTIGATE
		• Brainstorm three ethnic dishes as possible topics for this project. List them down on the *Topic Selection* worksheet. (See Figure 6.6)
		• Search three possible choices to determine interest and availability of resources. Based on information gathered, select a topic for project.
		• Utilize *Culture Concept Web* to help generate questions that will guide research on food, culture and country. Sample questions:
		  – What are the geographical features of this country?
		  – What are the traditional and modern diets like?
		  – Who commonly prepares the food in the family?
		  – What are some traditional dishes?
		  – When are these dishes prepared?
		  – How are foods prepared or preserved?
		  – What role does this food play in the country's economy?
		  – Why do people in a particular region eat certain dishes?
		  – What does the food tell us about the people or the country?
		• Gather information using print and online resources. Create a working bibliography of works used.
		• Find an individual representing that ethnic group to gain personal insight into the importance of food in a culture.
		• Contact interviewee. Generate questions for interview.
		• Complete interview with follow-up letter.
		• Continually reflect on self-progress. (See Figures 6.8 and 6.9)

Days 19-27	**CONSTRUCT/EXPRESS** • Review possible mediums for presentations (displays, video, PowerPoint). Explain written requirements for the essay. • Allot time for students to organize data and prepare the written piece and presentation. Also allow time for peer evaluations. (T)	**CONSTRUCT/EXPRESS** • Select format for final product. • Organize information by grouping notes into categories. Utilize research questions to assist with organization. Use *Organizing Data Worksheet*. (See Figure 6.10) • Create written component and presentation. Use *Rubric for Essay Writing*. (See Figure 6.12) • Submit draft for peer evaluations. Evaluate at least two drafts from peers using the *Peer Editing* worksheet. (See Figure 6.13) • Create presentations for the cultural fair. Use *Rubric for Presentation*. (See Figure 6.14)
	REFLECT • Monitor student progress through observation, self and peer reflection. Provide feedback when necessary. (T/LMS)	**REFLECT** • Practice presentation. Improve on work through self and peer reflection. Use *Reflection Doodles*. (See Figure 6.15)

continued

Time	Instructor's Tasks (LMS/T)	Student's Performance Tasks
Days 28-30	**CONSTRUCT/EXPRESS** • Invite school and community to attend cultural fair. (T/LMS) • Organize community panel to assess student projects using designed rubrics. (T/LMS)	**CONSTRUCT/EXPRESS** • Share presentations at school-wide cultural fair.
Day 31	**REFLECT** • Have students reflect upon process and product. (T/LMS)	**REFLECT** • Self-reflect on research process and product. Create a reflection journal answering the question, "How does food promote an appreciation of different world cultures?"

ASSESSMENT CHECKPOINTS

Figure 6.2 Project Assessment Plan

Checkpoints in the process	What is assessed	Who assesses	Assessment tool
Connect	Student participation and content understanding	Teacher Student	Observation
Wonder	Topic selection and creation of questions to focus research	Teacher Library media specialist Student	*Culture Concept Web* (See Figure 6.3) Questions
Investigate	Information seeking, access and retrieval, and the efficient and effective use of resource materials	Teacher Library media specialist Student	Observation *Topic Selection* (See Figure 6.6) *Progress Check* (See Figure 6.8) *Rubric for Assessing Notes* (See Figure 6.9) Self-reflection
Construct/Express	Evaluation, synthesis, and presentation of data in a clear manner	Teacher Library media specialist Student	Observation *Organizing Data* (See Figure 6.10) *Rubric for Essay Writing* (See Figure 6.12) *Peer Editing* (See Figure 6.13) *Rubric for Presentation* (See Figure 6.14) *Reflection Doodles* (See Figure 6.15)
Reflect/Assess	Assessment and evaluation of personal progress, making modifications for continued improvement	Community panel Teacher Library media specialist Student	Self-reflection Peer and community review

RESOURCES USED IN THE PROJECT

Asia Recipes.com. *AsiaRecipes.com.* 1999.1 Aug. 2007 <http://asiarecipes.com>.

British Broadcasting Company. *BBC Food Glossary.* 2007. 1 Aug. 2007 <http://www.bbc.co.uk/food/glossary>.

Condenet. *Epicurious Dictionaries.* 2006. 1 Aug. 2007 <http://www.epicurious.com/tools/fooddictionary>.

Davidson, Alan. *The Oxford Companion to Food.* Oxford: Oxford University Press, 1999.

The Epicentre. *Encyclopedia of Spices*. 2006. 1 Aug. 2007 <http://www.theepicentre.com/Spices/spiceref.html>.

Flandrin, Jean Louis, and Massimo Montanari. *Food: A Culinary History from Antiquity to the Present*. New York: Columbia University Press, 1999.

Food History News. 1999. 1 Aug. 2007 <http://foodhistorynews.com/index.html>.

Harada, Violet H., and Joan M. Yoshina. *Assessing Learning: Librarians and Teachers as Partners*. Westport: Libraries Unlimited, 2005.

Harada, Violet H., and Joan M. Yoshina. *Inquiry Learning through Librarian-Teacher Partnerships*. Worthington: Linworth Publishing, Inc., 2004.

Katz, Soloman (Ed.). *Encyclopedia of Food and Culture*. New York: Charles Scribner, 2003.

Kiple, Kenneth, and Kriemhild Ornellas (Eds.). *The Cambridge World History of Food*. Cambridge: Cambridge University Press, 2000.

Roy, Christian. *Traditional Festivals: A Multicultural Encyclopedia*. Santa Barbara: ABC-Clio, 2005.

Smithsonian Institution Traveling Exhibition Service. *Key Ingredients: America by Food*. Washington, DC: Smithsonian Institution. 2003. 1 Aug. 2007 <http://www.keyingredients.org/>.

Webb, Lois. *Multicultural Cookbook of Life Celebrations*. Phoenix: Oryx Press, 2000.

STANDARDS CITED

American Association of School Librarians, and the Association for Educational Communications and Technology. *Information Literacy Standards for Student Learning*. Chicago: American Library Association, 1998. 2 Aug. 2007 <http://www.ala.org/ala/aasl/aaslproftools/informationpower/InformationLiteracyStandards_final.pdf>.

American Council on the Teaching of Foreign Languages. *Standards for Foreign Language Education*. Alexandria: Author, n.d. 1 Aug. 2007 <http://www.actfl.org/i4a/pages/index.cfm?pageid=3392>.

International Society for Technology in Education. *National Educational Technology Standards: The Next Generation. National Educational Technology Standards for Students*. Washington, DC: Author, 2007. 2 Aug. 2007 <http://cnets.iste.org/students/s_stands.html>.

National Council of the Teachers of English, and International Reading Association. *Standards for the English Language Arts*. Urbana: International Reading Association, 1996. 2 Aug. 2007 <http//:www.ncte.org/about/over/standards/110846.htm>.

Task Force of the National Council for the Social Studies. *The Curriculum Standards for the Social Studies*. Silver Spring: National Council for the Social Studies, 1994. 2 Aug. 2007 <http://www.socialstudies.org/standards/>.

SAMPLES OF STUDENT WORK

FIGURE 6.4: CULTURE CONCEPT WEB (STUDENT EXAMPLE)

Criteria for evaluation of student work:

- Gathers accurate and relevant information from class discussions on the topic

- Includes relevant details on a country's history, diet, geography, beliefs, social customs, and people

FIGURE 6.7: TOPIC SELECTION (STUDENT EXAMPLE)

Criteria for evaluation of student work:

- Addresses all questions in the organizer
- Clearly states and logically explains all points made

FIGURE 6.11: ORGANIZING DATA (STUDENT EXAMPLE)

Criteria for evaluation of student work:

- Addresses all questions in the organizer
- Clearly explains the relationship between the dish and aspects of the culture

REFLECTION OF THE INSTRUCTORS

As library media specialists, we were asked by the foreign language teachers to assist in the development of this department-wide project. We began with a set of standards to address. The foreign language teachers agreed that more cultural aspects had to be incorporated in their present curriculum so students would appreciate the language and the people with whom they spoke. As a team, we decided that food was the "hook" of choice. Our planning consisted of face-to-face work sessions, phone conversations, email messages, and impromptu meetings in hallways.

We felt that the teachers and students truly valued our participation. During the planning phase, we helped to develop instructional strategies, strengthen research skills, retrieve needed resources, and assist in laying out the project calendar. During the implementation phase, we taught several lessons relating to information literacy skills, participated in the assessment of student products, and worked with teachers to continually assess student progress.

As a team, we realized that collaboration was an effective way to craft a standards-based curriculum. It offered us critical opportunities to solve problems and develop a collegial environment that fostered professional growth. Regular checkpoints during the project were essential for both instructors and students to constantly assess what students were able to do and identify where they needed more support and guidance. As a result, many adjustments were made to the timeline and instructional strategies in order to meet students' needs. By working together, we could share this work.

TEMPLATES AND RUBRICS FOR VARIOUS TASKS

Figure 6.3 Culture Concept Web

What can food tell us about a country and its culture? In groups, discuss this question then create a food concept web.

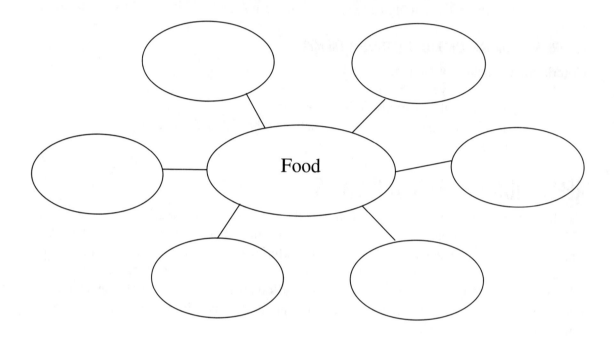

Figure 6.4 Culture Concept Web (Student Example)

Evaluation of student work: This student's web meets the assignment criteria. The sub-topics identified in this web accurately reflected class brainstorming sessions on the larger topic. The student was able to include at least one sub-topic for beliefs, diet, history, geography, social customs, and peoples.

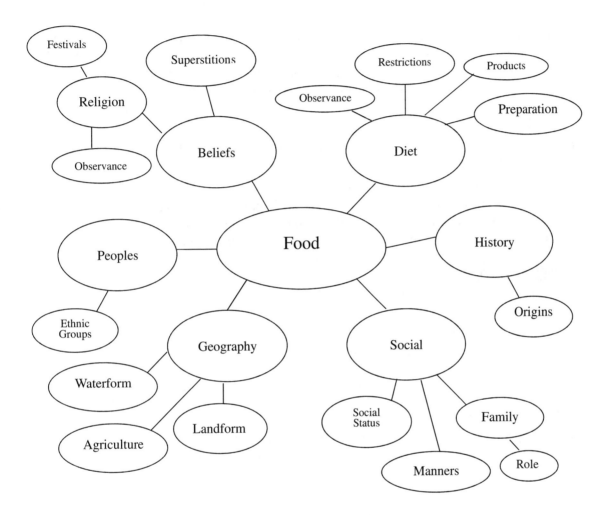

Figure 6.5 Student Project Instructions

You Are Invited!

The Foreign Languages and Social Studies Departments
cordially invite you to participate in a culinary cultural exchange program.

Congratulations! You've been selected to participate in a culinary cultural exchange program. This program is designed to bring deeper understanding and appreciation of a country and its culture through the study of food eaten by its inhabitants. What we eat, how we prepare it, and even when we eat it can explain a great deal about a person or group.

PROGRAM GOALS:

Students will demonstrate understanding of a country's geography, history, and culture through examination of food by:

- Researching the food and food traditions of a country.
- Interviewing someone from an ethnic group about his or her food traditions.
- Explaining how food is reflective of geography, history, and culture.
- Presenting data through an oral presentation and multimedia project or display.

OVERARCHING QUESTIONS:

- What is culture?
- What can a country's foods tell us about its:
  - Social customs
  - Religion, superstitions, and beliefs
  - Geography
  - Observances, festivals, and other special events
  - History
  - Diet and lifestyle
- Why and how is food an important aspect of culture?
- How can food facilitate cultural awareness and appreciation?

EXCHANGE REQUIREMENTS:

- Form a team of two to three members.
- Select a dish from a country that you are studying in your foreign language course.
- Divide project responsibilities among team members.
- Complete your research using a variety of sources to answer the overarching questions. Research both the country and the native dish.
- Interview an individual/group to gain personal insight into this specific food and culture.
- Create a written essay based on your research findings to answer overarching questions.
- Develop an oral presentation augmented by multimedia or video to document the knowledge gained, the accuracy and usefulness of sources, and the process you used to complete your project.
- Participate in a culinary cultural exchange fair.
- Continually reflect upon your process and performance.
- Reflect on process and product upon completion of the project.

Figure 6.6 Topic Selection

Select three potential topics and write them in the first column. Browse through various resources to add appropriate information in the remaining columns.

Potential Topic	I can use a variety of search strategies to find information.	I can find sufficient resources with information related to my topic.	My information will answer the overarching questions.
1.	YES NO Search strategies used:	YES NO Possible resources (list available resources):	YES NO Possible answer:
2.	YES NO Search strategies used:	YES NO Possible resources (list available resources):	YES NO Possible answer:
3.	YES NO Search strategies used:	YES NO Possible resources (list available resources):	YES NO Possible answer:

Based on your answers above, which topic will be the best choice for you?   Why?

Figure 6.7 Topic Selection (Student Example)

Evaluation of student work: This student received 10 on a 10-point scale. He was able to complete the table with appropriate responses for each block. He logically explained his topic selection based on the chart responses.

Potential Topic	I can use a variety of search strategies to find information.	I can find sufficient resources with information related to my topic.	My information will answer the overarching questions.
1. Mochi	YES NO Search strategies used: Boolean keywords: Mochi, rice, religion, history, Japan, planting, agriculture, Shinto	YES NO Possible resources (list available resources): Food Culture in Japan You Are What You Eat The Food Encyclopedia	YES NO Possible answer: Mochi is used at New Year and religious ceremonies. At New Year, mochi is made into flat discs like a mirror to represent the soul and is symbolic of the gods. Made out of rice, mochi is an important food product in Japan.
2. Miso	YES NO Search strategies used: Boolean keywords: Soybeans, seasoning, soup, soy	YES NO Possible resources (list available resources): Food Culture in Japan	YES NO Possible answer: Varieties vary based on regions. Historically, miso production was an annual activity tied to village events but now miso is bought in stores year round. It is served most often as soup at traditional meals.
3. Kelp (konbu)	YES NO Search strategies used: Boolean keywords: Seaweed, kelp, "marine vegetables", "ocean products"	YES NO Possible resources (list available resources): Food in Japan, The Visual Food Encyclopedia, Food Culture in Japan	YES NO Possible answer: Kelp is cultivated in cold waters off Hokkaido and NE Honshu. Shinto rituals involve food offerings including seaweed. They claim kelp helps stop absorption of cancer-inducing chemicals.

Based on your answers above, which topic will be the best choice for you?   Why?

The best choice will be mochi. I was able to find a lot of information on rice and rice products. There were also many references to mochi in religious ceremonies, festivals, and diet. As a rice product, it is very important to Japanese culture and history.

Figure 6.8 Progress Check

Use the chart below to assess your progress. Place a check in the appropriate column.

Criteria	Agree	Mostly Agree	Disagree
I completed my pre-search phase and selected my topic.			
I created a range of questions that address different aspects of the topic.			
I used quality sources and took notes on each source's usefulness.			
I took notes that answered my research questions.			
I used various search strategies to seek information.			
I organized my notes in an acceptable format.			

Comments/questions:

Figure 6.9 Rubric for Assessing Notes

Criteria	Exceeds (3)	Meets (2)	Approaches (1)	Score
My notes are accurate and complete.	✔ All information is accurate. ✔ Notes have enough details to support essential question. ✔ Information comes from reliable sources.	✔ All information is accurate. ✔ Notes include some information to address questions I asked. ✔ Notes have some details to support essential question.	✔ Some facts are accurate. ✔ Details aren't apparent. ✔ Notes do not help to answer the essential question.	
My notes relate to my topic and research questions.	✔ The notes answer all the questions I created. ✔ All the notes are about my topic and help to answer the essential question.	✔ The notes answer most of the research questions. ✔ Most of the notes are about my topic and help to answer the essential questions.	✔ The notes answer some of my questions. ✔ I don't know if my notes are helpful in answering the essential question.	
My notes come from a variety of sources.	✔ My resources include at least five sources; not more than half are electronic.	✔ I used at least four sources; not more than half are electronic.	✔ I used at least three resources.	
My notes are understandable to me.	✔ I always identify directly quoted material. ✔ I always put my research findings in my own words.	✔ I usually identify directly quoted material. ✔ I usually put my research findings in my own words.	✔ I sometimes identify directly quoted material. ✔ I sometimes put my research findings in my own words.	
My sources are properly cited.	✔ I kept a working bibliography of my resources. ✔ I always used the proper bibliographic format.	✔ I kept a list of most of the sources I used. ✔ I usually used the proper bibliographic format.	✔ I don't know where I got some of my information. ✔ I sometimes used the proper bibliographic format.	
			Total	

Rubric Scoring Guide:

Exceeded the standards	13 to 15 points
Met the standards	10 to 13 points
Approaching the standards	5 to 9 points
Not met	4 points and below

Figure 6.10 Organizing Data

Fill the boxes with information relating to your dish and country. Explain how the dish is representative of the country by drawing a line between the appropriate dish information and country categories. Then use the connections to answer the question at the end.

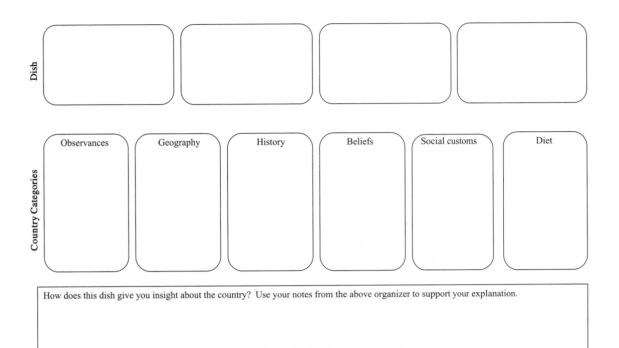

How does this dish give you insight about the country? Use your notes from the above organizer to support your explanation.

Figure 6.11 Organizing Data (Student Example)

Evaluation of student work: This sample met all the assessment criteria. The notes adequately covered all questions on the organizer and the student produced a clear and logical connection between mochi and its significance in Japan.

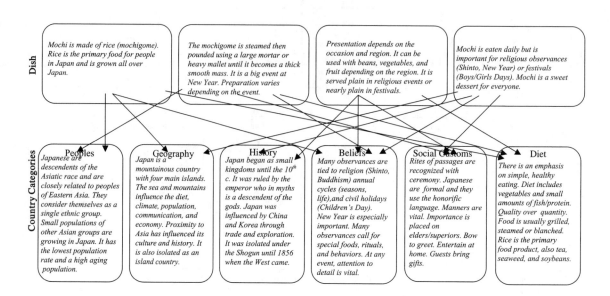

Dish

Mochi is made of rice (mochigome). Rice is the primary food for people in Japan and is grown all over Japan.

The mochigome is steamed then pounded using a large mortar or heavy mallet until it becomes a thick smooth mass. It is a big event at New Year. Preparation varies depending on the event.

Presentation depends on the occasion and region. It can be used with beans, vegetables, and fruit depending on the region. It is served plain in religious events or nearly plain in festivals.

Mochi is eaten daily but is important for religious observances (Shinto, New Year) or festivals (Boys/Girls Days). Mochi is a sweet dessert for everyone.

Country Categories

Peoples
Japanese are descendents of the Asiatic race and are closely related to peoples of Eastern Asia. They consider themselves as a single ethnic group. Small populations of other Asian groups are growing in Japan. It has the lowest population rate and a high aging population.

Geography
Japan is a mountainous country with four main islands. The sea and mountains influence the diet, climate, population, communication, and economy. Proximity to Asia has influenced its culture and history. It is also isolated as an island country.

History
Japan began as small kingdoms until the 10th c. It was ruled by the emperor who in myths is a descendent of the gods. Japan was influenced by China and Korea through trade and exploration. It was isolated under the Shogun until 1856 when the West came.

Beliefs
Many observances are tied to religion (Shinto, Buddhism) annual cycles (seasons, life),and civil holidays (Children's Day). New Year is especially important. Many observances call for special foods, rituals, and behaviors. At any event, attention to detail is vital.

Social Customs
Rites of passages are recognized with ceremony. Japanese are formal and they use the honorific language. Manners are vital. Importance is placed on elders/superiors. Bow to greet. Entertain at home. Guests bring gifts.

Diet
There is an emphasis on simple, healthy eating. Diet includes vegetables and small amounts of fish/protein. Quality over quantity. Food is usually grilled, steamed or blanched. Rice is the primary food product, also tea, seaweed, and soybeans.

How does this dish give you insight about the country? Explain using your notes from the organizer above.
Mochi is a by-product of one of the most important food products in Asia. Rice is grown across Japan no matter the geography. Eating mochi reaffirms the Japanese people's close ties to their history, beliefs, and environment. The Japanese are superstitious and continue to hold onto their traditional ways as seen in New Year's observances. Mochi is used in ceremonies to honor seasonal changes, rites of passages (marriage) and life in general (funerals). Mochi products vary according to regional agriculture and diet. The lengthy, careful preparation and presentation reflect the Japanese appreciation for quality over quantity, simplicity, and nature.

Figure 6.12 Rubric for Essay Writing

Criteria	Exceeds (3)	Meets (2)	Approaches (1)
Meaning	• Shows complete understanding of the topic. • Purpose is clear. • Expresses a firm opinion based on analysis of information, along with supporting reasons.	• Shows a basic understanding of the topic. • Purpose is clear. • Offers some analysis and explanation to support topic.	• Shows little or no understanding of the topic. • Purpose is vague. • Offers superficial analysis and explanation to support topic.
Content	• Information clearly relates to the topic. • All aspects of the topic are addressed. • Information is accurate and strongly supports conclusion. • Information comes from a wide variety of sources.	• Most information relates to topic. • Most aspects of the topic are addressed. • Accurate details and examples show some support of the conclusion. • Information comes from a limited range of sources.	• Information doesn't support topic. • Information is choppy and incomplete. • There are inaccuracies and details are not clearly connected to topic. • Information comes from one type of resource.
Organization	• Writing has a focus that is supported with detailed explanations and facts. • There is a seamless flow throughout the work. • Organization is logical.	• Writing has a focus that is usually supported by facts. • Transitions are sometimes choppy. • Organization is generally logical.	• Writing lacks a clear focus. • Ideas are not connected. • Organization is haphazard and disjointed.
Conventions	• Writing is clear, concise. • Work has been carefully proofed.	• Writing is generally clear, concise. • Work requires more careful proofing.	• Writing is vague. • Work requires extensive proofing.

Figure 6.13 Peer Editing

Evaluate your partner's draft and provide helpful feedback. Read each statement below and indicate the number that reflects your opinion.

Rating scale: 1 = Approaching   2 = Meets   3 = Exceeds

Criteria	Description	Rating	Comments
Meaning	• Shows complete understanding of the topic • Clearly states the purpose/focus • Expresses a firm opinion based on analysis of information, along with supporting reasons		
Content	• Information clearly relates to the topic • All aspects of the topic are addressed • Information is accurate and strongly supports topic and conclusion • Information comes from a variety of sources		
Organization	• Writing has a focus that is supported in detail with explanations and facts • Transitions among sentences, paragraphs, and ideas are seamless • Organization is effective and ideas flow		
Conventions	• Writing is concise, clear • Sentences vary in length and structure • Spelling, punctuation, grammar, and usage are correct		

Comments:

Figure 6.14 Rubric for Presentation

Criteria	Exceeds (3)	Meets (2)	Approaches (1)	Score
Coverage	Answers the basic questions of who, what, when, where, why, how with supporting information such as facts, examples or quotes.	Answers the basic questions of who, what, when, where, why, how with limited supporting information such as examples or quotes.	Attempts to answer the basic questions; however, information is lacking or incomplete.	
Organization	States thesis clearly. Presents ideas in a logical sequence with effective transitions.	States thesis clearly. Presents ideas in a logical sequence but transitions are sometimes choppy.	Lacks a thesis. Presents ideas in a haphazard manner with few if any transitions.	
Content	Clearly connects all information to the topic. Provides well-selected details that support the thesis.	Connects most information to the topic. Most details support the thesis.	Does not connect information to the topic. Few details support the thesis.	
Sources	Uses and cites a variety of print and online sources. Correctly cites all sources.	Uses and cites print and online resources. Correctly cites most sources.	Uses and cites only print or online resources, not both. Cites few sources correctly.	
Grammar, usage, and mechanics	Uses words, spelling, and punctuation correctly.	Uses words, spelling, and punctuation with minimal errors.	Numerous spelling, grammatical, and punctuation errors detract from the presentation.	
			Total	

Rubric Scoring Guide:

Exceeded the standards	14 to 15 points
Met the standards	10 to 13 points
Approaching the standards	6 to 9 points
Not met	5 points and below

Figure 6.15 Reflection Doodles

Name: _____ Topic: _____

In the space below, respond to the prompts by "doodling" your thoughts. You can draw your impressions—stick figures are fine. If you prefer, you can jot instead of draw.

At this point, how do you feel about your topic?	What challenges are you facing?
What are your next steps?	Comments?

Bad M.O.J.O.: A Forensic Approach to Scientific Inquiry

Authors' Note: M.O.J.O. stands for murder, offense, justice, and order.

COURSE: Physical Science, U.S. History
GRADES: 9-10
DURATION OF PROJECT: One quarter
STUDENT OUTCOMES
 CONTENT GOALS:
  Students will demonstrate scientific inquiry and inquiry learning skills
  as they unravel and solve a forensic mystery. Knowledge, technique,
  and experience gained will be the direct result of:

  - Observing, identifying, defining, and analyzing
   forensic evidence.
  - Researching the background and historical development
   of various forensic techniques.
  - Interviewing key individuals involved in the case.
  - Discovering patterns and connections among pieces
   of forensic and investigative evidence.
  - Persuasively communicating and supporting findings.

 PROCESS GOALS:
  Students will develop information literacy skills to retrieve, analyze,
  and synthesize information.

DESCRIPTION OF PRODUCT OR PERFORMANCE

Film, television, and media coverage of high-profile criminal cases has highlighted the
phenomenal technological advances in forensic science. Capitalizing on this national interest
in how crimes are solved, the M.O.J.O. project introduces students to various forensic
techniques as they conduct an investigation of their own.

First, students study a criminal case from the past and consider how the results might
have been different if current forensic techniques had been available. They then get involved
in a mock crime scene staged at the school. As the investigators, they evaluate the crime
scene and gather evidence. Through scientific inquiry and research, students collect and

analyze clues, uncover motives, and apprehend the suspect. They also participate in a mock trial where justice is administered based on the presentation of evidence and persuasive arguments. A student jury determines the verdict. Students will be responsible for:

- Recreating the sequence of events and analyzing the crime scene.
- Interviewing, gathering, and processing evidence.
- Synthesizing and evaluating collected information.
- Establishing links between evidence, motives, and possible suspects.
- Building and creating a case folder with documented findings and reports that determine motive and lead to a conviction.
- Presenting findings in a court of law to determine a verdict.

CONNECTION WITH STANDARDS

Standards from Language Arts, Social Studies, Science, Technology, and Information Literacy are integrated in this project.

LANGUAGE ARTS

Standards addressed in this unit deal with using language to communicate with various audiences, employing a range of writing strategies, applying language conventions, and conducting research using a variety of informational and technological resources. For more detailed information on the standards refer to <http://www.ncte.org/about/over/standards/110846.htm>.

SOCIAL STUDIES

Standards addressed in this unit focus on specific skills within broad thematic standards that deal with time, continuity, and change; science, technology, and society; and civic ideas and practices. For more detailed information on the standards refer to <http://www.socialstudies.org/standards/>.

SCIENCE

Standards addressed in this unit deal with the broad domains of science as inquiry, physical science, life science, science and technology, and the history and nature of science. For more detailed information on the standards refer to <http://books.nap.edu/html/nses/html/6e.html#ps>.

TECHNOLOGY

Standards addressed in this unit deal with basic operations and concepts; social, ethical, and human issues; technology productivity tools; technology tools for communication and research; and technology problem solving and decision making. For more detailed information on the standards refer to <http://cnets.iste.org/students/s_stands.html>.

INFORMATION LITERACY

Standards addressed in this unit focus on the access, evaluation, and use of information; appreciation for all forms of creative expression; development of self-reflection skills in knowledge acquisition; and social responsibility in working with information. For more detailed information on the standards refer to <http://www.ala.org/ala/aasl/aaslproftools/informationpower/InformationLiteracyStandards_final.pdf>.

OVERARCHING PROJECT QUESTIONS

- What do you know about forensic science? How do you know this?
- Why is forensic science so important to crime fighting in today's society?
- How have techniques in forensic science evolved over time?
- How would the outcome of historical cases be affected if they were re-examined using current forensic techniques?
- How might you solve a crime using different forensic techniques?

TIMELINE FOR PROJECT

Figure 7.1 Project Timeline

Time	Instructor's Tasks (LMS/T)	Student's Performance Tasks
Day 1	**CONNECT** • Discuss society's present fascination with forensic science. Utilize examples from movies, prime time television, and best-selling authors. (T)	**CONNECT** • Discuss what investigative procedures have been used by watching crime shows on television. Although dramatized, discern which are valid or purely fiction. Consider: — What do you know about forensic science? — How do you know this? • Create a list of these crime-fighting techniques.
Days 1-2	**WONDER** • Present details of the Massie Case. Discuss how the absence of standardized scientific collection and examination of evidence influenced the prosecution of the crime. (T) *Note: Other famous historical cases can be substituted for this one. The Massie Case was utilized due to its Hawaii ties and the availability of resources for this lesson.*	**WONDER** • Discuss how criminal cases were investigated prior to the introduction of current criminology techniques. • Discuss how points of view can be easily swayed in the absence of hard data. • Examine how key figures within the community influenced the outcome of the trial based upon their political and social status. • Formulate theories to address the following essential questions. Write responses in the form of an essay. Points should be backed by ideas developed in class. — Why is forensic science so important to crime fighting in today's society? — How would the outcome of historical cases be affected if they were re-examined utilizing modern crime lab techniques?

continued

Time	Instructor's Tasks (LMS/T)	Student's Performance Tasks
Days 3-4	**INVESTIGATE** • Using the file of forensic science techniques created on the first day of the unit, review findings with the class. Add to the list by introducing other methods that may have been missed. These may include the following: — Autopsy — Forensic entomology — Facial reconstruction — DNA matching — Dental records — Forensic anthropology — Blood analysis — Trace evidence analysis — Material evidence processing — Psychological profiling — Fingerprinting — Handwriting comparison — Voice recognition — Polygraph/body language interpretation — Toxicology — Artillery analysis (T) • Students select one method to research. To begin their research on the method, students are introduced to the library's print and online resources. Internet search techniques and keyword strategies are also reviewed and validating Web sites is strongly emphasized. (LMS)	**INVESTIGATE** • Answer the following prompt: — How might you solve a crime using different forensic techniques? • Select a technique to investigate. • Research a forensic topic. Gather information relating to its history, development, procedure, and practice. Think about: — How have techniques in forensic science evolved over time?
Days 5-6	**CONSTRUCT/EXPRESS** • Support students as they synthesize their gathered information. Students will create a factoid sheet to teach others in their class about their specific forensic topic. (T/LMS) • Compile factoid sheets into a crime investigation lab manual that will be issued to each student. (T/LMS)	**CONSTRUCT/EXPRESS** • Analyze research and select pertinent information that accurately describes the forensic method. • Complete and answer all the prompts on the factoid sheet. Provide history, overview, and process of the technique to teach others in the class. Use *Crime Scene Investigation Techniques* worksheet. (See Figure 7.3)
Days 7-11	**INVESTIGATE** • Introduce forensic skills and new resources to assist students in acquiring the criminal laboratory techniques. Allow students to develop mastery of each technique. Examples: — Trace evidence analysis — Material evidence analysis — Fingerprinting (T/LMS)	**INVESTIGATE** • Continue learning each of the forensic techniques and practicing them within the lab. Use the crime investigation manual as a reference tool throughout the process.
Day 12	**INVESTIGATE** • Presented with a crime, students demonstrate problem-solving skills and the knowledge of different criminology methods to solve the case. (T/LMS)	**INVESTIGATE** • Collect evidence from the crime scene by utilizing keen observation and problem-solving skills. Use *Collecting Evidence with Five Senses* to record significant findings. (See Figure 7.5) • Retrieve trace, material, and fingerprints to take to the criminal laboratory for analysis.

continued

Time	Instructor's Tasks (LMS/T)	Student's Performance Tasks
Day 13	**INVESTIGATE** • Instruct students in the art of interviewing. The aim is to coax the interviewee to divulge the information needed. Follow-up questioning is also practiced to extract additional information and develop greater detail and understanding of the crime. (LMS)	**INVESTIGATE** • Draw out details from witnesses and potential suspects utilizing good interviewing skills. To assist in this process, brainstorm and create open and closed-ended questions to utilize during the interview session. Use *Question Everyone to Get the Facts* worksheet. (See Figure 7.7)
Days 14-20	**CONSTRUCT/EXPRESS** • Conduct ongoing processing and evaluation of evidence in the lab. As results are developed, have students piece together the timeline of the crime and link evidence to a possible suspect. (T/LMS)	**CONSTRUCT/EXPRESS** • Process the evidence using the forensic techniques learned. Create a timeline of events that pieces together the crime (from beginning to end). Use the *Crime Rewind* worksheet. (See Figure 7.9) • Compile all laboratory results into a case portfolio. This folio will provide an orderly method to organize findings and build support for the apprehension and conviction of the culprit. • Identify a possible suspect based upon the results of the investigation.
Days 21-26	**CONSTRUCT/EXPRESS** • Stage a mock court proceeding. Suspect will be prosecuted based upon the analysis of the criminal data and the ability of the student teams to prosecute their defendant. (T) • Conduct cross examinations to challenge the teams' investigative prowess. This will be done by a panel consisting of the teachers and library media specialists. (T/LMS)	**CONSTRUCT/EXPRESS** • Create opening/closing statements and prepare to answer possible issues which will arise during rebuttal. All arguments should be clear, connected, and supported with forensic evidence. • Conduct a hearing regarding the presentation of evidence. Based upon findings, student teams prosecute their suspects and seek justice for the victim of the crime. • Reach a decision based upon the arguments presented and clarifying statements made during cross- examination. The jury will decide the verdict.
Day 27	**REFLECT** • Perform assessment to evaluate each student's court presentation. Use the *Criminal Court Presentation Rubric*. (See Figure 5.11) (T/LMS)	**REFLECT** • Conduct self-reflection and peer reviews to provide a means for student feedback.

ASSESSMENT CHECKPOINTS

Figure 7.2 Project Assessment Plan

Checkpoints in the process	What is assessed	Who assesses	Assessment tool
Connect	Student participation and content understanding	Teacher Student	Observation
Wonder	Higher-order thinking and ability to compare and contrast data	Teacher Student	Essay
Investigate	Information retrieval and the efficient and effective use of resources	Teacher Library media specialist Student	*Collecting Evidence with the Five Senses* (See Figure 7.5) *Question Everyone to Get the Facts* (See Figure 7.7) Observation Consultation
Construct/Express	Evaluation, synthesis, and presentation of data in a clear manner	Teacher Library media specialist Student	*Crime Scene Investigation Techniques* (See Figure 7.3) *Crime Rewind* (See Figure 7.9) *Criminal Court Presentation Rubric* (See Figure 7.11) Observation
Reflect	Assessment and evaluation of personal progress and modifications for continued improvement	Teacher Library media specialist Student	Self-reflection Peer review

RESOURCES USED IN THE PROJECT

Daniels, Maria (Ed.). "The Massie Affair." *American Experience*. PBS, 2005. 9 Aug. 2007 <http://www.pbs.org/wgbh/amex/massie/>.

Dias, Gary, and Robbie Dingeman. *Honolulu Homicide*. Honolulu: Bess, 2003.

Federal Bureau of Investigation. "Kid's Page." Washington, DC: U.S. Department of Justice, n.d. 8 Aug. 2007 <http://www.fbi.gov/fbikids.htm>.

Friedlander, Mark, Jr., and Terry Phillips. *When Objects Talk*. Minneapolis: Lerner Publications, 2001.

Owen, David. *Hidden Evidence*. Willowdale: Firefly, 2002.

Owen, David. *Police Lab*. Toronto: Firefly, 2002.

Rainis, Kenneth. *Crime-Solving Science Projects*. Berkeley Heights: Enslow, 2000.

Zwonitzer, Mark. "The Massie Affair." *American Experience*. PBS. Boston: WGBH, 2005.

STANDARDS CITED

American Association of School Librarians, and the Association for Educational Communications and Technology. *Information Literacy Standards for Student Learning*. Chicago: American Library Association, 1998. 2 Aug. 2007 <http://www.ala.org/ala/aasl/aaslproftools/informationpower/InformationLiteracyStandards_final.pdf>.

International Society for Technology in Education. *National Educational Technology Standards: The Next Generation. National Educational Technology Standards for Students.* Washington, DC: Author, 2007. 2 Aug. 2007 <http://cnets.iste.org/students/s_stands.html>.

National Committee on Science Education Standards and Assessment, National Research Council. *National Science Education Standards.* Washington, DC: National Academies, 1996. 2 Aug. 2007 <http://books.nap.edu/html/nses/html/6e.html#ps>.

National Council of Teachers of English, and International Reading Association. *Standards for the English Language Arts.* Urbana: International Reading Association, 1996. 2 Aug. 2007 <http://www.ncte.org/about/over/standards/110846.htm>.

Task Force of the National Council for the Social Studies. *The Curriculum Standards for Social Studies.* Silver Spring: National Council for the Social Studies, 1994. 2 Aug. 2007 <http://www.socialstudies.org/standards/>.

SAMPLES OF STUDENT WORK

FIGURE 7.4: CRIME SCENE INVESTIGATION TECHNIQUES (STUDENT EXAMPLE)

Criteria for evaluation of student work:

- Gathers accurate and relevant information from class discussions on the topic
- Collects accurate and relevant data from other credible resources
- Includes all information required on the fact sheet
- Provides sufficient information for classmates to understand the investigative method

FIGURE 7.6: COLLECTING EVIDENCE WITH THE FIVE SENSES (STUDENT EXAMPLE)

Criteria for evaluation of student work:

- Accurately documents information from the crime scene
- Provides sufficient data to begin a criminal investigation
- Addresses all questions in the organizer

FIGURE 7.8: QUESTION EVERYONE TO GET THE FACTS (STUDENT EXAMPLE)

Criteria for evaluation of student work:

- Effectively uses open-ended questions to uncover details that help in solving the crime
- Effectively uses closed-ended questions to uncover further details that help in solving the crime
- Addresses all questions in the organizer

FIGURE 7.10: CRIME REWIND (STUDENT EXAMPLE)

Criteria for evaluation of student work:

- Uses information gathered from analyzing the crime scene, interviewing suspects and witnesses, and processing evidence
- Demonstrates accurate analysis of data and effective problem-solving skills
- Produces a storyboard that is chronological and logical in sequence
- Completes a storyboard that is linked to the identified suspect and includes motive, criminal actions, and resulting felony

REFLECTION OF THE INSTRUCTORS

Various teams and academies on our campus have adapted this project because students are highly motivated and engaged when challenged to solve a crime involving forensic science. Because this unit can also be designed as standalone lessons to supplement classroom activities and discussion topics, we have used these materials to explore various historical and modern criminal cases as well as fictional crimes. One of our most popular and successful cases centered on the deaths of Shakespeare's Romeo and Juliet. Based on the evidence that students gathered through the "evidence" presented in the play and through re-enactment of the crime, they ultimately decided on a wrongful death suit in their mock court trial.

In the M.O.J.O. project, students asked for more time to contemplate and analyze the crime scene. To accommodate this request we made the scene available to them before, during, and after school. We also provided access to the crime scene through photos. This included an interactive 360-degree panoramic photo posted on our team's Web site.

We included additional technology by having students use presentation software to augment their court cases. They also used word processing applications to document their findings, create their final presentations, and compile their evidence into case portfolios.

As library media specialists, we played many different roles in this particular unit including that of the lead teacher, facilitator, technology instructor, and supporter. We constantly shifted the focus of our job descriptions to assist in the delivery of the lessons. This also held true for the other team members. When we took the lead in research skills instruction, the other members served as tutors and assistants, who reinforced the skills. By supporting each other, we felt that the students benefited from the personalized help and increased availability of instructors to aid them in their work.

All team members had to be flexible to cover the range of techniques and subjects that students had to master. For example, when we found that we needed additional time to introduce technology skills in the library, the team was willing to adjust the schedule even if it meant giving up time from some of the subject matter sessions. At the same time, when students picked up certain library-related skills faster than we anticipated, we could redistribute the time to other areas of instruction. As library media specialists, we frequently assumed a major role in conducting assessment activities. By analyzing the assessment data, we helped the team to pace the unit. In short, the complexity of the forensic work and the resulting need to collaborate as an instructional team made it critical that we understand and accept the importance of a fluid and evolving schedule in this project.

TEMPLATES AND RUBRICS FOR VARIOUS TASKS

Figure 7.3 Crime Scene Investigation Techniques

Solving a crime takes observation, skill, and ability to follow directions and protocol. In order to begin your training, your class will be responsible for researching and creating a laboratory manual to assist in collecting and processing evidence. Be as thorough as possible by utilizing a range of resources (print and online) to complete each of the points below.

Crime Scene Analysis Laboratory Manual
Investigation Technique: _____
Prepared by: _____

What are the major aspects of this criminology technique?

Summarize the historical development of this technique.

What should investigators be looking for at the crime scene? What type of evidence will be tested using this technique?

Describe the procedures that are followed during the following stages of analysis. Make sure to include who is responsible and the steps each should follow.

· Collection of evidence at the crime scene

· Testing at the crime laboratory

Figure 7.4 Crime Scene Investigation Techniques (Student Example)

Evaluation of student work: This example includes all of the requirements for this assignment. The data collected and interpreted from research resources are accurate. Information is complete and all prompts within the laboratory manual sheet have been addressed. Student's work exhibits a thorough understanding of the investigative technique.

Crime Scene Analysis Laboratory Manual
Investigation Technique: Fingerprinting
Prepared by: Joe Aloha

What are the major aspects of this criminology technique?

On each fingertip there are raised ridges of skin. Known as friction ridges, they provide a person the ability to grip and pick up objects. The only part of skin that does not allow hair growth are the fingertips. They grow in patterns and display any number of the following minutiae:

- Ridge ending-a ridge that ends abruptly
- Bifurcation-a single ridge that divides into two
- Lake or enclosure-a single ridge that bifurcates and reunites to continue as a single ridge
- Short or independent ridge-a ridge that starts, travels a short distance and then ends
- Dot-an independent ridge with approximately equal length and width
- Spur-a bifurcation with a short ridge branching off a longer ridge
- Crossover or bridge-a short ridge that runs between two parallel ridges

Identifying individuals through fingerprinting is based upon the principles of immutability and uniqueness. Regarding immutability, a person's ridge pattern does not change during his or her life span unless damaged in an accident. Each print pattern is unique and is composed of a variety of minutiae. No two patterns are identical.

Summarize the historical development of this technique.

The Chinese first practiced fingerprinting, also known as dermatoglyphics. Embedded in wax seals, they were recorded and commonly found on important state documents. Fingerprint identification is based upon a technique created by Sir Edward Henry (1850-1931). Focusing on the thumbprint, the system was implemented in Scotland Yard in 1900. In 1924, the Federal Bureau of Investigation (FBI) Identification Division was established. The FBI currently processes over 250 million sets of fingerprint records. The collection consists of both criminal and civil prints. Civil prints include government employees and applicants for federal jobs. A digital fingerprint analysis system (Automated Fingerprint Identification System) allows police officers to take suspects' prints using special electronic pads that immediately compare them with prints on file with the FBI.

What should investigators look for on a crime scene? How will the evidence be tested?

The fingertip's friction ridges consist of pores that continuously emit perspiration. When a person touches an object an impression is left. Called a latent fingerprint, the quality of visibility depends on the type of surface touched (e.g., metal, glass, plastic) and the environmental conditions (e.g., weather, moisture, dirt).

continued

Investigators at a crime scene should be looking for objects that seem out of place or have been moved. Each item that may contribute toward solving the felony can be dusted in powders that adhere to the print and cause it to be visible. These prints can then be recorded using photography or lifted off the object using adhesive tape. In certain conditions where the print is located on surfaces that are hard to read, special lighting, lasers, x-rays, and chemical reactions are used to bring the fingerprint into view. Direct prints are sometimes left behind. These are made when criminals have something on their hands such as blood, soot, ink or dyes. In this case, dusting and other processes to expose the print is not needed. Investigators process these prints by photographing them and taking the images to the lab.

Describe the procedures that are followed during the following stages of analysis. Make sure to include who is responsible and the steps that must be followed.

- **Collection of evidence at the crime scene**
  Crime Scene Investigator:
  Latent and direct fingerprints need to be collected. All objects that may have been touched by suspect(s) need to be gathered. Each item is dusted for prints. If it is a light surface, powdered graphite is applied with a brush to bring out the definition of the print. If it is a dark surface, talcum powder is applied in the same way. Once a print is visible, a picture is taken for evidence. The prints are then lifted off the object using adhesive tape and placed on a white card and sealed into an evidence collection bag. Evidence is then brought to the crime lab for fingerprint identification. A direct print is photographed and its location is recorded. If the object is moveable it is brought into the lab for analysis. If embedded within an object, a cast or clay molding may be used to preserve the print.

  Detective:
  After interviewing potential suspects, fingerprints are taken as a reference set for fingerprint analysis. Using an ink pad, an impression of each finger is rolled onto an index card and labeled. An impression of four fingers (together) is also taken from each hand.

- **Testing at the crime laboratory**
  Forensic Scientist:
  Prints are analyzed by examining their ridgeline detail. Each of the characteristics, known as minutiae (see above), form a unique pattern. Patterns that are commonly noted are the arch, loop, and whorl. The arch has ridgelines that start from one side of the fingertip, rise at the center, and exit on the other side. The loop has ridgelines that start and end on the same side of the fingertip. The whorl has ridgelines that are circular and do not begin or end on either side of the fingertip. Prints from the crime scene are compared to those taken from the suspects and from the fingerprint database. To make a positive match, prints need to have 8-12 points of similarity (ridgeline detail and position).

Figure 7.5 Collecting Evidence with the Five Senses

You have been called to the crime scene as a member of the investigative team. Your focus is collecting evidence to establish what has occurred during the course of the felony. Utilizing your five senses, document what seems out of place and might have contributed to the execution of the crime. Items and specimens gathered will be studied to link or clear potential suspects. Be thorough in your investigation. Your results will be used in court.

Looking over the scene, what do you see?

Listen carefully, can you hear anything?

Are there unusual odors?

Has the victim ingested anything (toxic or harmful)?

Did the victim touch anything or come into contact with anything suspicious?

Figure 7.6 Collecting Evidence with the Five Senses (Student Example)

Evaluation of student work: The student demonstrates a thorough understanding of the detailed observations necessary in analyzing a crime scene. The evidence reflects keen observation skills and provides adequate evidence to begin building a solid investigation.

Looking over the scene, what do you see?

The location is the 9th grade counselor's office. The room is ransacked. Pieces of furniture have been moved or thrown about the room. There is paper strewn everywhere and the filing cabinet of student records has been emptied. The counselor's wallet was taken; however, money collected for the prom was not touched. There was no sign of forced entry.

Listen carefully, can you hear anything?

Although the room is wired for an alarm it was not set during the lunch hour. The counselor's computer is setting off an alert signal. The warning is connected to a failed password attempt to log on and access the school's network. The phone still rings but the handset has been destroyed. Further investigation finds that the voice mail has been erased.

Are there unusual odors?

There are no toxic fumes present. However, there is a fruity scent in the air. The source: the counselor's hand lotion is found and it has been opened and spilled on the floor. Upon closely investigating the splatter, a partial shoe print is found. The print does not match the pair worn by the counselor.

Has the victim ingested anything (toxic or harmful)?

Although the victim was having lunch, it is ruled that the food had nothing to do with the crime. There is unfinished food left on the desk. There is an empty soda bottle found in the trash can; however, it is commonly known that due to a pre-existing medical condition, the counselor does not drink soda.

Did the victim touch anything or come into contact with anything suspicious?

The victim was knocked unconscious by a heavy object. Looking around the room there are several objects that might have been the weapon. Further investigation uncovers a trophy on the floor. There are traces of blood and hair on the object.

Figure 7.7 Question Everyone to Get the Facts

Interviewing all potential witnesses and suspects will allow investigators to retrieve facts that ultimately help to solve the case. To collect information that will be useful, a combination of closed and open-ended questions will be needed. To start you off, study the following tips for creating good questions. In the spaces provided formulate some opening queries to begin your dialog. Due to the dynamic nature of interviewing, answers need to be addressed by a series of follow-ups. After an opening query you will need to think on your feet and create additional questions to keep digging for more information.

 **Open-Ended Questions:** Open-ended questions are phrased so that the respondents are encouraged to explain their answers/reactions in depth from their point of view. Given the chance to elaborate, interviewers hope to draw out as much information from the subject as they possibly can. For example, "What did you witness?" requires participants to formulate a thoughtful answer.

 **Closed-Ended Questions:** Closed-ended questions limit answers to predetermined choices. These may include yes/no, true/false, multiple choice (with an option for "other" to be filled in), or ranking scale response options (statements are "ranked" according to degrees of agreement: I strongly agree, I somewhat agree, I have no opinion, I somewhat disagree, I strongly disagree). A commonly asked question such as "Do you feel that you can identify the suspect?" allows participants to respond with a succinct "yes" or "no."

 **Warning:** When developing queries be sure to avoid leading questions. In order for findings to be accurate and valuable, they must be the participants' genuine thoughts and feelings. Facilitators must be neutral and avoid questions that suggest any type of answer. For example, "How can you say that this was not the suspect?" may cause some to identify this person as the suspect even if they aren't sure how they feel.

Figure 7.8 Question Everyone to Get the Facts (Student Example)

Evaluation of student work: This completed sample fully exhibits the student's understanding of the concepts of open and closed-ended questions. Each query has been designed to elicit crucial details of the case and garner evidence that will be useful for solving the crime. The questioning has a logical flow that starts with drawing out simple answers from the interviewee. As the line of questioning progresses, there is a noticeable change in complexity and replies reflect critical details that contribute key pieces of information relating to the crime.

Open-Ended Questions: Open-ended questions are phrased so that the respondents are encouraged to explain their answers/reactions in depth from their point of view. Given the chance to elaborate, interviewers hope to draw out as much information from the subject as they possibly can. For example, "What did you witness?" requires participants to formulate a thoughtful answer.

- *How are you associated with the victim of this crime?*
- *When did you last see or come into contact with the victim?*
- *Who do you think may have a grudge against the victim?*
- *What events do you feel may have led to the crime?*
- *Where were you when the crime took place?*
- *What information might you have that could provide a lead in solving this case?*
- *What would anyone have to gain by committing this crime?*
- *What was the timeline of events that you have witnessed?*

Closed-Ended Questions: Closed-ended questions limit answers to predetermined choices. These may include yes/no, true/false, multiple choice (with an option for "other" to be filled in), or ranking scale response options (statements are "ranked" according to degrees of agreement: I strongly agree, I somewhat agree, I have no opinion, I somewhat disagree, I strongly disagree). A commonly asked question such as "Can you identify the suspect?" allows participants to respond with a succinct "yes" or "no."

- *Did you witness the events of the crime?*
- *Do you know the victim?*
- *Have you seen the victim today (or near the time of the crime)?*
- *Do you know the suspects?*
- *Are you directly connected to the crime?*
- *Did you notice anything unusual within the last two days (people, actions, and change in character)?*
- *Did the victim mention anything in conversation that might be useful in this case?*
- *Have the suspects been seen hanging around the scene of the crime?*
- *Have there been any other recent crimes that might be related to this one?*

Warning: When developing queries be sure to avoid leading questions. In order for findings to be accurate and valuable, they must be the participants' genuine thoughts and feelings. Facilitators must be neutral and avoid questions that suggest any type of answer. For example, "How can you say that this was not the suspect?" may cause some to identify this person as the suspect even if they aren't sure how they feel.

Figure 7.9 Crime Rewind

Hey, super sleuth! Based on the data you have gathered, piece together the elements of the crime. Use the storyboard below to construct a timeline to document the events. Include suspicious actions that led to, occurred during, and after the criminal act. Make sure to include the date, time, location, and people involved. Remember to be as thorough as possible. Your completed sequence of events will assist you in your continuing investigation. Feel free to use additional pages as needed.

Date:	People involved:
Time:	Sequence of events:
Location:	

Date:	People involved:
Time:	Sequence of events:
Location:	

Date:	People involved:
Time:	Sequence of events:
Location:	

Figure 7.10 Crime Rewind (Student Example)

Evaluation of student work: The finished storyboard paints an accurate retelling of the crime from the first suspicious activity to the end. Based upon evidence collected, each frame of the storyboard provides all of the detailed data for each of the prompts. The frames are assembled in chronological order and show a logical flow of events. The completed assignment also reflects critical-thinking and problem-solving skills employed to analyze and interpret clues and events to solve the crime.

Date: March 14, 2007	People Involved: 9th grade counselor and a student failing in one or more classes
Time: 8:26 AM	Sequence of Events: Students, who were failing in more than one course, were notified that they were in jeopardy and would probably repeat the 9th grade. Because this notification came right before the spring break trip, many students were not going to be able to attend the trip. They were not only taken by surprise, they were very angry.
Location: 9th grade counselor's office	

Date: March 15, 2007	People Involved: 9th grade counselor and three of the failing students
Time: 2:25 PM	Sequence of Events: Students went in to discuss their situation with the counselor. They tried to convince her that due to teacher's grading errors and extra credit assignments that were not applied in time, their failure status was inaccurate. If this was corrected they should be able to go on the trip. Counselor refused to change the decision and a heated exchange of words occurred.
Location: 9th grade counselor's office	

Date: March 16, 2007	People Involved: 9th grade counselor
Time: 12:00 - 12:25pm	Sequence of Events: While the counselor was having lunch, someone entered her office and knocked her unconscious with a trophy that was located near the door. The office was then ransacked. Upon closer inspection, student records were discovered missing.
Location: 9th grade counselor's office	

Figure 7.11 Criminal Court Presentation Rubric

Criteria	Exceeds (3)	Meets (2)	Approaches (1)	Score
Opening statement	Properly introduces team to the court. Engages the interest of the audience. Presents a thorough, well-organized introduction of arguments and evidence.	Properly introduces team to the court. Although presentation may consist of arguments and evidence, it is not thorough and consistent in generating the interest of the court.	Does not properly introduce team to the court. Statement may include argument and evidence; however, it is incomplete and not organized. Presentation is not engaging.	
Effective use of forensic evidence	Demonstrates a thorough understanding of the evidence and effectively uses the data to support all arguments. All connections and interpretations clearly support the points being made.	Demonstrates an understanding of the evidence. Most connections and interpretations clearly support the points being made.	Does not demonstrate an understanding of the evidence and does not support arguments with data. Most connections and interpretations do not clearly support the points being made.	
Rebuttals	Responds accurately and logically to all issues raised by opposing side. Effectively questions opponents with strong arguments and appropriate evidence.	Responds accurately and logically to most of the issues raised by the opposing side. Questions opponents but supporting arguments and evidence may be superficial.	Unprepared in responses to issues raised by opponents. Responses are often vague and illogical. Little or no attempt to challenge opposing arguments.	
Closing statements	Presentation is thorough, well organized. Clearly presents arguments and evidence. Leaves no unanswered issues and is a complete summation of remarks made during the trial.	Although statement shows organization, some points and evidence are minimally supported. Majority of questions are answered. Statement attempts to sum up activities made during trial.	Arguments are unorganized, incomplete, and weakly supported. Statements do not adequately sum up activities during the trial and leave questions unanswered.	
			Total	

Rubric Scoring Guide:

Exceeded the standards	10 to 12 points
Met the standards	7 to 9 points
Approaching the standards	4 to 6 points
Not met	3 points and below

8 Helping Our Environment, Helping Ourselves

COURSE: Biology, Economics, Language Arts
GRADES: 11-12
DURATION OF PROJECT: One semester
STUDENT OUTCOMES
CONTENT GOALS:

Students will demonstrate inquiry learning and decision-making skills as they develop a strategy for environmental sustainability. Knowledge, technique, and experience gained will be the direct result of:

- Identifying ideas for economic growth, environmental protection, and social equity as keys to sustainable development.
- Defining and applying economic concepts of scarcity, sustainable development, and natural resources and growth.
- Developing background knowledge and an overview of various environmental issues.
- Selecting an issue impacting sustainable development in the community.
- Constructing a plan to deal with the community issue.

PROCESS GOALS:

Students will develop information literacy skills needed to foster complex and higher-order thinking.

DESCRIPTION OF PRODUCT OR PERFORMANCE

While the earth's population has been growing, so has the need for natural resources to sustain the burgeoning world population. Increased demand for land and natural resources from over-fishing in Asia to the deforestation of the Amazon Basin has clearly impacted the environment. If this trend continues, humans will destroy the goods needed for their own survival. Individuals can reverse this trend and make a difference in their communities.

In this unit of study, students will gather information on an environmental issue relating to sustainability in their own communities. They will develop possible alternatives to address the issue and design and implement their strategies. Students will be responsible for:

- Understanding the economic concepts of scarcity, natural resources, and sustainable development and growth.
- Gathering and analyzing information on an issue impacting the community and its future.
- Using a decision-making process to design and implement an activity or program impacting the community's sustainable development.
- Presenting information and ideas on an issue affecting the environment, economy, and people of the community.
- Reflecting on the learning process by completing evaluations and journal logs and sharing these reflections with peers.

CONNECTION WITH STANDARDS

Standards from Language Arts, Social Studies, Economics, Science, Technology, and Information Literacy are integrated in this project.

LANGUAGE ARTS

Standards addressed in this unit deal with using language to communicate with a variety of audiences; employing a range of writing strategies; conducting research through question generation and problem-solving on issues and interests; and using a variety of informational and technological resources. For more detailed information on the standards refer to <http//: www.ncte.org/about/over/standards/110846.htm>.

SOCIAL STUDIES

Standards addressed in this unit focus on specific skills within broad thematic standards that deal with time, continuity and change; and civic ideals and practices. For more detailed information on the standards refer to <http://www.socialstudies.org/standards/>.

ECONOMICS

Standards addressed in this unit focus on the concepts of scarcity and marginal cost/benefit. For more detailed information on the standards refer to <http://ncee.net/ea/standards/>.

TECHNOLOGY

Standards addressed in this unit deal with basic operations and concepts; social, ethical, and human issues; technology productivity tools; and technology tools for communication and research. For more detailed information on the standards refer to <http://cnets.iste.org/ students/s_stands.html>.

SCIENCE

Standards addressed in this unit deal with the broad domains of life science, and science from personal and social perspectives. For more detailed information on the standards refer to <http://books.nap.edu/html/nses/html/6e.html#ps>.

INFORMATION LITERACY

Standards addressed in this unit focus on the access, evaluation, and use of information; appreciation for all forms of creative expression; development of self-reflection skills in knowledge acquisition; and social responsibility in working with information. For more detailed information on the standards refer to <http://www.ala.org/ala/aasl/aaslproftools/informationpower/InformationLiteracyStandards_final.pdf>.

OVERARCHING PROJECT QUESTIONS

- How can we conserve the earth's resources?
- How can we balance economic growth, environmental protection, and social equity to create sustainable development?
- How can we motivate people to care for their environments?
- To what extent can we personally impact our community's sustainable future?

TIMELINE FOR PROJECT

Figure 8.1 Project Timeline

Time	Instructor's Task (LMS/T)	Student Performance Tasks
Days 1-2	**CONNECT** • Create a gallery of historic and current photos from the community to engage student interest. (LMS/T) • Facilitate discussion on group reaction to photographs. Follow with discussion on relationship between environment, economy and society. (T)	**CONNECT** • Walk through the gallery of historic and current area photos. • Address the question: "What do the photographs explain about the environment, economy and society of our community?" Write responses, questions, and comments. • Discuss reaction to the photographs in small and large groups. Respond individually to the prompts by writing a reflection on the following: • If we continue with our current practices, what will the environment, economy, and society of our community look like in the future? • What would we like our community to look like in an ideal future?

continued

Time	Instructor's Task (LMS/T)	Student Performance Tasks

Days 2-4	**WONDER**
	• Summarize class responses to previous lesson's prompts. Focus discussion on:
	  – How will the likely future impact our lives?
	  – What action is needed to produce the desired future? (T)
	• Discuss concept of sustainable development and the relationship between economics, environment, society, and politics. Key economic concepts for each area will need to be discussed including:
	  – Natural resources
	  – Scarcity
	  – Stewardship
	  – Supply/demand
	  – Growth
	  – Green economics (T)
	• Introduce Sustainable Development Movements including:
	  – Agenda 21
	  – World Millennium Project
	  – UN Earth Day Summit
	  – Kyoto Protocol (T)
		WONDER
		• Discuss similarities and differences between likely and desirable futures.
		• Develop an individual definition of sustainable development based on the discussion regarding economics, environment, society, and politics.
		• Explain what sustainable development might look like in our community.
		• Respond to prompts based on information given:
		  – What do these items say about sustainable development?
		  – What is the vision for our future?
		• Apply new information to predict a response to the essential question: "How can we balance the needs of people and nature to move towards a sustainable future?"

Day 5	**CONNECT** • Discuss local environmental and related economic issues based on student logs and responses. Highlight key economic concepts in each issue. (T) • Inform students they will become empowered citizens by creating a program or project addressing a local issue impacting various economic, environmental, social, and political stakeholders. (T)	**CONNECT** • Identify community issues by viewing the local television news or reading the local newspaper for three days. Keep a log of issues reported. Use *What's News* worksheet. (See Figure 8.3) • Discuss environmental issues and how key economic concepts figure into these issues.

Days 6-8	**WONDER**
	• Demonstrate Internet searches using keywords and search strategies. (LMS)
	• Help students apply criteria for evaluating Web sites. (LMS)
	• Have students search for general information regarding possible topics relating to the community's environment, society, and economy. (LMS)
	• Have students decide on a topic based on their pre-search. (T)
	• Create chart of students' choices by having students submit their selected topic. (T)
	• Have students form small teams of two or three members, who are also interested in the same topic. (T)
		WONDER
		• Select several environmental issues and gain an overview in order to decide on a topic.
		• Apply criteria for selecting and evaluating Web sites.
		• Write responses based on pre-searching section.
		  – What search engine(s) did I use? What search words did I try?
		  – How did I decide which information was relevant and essential to my understanding of the topic?
		• Select a topic for deeper investigation based on your research and interest. Share choice with class. Find two or three classmates, who are interested in the same topic, to form a team.

continued

Time	Instructor's Task (LMS/T)	Student Performance Tasks
Days 9-14	**INVESTIGATE** • Explain need for focus questions to guide research for deeper investigation. (LMS) • Provide access to and instruction on a variety of possible print and online resources. (LMS) • Help students develop questions for stakeholder groups. (LMS/T) • Connect students with community resources relating to their topics. (LMS). • Encourage students to go on-site if possible to get a visual first-hand account. (T) • Continue to monitor student projects through observation, interview questions, and written progress reports. (LMS/T) *Note: Students will need additional time to complete interviews.*	**INVESTIGATE** • Use *Finding a Focus* worksheet (See Figure 8.5) to create questions that will guide the research. • Research the issue including role of the following: history, stakeholders, location, areas of concern, impact on economy, environment, society, and politics. Divide responsibilities among team members. • Interview or survey stakeholders on the issue. • Visit locale if possible to get a visual first-hand account. • Respond to questions: – What resources have you utilized? – Have you encountered any difficulties finding information? How did you address this problem? – What are your next steps?
Days 15-23	**CONSTRUCT** • Allot time for students to analyze information and prepare presentation. (T) • Introduce people who made a difference in their communities as role models. Possible individuals: – Ryan Ellison and Ocean Robbins (Youth for Environmental Sanity) – Nevada Dove, Fabiola Tostado and Maria Perez (fight against industrial development near schools) – Simon Jackson (letter writing campaign to save the white Kermode bear) – Chou Yu-sheng (neighborhood recycling) – Pattonville High School, MS (methane heating) – Wangari Maathai (Green Belt Movement) (LMS) • Have students brainstorm possible projects to address their issue. (T) • Review decision-making process with teams. Direct students to explain why a particular project was chosen in order to assess their decision-making rationale. (T) • Observe student teams. Provide feedback and comments. (T/LMS) • Explain rationale for action plan and worksheets used to create an action plan. Provide ample time to create the plan. (T/LMS) – Conference with students on possible projects. (T/LMS) • Allot time to work on presentation. (T) • Conduct ongoing assessment to evaluate students' progress through conferencing, journals and progress reports. (T/LMS) • Provide coaching sessions and individual assistance and guidance as projects develop. (T/LMS)	**CONSTRUCT** • Analyze responses to interview/survey. Identify major objectives and concerns of each stakeholder group. • Compile information gathered for a comprehensive review of the situation. Use *Piecing It Together* worksheet. (See Figure 8.7) • Identify and select the environmental, societal, political, and economic aspects of the issue the team may want to address in their project. *Note: These aspects may change as students examine more data.* • Study people who have impacted their communities to gain ideas and inspiration. • Brainstorm possible projects or programs addressing chosen issue. Students may change their minds about the projects as they explore possibilities. • Create a matrix to address the pros and cons of each possible activity to decide on the most feasible and effective option. Use *Deciding on a Project* matrix. (See Figure 8.9) • Based on the comparison matrix created, assess each possible activity for relevance, feasibility, and effectiveness. Select one for implementation. • Confer with instructors to explain team's rationale for project choice. Tentatively explain possible project. • Formulate an action plan for project or program. Submit to instructors for review. Use *Action Plan* organizers. (See Figures 8.11, 8.13, 8.15, and 8.17) • Create presentation to class explaining the issue and the plan you have developed. The goal is to gain support for your plan from peers. • Confer with instructors for feedback on project and action plan. • Provide progress reports on planning of project.

continued

Time	Instructor's Task (LMS/T)	Student Performance Tasks
Days 24-26	**EXPRESS** • Organize schedule for presentations. Arrange for equipment if needed. (T)	**EXPRESS** • Present the issue as well as the plan and persuade class to volunteer for cause. Use *Presentation Rubric.* (See Figure 8.19)
Days 27-80	**CONSTRUCT/EXPRESS** • Continue to allot planning time for project implementation. (T) • Conduct ongoing assessment to evaluate students' progress through conferencing, journals, and progress reports. (T/LMS) • Provide coaching sessions and individual assistance and guidance as projects develop. (T/LMS)	**CONSTRUCT/EXPRESS** • Participate and implement program or project. • Develop a short presentation to share the project results and reflections. • Confer with instructors for feedback on project and action plan. • Provide progress reports on planning of project.
Days 81- 88	**REFLECT** • Have students reflect on process and product. (T/LMS) • Allot time for sharing of projects and reflections. (T/LMS)	**REFLECT** • Conduct self-reflection, peer, and community reviews to provide feedback on project's success. • Share with class the results of the projects and reflections.

ASSESSMENT CHECKPOINTS

Figure 8.2 Project Assessment Plan

Checkpoints in the process	What is assessed	Who assesses	Assessment tool
Connect	Student participation and content understanding	Teacher Library media specialist Student	Observation Written reflection *What's News* (See Figure 8.3)
Wonder	Student participation and concept understanding	Teacher Library media specialist Student	Observation Written reflection *Finding a Focus* (See Figure 8.5)
Investigate	Information seeking, access, and retrieval Effective and efficient use of information	Teacher Library media specialist Student	Observation Research questions Reflections
Construct/Express	Evaluation, synthesis, presentation of project, and project implementation	Teacher Library media specialist Student	Observation Conferencing *Piecing It Together* (See Figure 8.7) *Deciding on a Project* (See Figure 8.9) *Action Plan* (See Figures 8.11, 8.13, 8.15, 8.17)
Reflect	Assessment and evaluation of personal progress and modifications for continued improvement	Teachers Library media specialist Student	Reflection Peer review *Presentation Rubric* (See Figure 8.19)

RESOURCES USED IN THE PROJECT

Division for Sustainable Development. New York: United Nations, 2004. 1 Aug. 2007 <http://www.un.org/esa/sustdev>.

"Economic Concepts High School Graduates Should Know." *Economic Education Web*. Omaha: University of Nebraska-Omaha, 2007. 1 Aug. 2007 <http://ecedweb.unomaha.edu/ec-cncps.cfm>.

Environmental Literacy Council. Washington, DC: Author, 2002. 2 Aug. 2007 <http://www.enviroliteracy.org/>.

Hawaii 2050 Sustainability Task Force. *Hawaii 2050*. Honolulu: State of Hawaii, 2006. 2 Aug. 2007 <http://hawaii2050.org/>.

Kay, Jane. "The Plastic Garbage Pits of the Pacific/Trash Particles, Looking Like Food, Imperil Sea Life." *San Francisco Chronicle*. Newspaper Source. Kapolei High School Library. 1 Aug. 2007 <http://search.ebscohost.com>.

Mongillo, John. *Creating a Sustainable Society*. Westport: Greenwood Press, 2004.

Mongillo, John. *People and Their Environments*. Westport: Greenwood Press, 2004.

Millennium Project. "Millennium Development Goals: What They Are." New York: United Nations, 2006. 1 Aug. 2007 <http://www.millenniumproject.org/goals/index.htm>.

National Center for Environmental Decision-Making Research. "Cost-Benefit Analysis and Environmental Decision Making: An Overview." Knoxville: University of Tennessee, 2004. 1 Aug. 2007 <http://www.sunsite.utk.edu/ncedr/tools/othertools/costbenefit/overview.htm>.

Sustainable Tourism Project. Honolulu: Department of Business, Economic Development and Tourism, State of Hawaii, 2006. 2 Aug. 2007 <http://www.hawaii.gov/dbedt/info/visitor-stats/sustainable-tourism-project/overview>.

STANDARDS CITED

American Association of School Librarians, and the Association for Educational Communications and Technology. *Information Literacy Standards for Student Learning*. Chicago: American Library Association, 1998. 2 Aug. 2007 <http://www.ala.org/ala/aasl/aaslproftools/informationpower/InformationLiteracyStandards_final.pdf>.

International Society for Technology in Education. *National Educational Technology Standards: The Next Generation. National Educational Technology Standards for Students*. Washington, DC: Author, 2007. 2 Aug. 2007 <http://cnets.iste.org/students/s_stands.html>.

National Committee on Science Education Standards and Assessment. *National Research Council. Science Content Standards 9-12*. Washington, DC: National Academies, 1996. 2 Aug. 2007 <http://books.nap.edu/html/nses/html/6e.html#ps>.

National Council on Economic Education. *Voluntary National Content Standards in Economics*. New York: Author, 2007. 2 Aug. 2007 <http://www.ncee.net/ea/standards/>.

The National Council of Teachers of English, and International Reading Association. *Standards for the English Language Arts*. Urbana: International Reading Association, 1996. 2 Aug. 2007 <http://www.ncte.org/about/over/standards/110846.htm>.

Task Force of the National Council for the Social Studies. *The Curriculum Standards for the Social Studies*. Silver Spring: National Council for the Social Studies, 1994. 2 Aug. 2007 <http://www.socialstudies.org/standards/>.

SAMPLES OF STUDENT WORK

FIGURE 8.4: WHAT'S NEWS (STUDENT EXAMPLE)

Criteria for evaluation of student work:

- Gathers accurate and relevant information from local news resources
- Addresses all areas and questions noted on the news organizer
- Provides sufficient information for an overview of the issue

FIGURE 8.6: FINDING A FOCUS (STUDENT EXAMPLE)

Criteria for evaluation of student work:

- Collects accurate and relevant data from credible resources
- Addresses all areas and questions noted on the news organizer
- Provides sufficient information for an overview of the issue
- Clearly states personal opinion and backs it with accurate details that support decisions and conclusions

FIGURE 8.8: PIECING IT TOGETHER (STUDENT EXAMPLE)

Criteria for evaluation of student work:

- Provides adequate data to begin a deeper investigation
- Addresses all questions in the organizer
- Bases reflection on a careful analysis of information collected

FIGURE 8.10: DECIDING ON A PROJECT (STUDENT EXAMPLE)

Criteria for evaluation of student work:

- Poses activities that are relevant, feasible, and logical
- Presents information that addresses all required areas

FIGURES 8.12, 8.14, 8.16, AND 8.18: ACTION PLAN FOR SUCCESS, PARTS 1-4 (STUDENT EXAMPLES)

Criteria for evaluation of student work:

- Demonstrates an equitable sharing of responsibilities among all team members
- Bases decisions on analysis and synthesis of the information presented
- Produces a logical plan of action
- Identifies an activity that is feasible and related to the community's sustainable development

REFLECTION OF THE INSTRUCTORS

The geographic isolation of our state has created challenging economic and social situations for our unique island environment. A burgeoning population and the concomitant demands of growing urbanization have further taxed our limited natural resources. For these reasons, we have adopted the sustainability of the environment with a focus on the welfare of local communities as one of the themes for our school curriculum. Our academies often require service learning from their juniors and seniors to promote community awareness and civic engagement.

As library media specialists, we served in various roles throughout this project, e.g., lead teacher, information specialist, and volunteer. We worked with the teachers for several individual lessons and constantly partnered to assess students' progress, reinforce skills, and facilitate reflections. The teaming worked well as students were able to get more personalized attention and immediate feedback with the larger number of instructors.

Students chose topics that included marine debris, endangered native species, soil erosion, recycling, and water conservation. Groups sometimes joined together to implement their projects. For example, the group planning a beach clean-up worked with a group focusing on area reclamation. The groups merged their topics into a larger and longer event starting with cleaning the beach followed by activities to sustain the area's environment.

The teachers were forced to be flexible in planning and scheduling because of the range of projects and the skills needed to complete them. For instance, students required more planning time to develop an activity impacting sustainable development; consequently, two groups actually implemented their projects after the quarter ended. As a teaching team, we discovered that these types of projects might require adjustments to the project's timeline depending on the focus and the nature of the activity.

TEMPLATES AND RUBRICS FOR VARIOUS TASKS

Figure 8.3 What's News

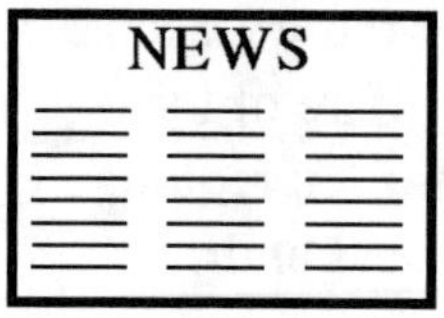

NEWS

Won't you be an informed neighbor? For the next three days view the local television news or read the local newspaper to find three issues impacting your community's people, economy, and environment. Identify and note the important information on each issue on the chart below.

	Story #1	Story #2	Story #3
Issue?			
Who?			
What?			
Where?			
When?			
Why?			

Figure 8.4 What's News (Student Example)

NEWS

Evaluation of student work: Sample exceeded the assessment criteria. The student did a good job of summarizing (1) the issues as well as their importance, (2) the agencies involved, and (3) information about the locations and timelines.

	Story #1	Story #2	Story #3
Issue?	Reforestation of the forest reserve	Marine debris from trash endangering animals	Greenhouse emissions bill
Who?	Department of Land and Natural Resources (DLNR)	National Oceanic and Atmospheric Administration, University of Hawaii, volunteers, fishing industry, public	Legislature, environmental groups, public
What?	The DLNR wants to clear debris from wildfire, fix roads damaged from firefighting, repair/install fences to keep animals out, and replant native trees/plants in destroyed area. They are requesting $2.64 million from the legislature.	Marine debris from littering, fishing nets, and cruise ships are harming and killing the fish, birds, animals, coral reefs, and even people. Scientists and volunteers are working to clean debris from the island beaches and waters.	The state legislature passed a bill to reduce greenhouse emissions that cause global warming. Bill gives money ($500,000) and focus to the problem. Hawaii is the second state to address the problem with laws.
Where?	Kula Forest Reserve on Maui.	Worldwide but on local beaches, Northwest Hawaiian Islands, oceans	Entire state
When?	The department would like to start as soon as possible. The clean up would begin in summer and continue until June 2009.	Daily. It is an ongoing battle.	Emissions to be reduced by 2020. Program will begin in 2008.
Why?	The hope is to create a native forest ecosystem. DLNR also wants to prevent massive erosion and clear and plant in burned areas before they grow back with invasive weeds and grasses.	Seven Asian nations that fish in islands don't take damaged nets back for repair but dump them in the ocean. This damages the reefs and entangles animals. Trash is eaten by animals that die from poisoning, starvation from trash in their bellies that clog their stomachs. Some animals are endangered.	The bill reduces emissions to stop global warming that cause worldwide problems. The bill is symbolic of Hawaii's commitment to the environment.

Figure 8.5 Finding a Focus

In order to bring deeper meaning and greater impact to a cause you must be knowledgeable and interested in the issue. Take time to look into possible issues that interest and motivate you. Select three issues in our community impacting the environment, economy, and people. Quickly research the who, what, when, where, why, and how for each of the topics. Based on the information collected, determine which issue might be the best to research in depth.

ISSUE #1:

WHO	WHAT	WHEN	WHERE	WHY

ISSUE #2:

WHO	WHAT	WHEN	WHERE	WHY

ISSUE #3:

WHO	WHAT	WHEN	WHERE	WHY

After critically looking at the data I've collected, I chose issue # ___ because:

Figure 8.6 Finding a Focus (Student Example)

Evaluation of student work: Sample met the assessment criteria. The student has identified critical issues and described each one with relevant information that provides an adequate overview of the different topics. He has also justified selection of an issue for further study.

ISSUE #1: Marine debris

WHO	WHAT	WHEN	WHERE	WHY
Public, National Oceanic and Atmospheric Administration	Trash in the ocean is damaging the environment (coral reefs, pollution) and animals (fish, turtles, seals, whales, birds).	Daily	Throughout the ocean, but the current brings a lot of debris to the center of the Pacific.	Fishing boats don't take back nets to repair but dump nets in the ocean.

ISSUE #2: Curbside recycling

WHO	WHAT	WHEN	WHERE	WHY
Public, city council, environmental groups	City wants to try island-wide curbside recycling again. There are no firm plans as to how it will be implemented.	July 2007	First tried in the Mililani community but failed due to high cost and low participation.	Landfills and trash are increasing with no solution.

ISSUE #3: Reduce greenhouse emission

WHO	WHAT	WHEN	WHERE	WHY
State, Sierra Club, public	A bill to lower greenhouse emissions to 1990 levels by 2020. It appropriates $500,000 for the next two years. It sets a limit on the amount of emissions in Hawaii.	Bill passed by the legislature. It needs to be signed by the Governor.	Entire state	To commit to addressing the global warming problem in Hawaii and the world. The bill is symbolic and Hawaii is the second state to pass such a bill.

After critically looking at the data I've collected, I chose issue # _1_ because I live near the beach and I see the trash littering the sand. I also go to the beach a lot and feel it's a valuable place for everyone. I can exercise, socialize with my friends, and relax there. It provides everyone with food, energy, beauty, recreation, and cool animals. Trash harms the ocean environment and its animals and plants. In turn, this hurts all of us. Ocean pollution and destruction of ecosystems must be stopped.

Figure 8.7 Piecing It Together

How does all the information fit together? Compile the information you've gathered. As each group member shares his or her information, organize your notes using the diagram below by identifying the main points for each of the areas. Examine the information to construct a personal response to the question in the box below.

Location/Area	History

Stakeholders	Key Concerns

Possible Solutions	Other

Is there sufficient information for me to become an "expert" on this topic? What are my next steps?

Figure 8.8 Piecing It Together (Student Example)

Evaluation of student work: Sample exceeded the assessment criteria. The student provided sufficient information to launch a deeper study. She completed all portions of this organizer with relevant information and provided a thoughtful reflection based on the information she had gathered.

Location/Area

Main Hawaiian Islands and Northwest Hawaiian Islands (NWHI). In 1909, T. Roosevelt designated several remote NWHI as a wildlife refuge.
Islands with big problems are French Frigate Shoals and South Point, Big Island. In the community, frequently used beaches, populated coastal areas, and fishing spots are affected. However, it is a worldwide problem.

History

Marine debris had always been a problem. Dumping land trash into the ocean was controlled internationally in 1973 (London Convention). In 1978, dumping from sea vessels was addressed. In 1987, the Environmental Protection Agency began monitoring storm drain and sewer run-offs. In 2006, Pres. Bush proclaimed the NWHI a national monument.

Stakeholders

Everyone around the world is affected, especially those along coastal areas. Locally, the Department of Land and Natural Resources and local environmental groups are working to prevent marine pollution and protect marine ecosystems. Visitors, hotels, beach users, recreational businesses, and fishermen are affected by ocean debris.

Key Concerns

o   Difficult to enforce violations
o   Danger to animals (disease, sickness, starvation, malnutrition)
o   Loss of coral reef habitats
o   Interference with navigation of ships
o   Economic impact to shipping, fishing, coastal business, tourism
o   Health concerns for humans from eating marine animals/plants, water pollution

Possible Solutions

o   Increased awareness campaigns with public and government
o   Stricter enforcement of punishment for violators at all levels
o   Government working with business/industries to prevent pollution
o   Clean ups of existing trash
o   Creation of more educational programs

Other

Marine debris is any man-made object discarded in the ocean. It can come from fishing boats, cargo ships, storm drain run-off, littering, and natural disasters. Most debris are plastics, glass, metals, and trash. Fishermen, beach goers, recreational businesses must be more diligent about their actions. More than 7,000 animal species are affected in the NWHI, at least 25% are native to Hawaii.

Is there sufficient information for me to become an "expert" on this topic? What are my next steps?
There is a lot of information on marine debris especially for the NWHI; but not as much on the main Hawaiian Islands. We must look for information on trash in our community. We found a local chapter of a national organization that focuses on the ocean that we can contact. We will also contact the Visitors' Bureau to find data about visitor numbers and visitor impact on the environment and economy. We are waiting for a call back from our community's city council member and state representative. We are trying to think of other possible ideas to address this problem.

Figure 8.9 Deciding on a Project

At this point, you've gained an understanding of an important issue concerning your community's sustainability. It's time to brainstorm possible activities to address this issue. Remember: little projects can have a big impact on those around you and can grow in time. Identify activities that are feasible given the time you have to complete the work, then decide which possibility will best fit your needs and have the greatest impact. In the chart below, brainstorm several activities and the steps needed to implement them. List the pros and cons for each one.

Possible Activity & Implementation Steps	Pros	Cons

Figure 8.10 Deciding on a Project (Student Example)

Evaluation of student work: Sample exceeded the assessment criteria. The activities listed are plausible and relevant. Steps are outlined. The pros and cons are clearly identified and articulated.

Possible Activity & Implementation Steps	Pros	Cons
Beach clean-up • Set location, time • Determine scope of clean-up • Supplies needed • Publicity	• Many beaches in nearby areas • Closer clean-up for volunteers • Familiar with area • Partner with local group	• Common, not a unique activity • Dependent on volunteers • Area selected needs to be easily accessible and safe
Storm Drain Cleaning /posting signs • Set area • Determine need for cleaning, posting signs • Permission of city • Supplies and volunteers • Publicity	• Not a common activity • Important to homeowners • Would prevent flooding • May require walking in neighborhood • No need to leave school area	• Can't enter storm drains • Need to get into drainage ditches or streams • Not as picturesque as beach • May be difficult to get volunteers since it's not a popular or familiar place
Education presentation to elementary or middle school • Find a school and teacher • Develop materials with teacher for appropriate age • Supplies • Publicity	• Cooperation with other schools in the neighborhood • Requires only a small group depending on project	• Coordination with teacher and principal • Need a simple topic • Setting up date and time may be difficult • Need to become familiar with learning level of children
Set up recycling program in community • Research what can be recycled • Set scope of area • Recruit help from volunteers, businesses • Publicity and permits	• Can be focused on our community • An issue people recognize • Items can be limited to specific ones	• Not everything can be recycled • Transporting to recycling plant may be hard • Need to be specific about what will be accepted • May require storage space
Coastal habitat restoration • Research habitat restoration in area • Contact National Oceanic & Atmospheric Administration office for information and partnership possibilities • Set scope of restoration • Supplies and volunteers • Publicity and permits	• Can form community partnership to expand scope of project and receive expert assistance • Unique project for students • Connected to topics studied in classes • Long-lasting impact • Can be a long-term class project	• Will need to coordinate with outside agency • Difficult to establish connections • May require lots of funding • Getting volunteers may be difficult • Might require more in-depth research • Can't be done in one day

Figure 8.11 Action Plan for Success, Part 1: Organizing the Team

Now that you are knowledgeable about the issue, devise a plan to tackle this problem. An action plan can get you organized and on your way. Work with your group members to plan your event or movement. Be as clear and detailed as possible. This will help you persuade others to join your efforts. Good luck!

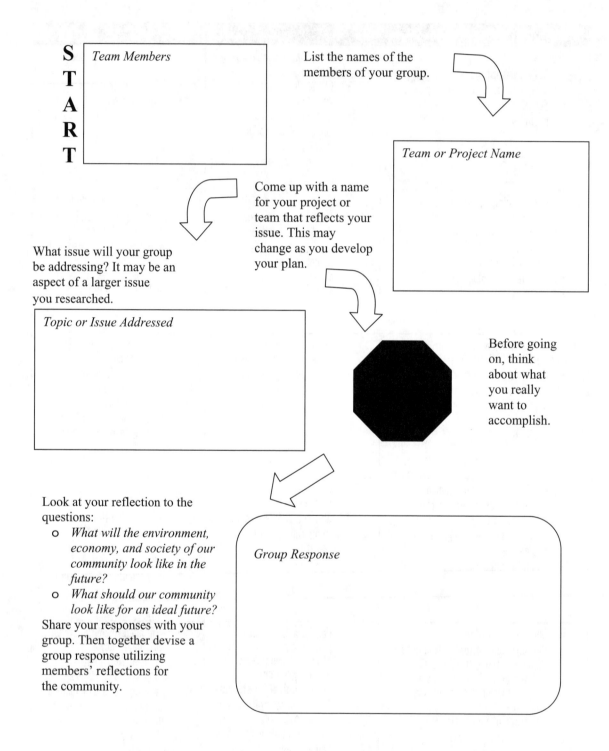

Figure 8.12 Action Plan for Success, Part 1: Organizing the Team (Student Example)

Evaluation of student work: The team met the assessment criteria. Members have focused on an issue and started to formulate a team response regarding the relevance of the beach restoration project.

**S
T
A
R
T**

Team Members
Joe Aloha
Pam Mahalo
Glenn Miyashiro
Sandy Birch

List the names of the members of your group.

Team or Project Name

Restoring the Beach

Come up with a name for your project or team that reflects your issue. This may change as you develop your plan.

What issue will your group be addressing? It may be an aspect of a larger issue you researched.

Topic or Issue Addressed
Land and sea pollution harms the marine environment, which impacts marine plants and animals, recreational ocean users, fisher folk, and visitors. Restoring the coastal environment encourages preservation of both land and ocean resources for future generations.

Before going on, think about what you really want to accomplish.

Look at your reflection to the questions:
  o *What will the environment, economy, and society of our community look like in the future?*
  o *What should our community look like for an ideal future?*
Share your responses with your group. Then together devise a group response utilizing members' reflections for the community.

Group Response
The people in our community will have a better quality of life if we work together to protect our environment for economic survival and the preservation of our cultural heritage. There will be open spaces and clean oceans for all to enjoy. By conserving our environment, we also positively affect the economy of our state.

Figure 8.13 Action Plan for Success, Part 2: Selecting an Activity

Now that you have brainstormed activities it's time to select one to implement. You will need the list of possibilities that your group originally brainstormed. Consider which project might be most feasible, effective, and relevant to address your chosen issue. Carefully assess each activity and analyze its pros and cons in order to make a group decision.

Our group decided the best project in the given time frame would be:

This is the best project because:

Our tentative steps to implement this project are:

We will know if our project is successful if:

Evaluation of student work: The team exceeded the assessment criteria. They were able to provide a sound rationale for undertaking this activity, outline critical steps to implement the activity, and articulate strategies to assess the effectiveness of their work and the outcome of the activity.

Our group decided the best project in the given time frame would be:
Restoring the beach

This is the best project because:
Many of our students are avid beach users. Several of our classmates work in the visitor industry, which is impacted by the marine debris on the beach. A littered beach negatively influences tourism and food resources for restaurants. Importantly, it endangers the marine life. We plan to do this project during February on the south shore of Oahu. This will fall within the project's timeline and still give us at least three months to plan, especially over the school break. If our plan is successful, it will generate enough interest and support among community members and students that it might become a sustainable event.

We plan to solicit support from businesses and community leaders to restore the beach. We will need the assistance of an organization like the National Oceanic and Atmospheric Administration (NOAA). This type of partnership will allow for more participation from all stakeholders in the community. In turn, such a project will touch more citizens, impact a larger area, and lighten the workload for individuals.

Our tentative steps to implement this project are:
- Set our goals and objectives
- Contact local organizations for support and participation in the event
- Research and designate an area for clean-up
- Establish a tentative start date
- Research other local projects similar to this one
- Research need for any permits necessary for event
- Research any possible health hazards and ways to prevent them
- Estimate the number of volunteers needed and how to organize and schedule them
- Estimate the supplies needed for the clean up
- Create a plan to effectively dispose of the waste collected
- Publicize event to create excitement, awareness, and recruit volunteers
- Clean and restore!
- Evaluate success of project
- Create means to sustain the project and continued restoration in the impacted area

We will know if our project is successful if:
- We can obtain the assistance of outside agencies
- We can gain support from community groups in terms of volunteers and supplies
- We can create a plan that works
- We can actually have the restoration done
- We can sustain the restoration and adopt it as a long-term school project

Figure 8.15 Action Plan for Success, Part 3: Designing the Activity

You are ready to design the activities needed to meet your objectives. List the tasks and the roles and responsibilities for each activity or task. Also decide on the location and time of the event, then complete this section by establishing a timeline for each activity. Add more sheets if necessary.

Tasks	Who	When	Where	Notes

Figure 8.16 Action Plan for Success, Part 3: Designing the Activity (Student Example)

Evaluation of student work: The team exceeded the assessment criteria. Their plan shows that they will use a range of critical resources. They are sharing responsibilities. They recognize the importance of starting immediately to get their project underway.

Tasks	Who	When	Where	Notes
Research other local restoration projects Contact people who took part in them	Glenn Joe	As soon as possible	Check the local papers, ask science teachers, search the Internet (check NOAA Web site or University of Hawaii)	
Contact possible local environmental organizations for information and assistance	Sandy Pam	As soon as possible	Check phone books, local newspapers, Internet, ask biology teacher	Ms. G volunteers with the Nature Conservancy (ask her) Mr. W worked with the university on a bird tagging project
Find out if we need permits and if we do, how to obtain them	Sandy	After talking to environmental groups	Ask local officials and groups who have done similar projects	
Find a location near the school for the restoration project Find out more specifics about what we can do	Pam Glenn	After talking to environmental groups	Ask local groups Speak to teachers and librarians	If a nearby site is not possible, can we go elsewhere? Or can we assist with a project developed by a local group?
List and estimate necessary supplies and equipment needed for restoration	Joe	As soon as possible	Ask local groups Check library resources on coastal plants and community Interview a scientist	Cost may be high; the project might need to be scaled down Might need to get sponsors

Figure 8.17 Action Plan for Success, Part 4: Budget and Supplies

For the activity you are planning, what supplies will you need? Decide what is needed. Then determine if it is owned or must be borrowed or purchased. List where the item can be found and when it is needed.

Item	Qty	Where to obtain	Who obtains	Estimated cost	When needed

Estimated Total:

Figure 8.18 Action Plan for Success, Part 4: Budget and Supplies (Student Example)

Evaluation of student work: The team exceeded the assessment criteria. They prepared a comprehensive list of items needed. They have done their homework regarding how to acquire the items, who will be responsible for the acquisition, and how much needs to be budgeted for this activity.

Item	Qty	Where to obtain	Who obtains	Estimated cost	When needed
Paper for publicity: colored and white	1 pack each	Office supply store	Pam	$20	ASAP — need to start advertising
Gardening supplies: shovels, picks, weeders, water cans	Depends on # of volunteers	Agriculture Department Parents, volunteers can bring their own	Glenn	Borrow	Two days before event
Refreshments: water and snacks	Depends on # of volunteers	Area businesses	Sandy	Donations	Pick up day before or day of event
Garbage bags, plastic gloves	40 bags 100+ pairs of gloves	Warehouse donations	Pam	$25	Pick up at least one day before event
Coastal plants	As many as possible	University Agriculture Program, Sierra Club	Pam Glenn	Obtain donations	Pick up day of or before event
Coolers and ice for refreshments	4 coolers	Athletics (2) Joe (1) Sandy (1)	Sandy	Free	Day of event, arrange with Athletics to get ice from snack bar
Tents or coverings for shade	4-6 tents	Athletics (2) Mrs. G (1) Mr. K (1) Others?	Joe	Free	Day of event
Tables	3 tables	Sandy's mom (2) Pam's uncle (1)	Joe	Free	Day of event
Stamps	100 stamps	Post office	Sandy	$39	Right away for donation letters, thank you's

Estimated Total: $185

Figure 8.19 Presentation Rubric

Criteria	Exceeds (3)	Meets (2)	Approaches (1)	Score
Coverage	Provides all necessary background information. Displays extensive knowledge. Answers all class questions with explanations and elaboration.	Provides most of background information. Answers most questions but lacks elaboration on some of them.	Provides sketchy information. Appears uncomfortable with questions and able to answer only rudimentary questions.	
Organization	Presents all information in a logical and interesting manner. Ideas flow clearly from one point to the next.	Presents most of the information in a logical sequence. Has a satisfactory organization but needs better transitions.	Has a vague thesis. Presents most of the information in a disjointed fashion that does not flow logically.	
Content	Presents an abundance of information clearly related to topic. Includes clear details and examples that support the overall message.	Presents sufficient information that relates to topic. Some details and examples could be better connected to overall message.	Thesis is not clear. Provides information that does not support the thesis.	
Sources	Uses and cites a variety of print and online sources.	Uses a limited number of resources. Most references are correctly cited.	Uses only 1 or 2 resources. References are not correctly cited.	
Grammar, usage and mechanics	No errors found.	Has minimal errors in a few areas.	Has numerous errors in many areas.	
Delivery	Speaks directly and clearly throughout presentation. Does not rely on notes.	Speaks directly and clearly through most of the presentation. Relies infrequently to notes.	Does not speak directly or clearly through most of the presentation. Relies heavily on notes.	
			Total	

Rubric Scoring Guide:

Exceeded the standards	16 to 18 points
Met the standards	12 to 15 points
Approaching the standards	6 to 11 points
Not met	5 points and below

Lei of A.L.O.H.A.: An Appreciation of Cultures

Authors' Note: The themes of conflict resolution, tolerance, and acceptance of individual differences are universal. Although this unit utilizes Native Hawaiian icons and references, it can be effectively adapted to other ethnic cultures including Hispanic-American, Native-American, African-American, Middle Eastern-American, European-American, and Asian-American groups. We invite readers to modify examples to make lessons relevant for their student populations.

COURSE: Social Studies, Guidance and Counseling
GRADES: 9-12
DURATION OF PROJECT: Two weeks
STUDENT OUTCOMES
CONTENT GOALS:
Students will demonstrate an understanding of multicultural differences and their contributions to the "Hawaiian culture" by:

- Identifying, defining, and analyzing cultural characteristics.
- Presenting data on the societal impact of immigration.
- Discussing and sharing different ethnic traditions and cultural practices.
- Discovering connections with other cultures to appreciate how diversity enriches our communities.

PROCESS GOALS:
Students will develop information literacy skills needed to foster complex and higher-order thinking.

DESCRIPTION OF PRODUCT OR PERFORMANCE

Recent changes in the demographics of high school populations have had a tremendous impact on students' social behaviors. Cliques, fighting, and problems originating from *My Space* have been traced back to misunderstandings resulting from culture shock. These problems stem from students not being aware of cultural differences and not knowing how different ethnic groups contribute to the success of a community. In this project, students will identify and study how different ethnic groups shape the multicultural tradition that defines

Hawaii today. By undertaking this project, we hope to sensitize students to the human values of tolerance, cooperation, respect, and kindness. Students will be responsible for:

- Gathering, analyzing, and presenting information on different cultures.
- Determining the cultural and historical impacts of immigration on contemporary American society.
- Creating a scrapbook anthology of journal entries and artifacts to showcase unique personal histories and connections to ethnic and cultural roots.
- Participating in a culminating discussion and problem-solving exercise that results in suggestions for resolving conflicts, building character, overcoming differences, and accepting other cultures.

CONNECTION WITH STANDARDS

Standards from Language Arts, Guidance and Counseling, Social Studies, Technology, and Information Literacy are integrated in this project.

LANGUAGE ARTS

Standards addressed in this unit deal with using language to communicate with various audiences, employing a range of writing strategies, applying language conventions, and conducting research using a variety of informational and technological resources. For more detailed information on the standards refer to <http://www.ncte.org/about/over/standards/110846.htm>.

GUIDANCE AND COUNSELING

Standards addressed in this unit encourage the acquisition of attitudes, knowledge, and interpersonal skills to help students understand and respect self and others; contribute to effective learning in school and beyond. For more detailed information on the standards refer to <http://www.schoolcounselor.org/files/NationalStandards.pdf>.

SOCIAL STUDIES

Standards addressed in this unit focus on specific skills within broad thematic standards that deal with culture, individual development, and identity; individuals, groups and institutions; and global connections. For more detailed information on the standards refer to <http://www.socialstudies.org/standards/>.

TECHNOLOGY

Standards addressed in this unit deal with basic operations and concepts; social, ethical, and human issues; technology productivity tools; and technology tools for communication and research. For more detailed information on the standards refer to <http://cnets.iste.org/students/s_stands.html>.

INFORMATION LITERACY

Standards addressed in this unit focus on the access, evaluation, and use of information; appreciation for all forms of creative expression; development of self-reflection skills in knowledge acquisition; and social responsibility in dealing with information. For more detailed information on the standards refer to <http://www.ala.org/ala/aasl/aaslproftools/informationpower/InformationLiteracyStandards_final.pdf>.

OVERARCHING PROJECT QUESTIONS

- How have conflicts among students impacted the general school climate?
- What causes these conflicts on campus?
- How have these conflicts affected you and your personal learning environment?
- How can students from many different cultural backgrounds coexist harmoniously?
- How do our ethnic and family backgrounds contribute to our individual uniqueness?
- How do different cultural practices enrich our lives?
- What elements of "local Hawaiian culture" have you and your family adopted that have originated from other ethnic groups?
- How can we better understand and accept perceived cultural differences within our school community?

TIMELINE FOR PROJECT

Figure 9.1 Project Timeline

Time	Instructor's Tasks (LMS/T)	Student's Performance Tasks
Day 1	**CONNECT** • Discuss the school's present situation regarding the rise in social conflicts. Cite examples and data taken from recent discipline reports/statistics. (T)	**CONNECT** • Discuss incidents that have occurred on campus. — How have conflicts among students impacted the general school climate? — How have these conflicts affected you and your learning environment?
Days 1-2	**WONDER** • Brainstorm possible reasons for conflicts on campus. Focus on the following areas of discussion: — Changes in school demographics — Cliques and socialization problems — Ethical use of technology (T)	**WONDER** • Create a list of possible reasons for disputes. Compile the class response to the following: — What causes these conflicts on campus?

continued

Time	Instructor's Tasks (LMS/T)	Student's Performance Tasks

Day 2	**CONNECT**
	• Identify common ideas that have been generated from the list. Categorize them under "problem" topic headings. Some suggestions include:
	  — Intolerance
	  — Miscommunication or communication breakdown
	  — Ethnic/individual differences
	  — Ignorance
	  — Teen issues (T)
	• Focus on ethnic/individual differences as the focal point for discussion. Emphasize that according to school investigations and survey results, a majority of disputes are rooted in misunderstanding among and ignorance of different cultures. (T)
		CONNECT
		• Categorize responses under common topic headings. Create connections to determine root causes for campus disputes and possible remedies. Discuss:
		  — How can students from many different cultural backgrounds coexist harmoniously?
		• Share your ethnicity and culture within small groups. While getting familiar with team members, concentrate discussion on the following driving question:
		  — How do our ethnic and family backgrounds contribute to our individual uniqueness?

Day 3	**INVESTIGATE** • Introduce different print and online resources. Reinforce the use of the library's online public access catalog, e-books, and online reference subscriptions. (LMS)	**INVESTIGATE** • Complete a mini-research assignment. The goal is to find and share important discoveries regarding your ethnic roots. • Locate at least three key contributions originating from your country of study. • Preface your findings with "Did you know...?" Facts can include but are not limited to science, technology, history, sociology, and politics.
Day 4	**CONSTRUCT/EXPRESS** • Compile results that students share in a matrix. (T/LMS) • List each of the ethnicities that students represent and record the facts that they have located through their research. (T/LMS) • End with a comprehensive visual representing the range of the class's ethnic origins. (T/LMS)	**CONSTRUCT/EXPRESS** • Present three bits of information that you collected through research. • Contribute findings to the ethnicity matrix.
	CONNECT • Share how sugar and pineapple plantations in nineteenth and early twentieth century Hawaii influenced the multicultural mix of this state. (LMS) • Explain how more contemporary waves of immigrants have contributed to an increasingly diverse state population. (LMS) • Link this history to the uniqueness of Hawaii's culture. (LMS) • Emphasize that as new ethnicities bring their cultures to the islands, aspects of each become blended and accepted as part of the local tradition. (LMS)	**CONNECT** • Brainstorm how each individual culture listed on the matrix has contributed to the "Hawaiian Culture." List individual ideas down in preparation for the journaling activity to follow. • Look over the *Hawaiian Symbology* handout to read about examples of icons that have been contributed by other cultures. (See Figure 9.3)

continued

Time	Instructor's Tasks (LMS/T)	Student's Performance Tasks
Day 5	**INVESTIGATION** • Introduce primary resources. Focus on the characteristics that define a resource as "primary" and provide examples of different genres that can be used. (LMS)	**INVESTIGATION** • Create a list of potential primary resources that can be used in the scrapbook project to follow. Check to see that the items listed fall within the parameters of "primary resources" and that they will be useful in your research.
	CONSTRUCT/EXPRESS • Introduce the scrapbook project. Explain the overall purpose of the assignment, i.e., to produce an increased awareness of each of our cultures, traditions, and values. (T) • Teach journaling techniques. Stress the importance of including details, analysis, and thoughtful reflection. (T/LMS)	**CONSTRUCT/EXPRESS** • Complete the *Journaling Your Heritage* worksheet. (See Figure 9.4) Respond to all prompts and driving questions. • Remember to include a list of primary resources that will be used to illustrate key points. The following queries should be addressed in the entries: — How do different cultural practices enrich our lives? — What elements of Hawaiian culture have you and your family adopted that have originated from other ethnic groups?
Days 6-7	**CONSTRUCT/EXPRESS** • Invite a guest speaker who is a scrapbook expert. Demonstrate effective page layout techniques and craft skills that can be creatively used to highlight information being presented. (LMS) • Teach technology skills needed to construct the scrapbook. Include instruction in digital photography, scanning, word processing, and the use of publishing software. (T/LMS)	**CONSTRUCT/EXPRESS** • Create scrapbook pages that include information gleaned from the journaling worksheet and the collection of primary resources. • Using the techniques introduced by the guest speaker and through the technology workshop, compose pages that address the driving questions and meet the goals of the project.
Day 8	**REFLECT** • Have students share their completed scrapbooks. (T/LMS) • Have students present their responses to each of the driving questions as they share the projects. (T/LMS)	**REFLECT** • Share scrapbooks with classmates. • Create a list of new information that you are learning regarding the ethnicity, culture, traditions, and values of different cultures as you listen to the projects being presented. • Debrief as a class, discussing all of the projects presented. Add new information collected to the ethnic matrix begun at the onset of the unit.
Day 9	**WONDER** • Looking over the matrix that the class has created, note the large range of ethnicities and cultures represented. (T/LMS) • Revisit the initial problem raised regarding misunderstandings related to ethnic/individual differences. (T/LMS)	**WONDER** • Knowing it takes more than understanding the differences in cultures for acceptance of others to occur, suggest ideas for character education. • Use *The True Meaning of A.L.O.H.A.* worksheet to contribute ideas for each of the behavior elements. (See Figure 9.7). Ideas should address the following driving question: — How can we better understand and accept perceived cultural differences within our school community?
	CONSTRUCT/EXPRESS • Construct the "Lei of A.L.O.H.A." using the suggestions contributed by each of the students. (T/LMS)	**CONSTRUCT/EXPRESS** • Create flowers using the *Lei of A.L.O.H.A.* template. (See Figure 9.9) • List each idea on a separate flower, labeling it with the area it addresses and the suggestion for actions by classmates. • Place each blossom on the "Lei of A.L.O.H.A." template posted in the classroom. • Discuss the completed lei. Reflect on how each student can contribute towards making the lei a reality through daily practice.

ASSESSMENT CHECKPOINTS

Figure 9.2 Project Assessment Plan

Checkpoints in the process	What is assessed	Who assesses	Assessment tool
Connect	Student participation and content understanding	Teacher Library media specialist Student	Observation Group discussion
Wonder	Higher-order thinking and ability to make connections to prior experiences	Teacher Student	Group discussion *True Meaning of A.L.O.H.A.* graphic organizer (See Figure 9.7) Journal entry
Investigate	Information retrieval and the efficient and effective use of resource materials	Library media specialist Student	Mini-library research Collection of primary sources Observation Consultation
Construct/Express	Evaluation, synthesis, and presentation of findings in a clear manner	Teacher Library media specialist Student	*Journaling your Heritage* (See Figure 9.4) Scrapbook Lei of A.L.O.H.A. activity Observation
Reflect	Assessment and evaluation of personal progress and modifications for continued improvement	Teachers Library media specialist Student	Self-reflection *Scrapbook Rubric* (See Figure 9.6) Lei of A.L.O.H.A. class discussion Observation Group discussion

RESOURCES USED IN THE PROJECT

Danico, Mary Yu. *The 1.5 Generation: Becoming Korean American in Hawaii.* Honolulu: University of Hawaii Press, 2004.

Dorrance, William H., and Francis S. Morgan. *Sugar Islands.* Honolulu: Mutual Publishing, 2000.

James, Robert. *What Is This Thing Called Aloha.* Waipahu: Island Heritage, 2002.

Massey, Brent. *Culture Shock! A Survival Guide to Customs and Etiquette.* Tarrytown: Marshall Cavendish, 2006.

Namkoong, Joan. *Family Traditions in Hawaii: Birthday, Marriage, Funeral and Cultural Customs in Hawaii.* Honolulu: Bess Press, 1994, 2004.

Nordyke, Eleanor C. *The Peopling of Hawaii.* 2nd ed. Honolulu: University of Hawaii Press, 1989.

Ogawa, Dennis M. *Jan Ken Po: The World of Hawaii's Japanese Americans.* Honolulu: University of Hawaii Press, 1973.

Provenzano, Renata. *A Little Book of Aloha: Hawaiian Proverbs and Inspirational Wisdom.* Honolulu: Mutual Publishing, 2001.

Rayson, Ann. *Modern History of Hawaii.* Honolulu: Bess Press, 2004.

Ronck, Ronn (Ed.). *Firsts and Almost Firsts in Hawaii.* Honolulu: University of Hawaii Press, 1995.

Takaki, Ronald. *Pau Hana: Plantation Life and Labor in Hawaii 1835-1920.* Honolulu: University of Hawaii Press, 1983.

STANDARDS CITED

American Association of School Librarians, and the Association for Educational Communications and Technology. *Information Literacy Standards for Student Learning.* Chicago: American Library Association, 1998. 2 Aug. 2007 <http://www.ala.org/ala/aasl/aaslproftools/informationpower/InformationLiteracyStandards_final.pdf>.

American School Counselor Association. *ASCA National Standards for Students.* Alexandria: American School Counselor Association, 2004. 12 Aug. 2007 <http://www.schoolcounselor.org/files/NationalStandards.pdf>.

International Society for Technology in Education. *National Educational Technology Standards: The Next Generation. National Educational Technology Standards for Students.* Washington, DC: Author, 2007. 2 Aug. 2007 <http://cnets.iste.org/students/s_stands.html>.

The National Council of Teachers of English, and International Reading Association. *Standards for the English Language Arts.* Urbana: International Reading Association, 1996. 2 Aug. 2007 <http://www.ncte.org/about/over/standards/110846.htm>.

Task Force of the National Council for the Social Studies. *The Curriculum Standards for Social Studies.* Silver Spring: National Council for the Social Studies, 1994. 2 Aug. 2007 <http://www.socialstudies.org/standards/>.

SAMPLES OF STUDENT WORK

FIGURE 9.5: JOURNALING YOUR HERITAGE (STUDENT EXAMPLE)

Criteria for evaluation of student work:

- Collects accurate and relevant information from the interview
- Gathers additional relevant data from the research
- Uses primary sources appropriately
- Addresses all components of the scrapbook planning sheet
- Effectively communicates information for classmates to understand a particular ethnic culture and heritage

FIGURE 9.8: THE TRUE MEANING OF A.L.O.H.A. (STUDENT EXAMPLE)

Criteria for evaluation of student work:

- Provides responses that represent all of the attributes linked to the term A.L.O.H.A.
- Identifies actions that are thoughtful and reasonable for students to perform
- Addresses all the elements of A.L.O.H.A. on the planning sheet
- Presents suggestions to promote positive relationships

REFLECTION OF THE INSTRUCTORS

As library media specialists, we were truly challenged to help the teachers develop a unit that addressed the needs of the school community. Character education was not only an unusual subject for collaboration; it was uncharted territory. Thinking outside of the box, we suggested a creative outlet for this project: a personal scrapbook and a Lei of A.L.O.H.A. as culminating activities. The team was able to teach the value of conflict resolution by engaging the students in these personally relevant tasks.

From all accounts, students were very motivated and responsive to this unit because they connected with the activities and realized its link to a real issue, i.e., conflicts in school. They engaged in open and candid communication and developed critical skills in dialoging with classmates to promote a collegial atmosphere built on trust and understanding.

We have used ideas from this project to teach other students the use of primary sources. We have also incorporated character education and cultural tolerance in other subject areas. By having students design and create a personal scrapbook, we capitalize on each student's unique abilities and talents. If time is short, in lieu of creating the scrapbook we have the students compose short biographies with historical artifacts (links to ethnicity or family) and share them in small groups or with the entire class. A caveat: when we did a shortened version of this unit, students didn't spend enough time with primary resources. Consequently, they didn't fully understand the value of using them in subsequent work.

Although this specific project uses Hawaiian icons and references to local history, it can be adapted for use elsewhere. Teaching teams can substitute icons and symbology from their own regions. No matter what examples are used, the message of Aloha can be used to bridge differences and create understanding.

TEMPLATES AND RUBRICS FOR VARIOUS TASKS

Figure 9.3 Hawaiian Symbology

Note: Hawaiian symbology refers to Island icons contributed by other cultures

The Hawaiian Aloha Shirt

Known as one of the "visual symbols" of Hawaii, the Aloha shirt originated in the 1930s. Although the exact maker is not known, historically many say that immigrant Japanese tailors created the first shirts.

In 1947, the City and County of Honolulu encouraged its workers to wear Hawaiian attire between June and October as a way to beat the summer heat. The original designs were made from silk or cotton and often had floral patterns with coconut shell buttons. Over the years, the market has changed and shirts are now produced in brighter hues and bolder designs (e.g., hula girls and surfers). The Aloha shirt gained popularity as tourism grew in the islands in the 1960s. It is now a sought after souvenir among visitors and an integral part of island attire for local folk.

The Macadamia Nut

Although commonly linked to Hawaii, immigrants first introduced macadamia nuts to the islands in 1881 from Australia. These plants were mainly used as part of a reforestation project to prevent erosion.

The nuts were not commercially planted until 1921. Many farms were established on the islands of Oahu and the Big Island (Hawaii). Nuts were shelled, roasted, salted, bottled, and marketed.

Chocolate covered macadamia nut candies became popular a few years later. By the middle of the 1930s, sales of the confections skyrocketed and they became a time honored "gift of aloha." Today, boxes of this delicious Hawaiian treat can be found in grocery aisles around the world.

Figure 9.4 Journaling Your Heritage

 Each one of us is unique. We are characterized by the environment in which we have been raised and by the people who have influenced our upbringing. Members of our family help to shape our cultural practices, beliefs, and values. Many of them continue to practice customs dating back many generations. If you can trace your roots to ancestors both in this country and from your country of origin, you will discover a personal history rich in traditions that are still followed today.

We all have a story to tell. Let's share these experiences with one another so that we may appreciate one another's unique ethnic heritages. Respond to the following driving questions utilizing journaling techniques. Remember to address each of the queries in its entirety. Include as many details as possible and provide concrete details to answer the five W's (who, what, when, where, and why). To support each of your entries, also list available primary sources that help to illustrate your points (e.g., photographs, maps, artifacts, newspaper articles, diary entries, letters, audio/video recordings, oral histories, postcards). The completed sheet will provide you with valuable content for your scrapbook.

What is your ethnic background? Which ethnic group do you strongly identify with?

How does your ethnic and family background contribute to your individual uniqueness?

Looking at the members who comprise your family tree, profile one of your earliest ancestors. Include information regarding ethnicity, dates of birth/death, profession, interests, accomplishments, and adventures. Include a list of related primary resources and their historical importance.

How did this relation make an impact on you and the outcome of your ancestral heritage?

What factors led your ancestors to immigrate to the United States? Why did they choose to settle in Hawaii?

Are there any cultural practices/traditions that are still observed by you and your family? Describe them and provide primary resources that will further illustrate your observances.

How do these cultural practices enrich your life?

Which elements of the "Hawaiian Culture" have you and your family adopted? Which ethnic groups did they originate from?

Figure 9.5 Journaling Your Heritage (Student Example)

Evaluation of student work: This example demonstrates all of the requirements for this assignment. The data collected and interpreted show in-depth reflection. Information is complete and all prompts within the journaling sheet have been addressed. Student's work exhibits a clear understanding of primary resources and the historical value of the cultural information being presented.

What is your ethnic background? Which ethnic group do you strongly identify with?

I am Caucasian. My family is made up of so many different races that no one is 100% sure of all of them. My best guess is that I am of English, German, and Scandinavian descent.

How does your ethnic and family background contribute to your uniqueness?

I come from a close-knit family. Our ethnic culture plays a strong role in this. There are many traditions that we observe. We celebrate holidays, birthdays, and anniversaries together. Church has also played a strong role in my upbringing. We are Catholics. On both sides of my family we follow the same religion and have for at least three generations. My parents are both working professionals. My father is an accountant while my mother is a nurse. They are both college graduates, and due to this, our family strongly believes that education is an important part of our lives. Because of this I work hard and try to excel in all of my coursework and serve as a member of the science club. My grandfather played Lacrosse and my father is a soccer coach. I am a goalie and a golfer. I am a member of our school's soccer team and attend practice every day. These are all national sports played in England. I think the love of these sports is in our blood.

Create a profile of one of your earliest ancestors. Include information regarding ethnicity, dates of birth/death, profession, interests, accomplishments, and adventures. Include a list of related primary resources and their historical importance.

I would like to profile my great-great grandfather. He was born in London, England, on August 8, 1899. He was a sailor and worked for a shipping company transporting cargo from England to countries around the world. His interests included whittling and magic. According to his ship journals he would entertain his crew with "sleight of hand" tricks. It was something that he did to make long journeys at sea enjoyable. He was also a musician. He was a master of the harmonica. One of the most interesting tales that he told us was his encounter with pirates. While sailing to Asia his crew ran into a ship that attempted to commandeer their vessel. The crew had to fight to keep the pirates from boarding and stealing their cargo. They managed to shoot at the invaders and with full sails billowing, outran their assailants. Primary sources I used: picture of great-great grandfather, sailor's compass/sextant, harmonica, and ship's journal.

How did this ancestor affect your life today?

My great-great grandfather was a strong man and a hard worker. He served as a cabin boy and after dedicated years of service became captain of his own vessel. His adventures are logged in his personal journals and the logs show that he was truly a "man of the sea." His love of travel was deep rooted and I believe it is something I have in common with him. He married several times and his wives were from different countries that he visited on his travels. Therefore, I have relatives scattered throughout the globe.

Why did your ancestors immigrate to the U.S.? Why did they settle in Hawaii?

My great-great grandfather immigrated to America when he retired from the shipping business. Although he gave up his commission as captain, he was offered a position in Massachusetts as a shipping administrator. He moved and started his second career there. The move to Hawaii did not happen until my generation. My father is a retired army officer. When he decommissioned from military service, we decided to move to Hawaii. We were tired of the snow and unpredictable climates that we had experienced throughout our lives. My dad decided that Hawaii would be a much more inviting environment to live in.

Are there any cultural practices/traditions that you still observe? Describe them and provide primary resources that provide more details.

We celebrate various English traditions that have been passed down through the generations. We enjoy the food associated with England. For dinner we commonly have Shepherd's Pie. It's made from a recipe that has been in our family for at least three generations. On Saturdays, we observe time for tea. Together we create delicious finger sandwiches and scones. At Christmas my mom bakes and decorates a Yule log. We all join dad around the piano and sing carols.

Primary resources: Shepherd's Pie recipe, picture of our family at tea, Christmas carol music sheets (English origin).

Which elements of the "Hawaiian Culture" have you and your family adopted? Which ethnic groups did they originate from?

Living in Hawaii we have been exposed to many different cultures. Our family has adopted hula and Hawaiian food. My sister is a member of the local hula troop (halau) and has been dancing for many years. Whenever we have a chance we order Hawaiian foods such as pork laulau and lomi salmon. In the summer we often go to the local Bon Dances. This is a Buddhist tradition that celebrates a memorial for the dead. These festivities include hours of dancing to taiko drums and Japanese music. Every February we also observe Chinese New Year. We take a trip to Chinatown and watch the lion dances. We feed the "lions" money wrapped in red paper for good luck. We eat dim sum pastries, jai soup, and almond cookies.

Figure 9.6 Scrapbook Rubric

Criteria	Exceeds (3)	Meets (2)	Approaches (1)	Score
Individual characteristics and ethnic heritage connections	Effectively introduces students and their unique characteristics to their peers. Includes references to ethnic heritage, culture, and values that reflect the shaping of character and upbringing.	Introduces students to the class but does not fully reflect their individual qualities and characteristics. Makes ethnic heritage connections but the impact on upbringing is not always clear.	Does not introduce student's unique individual qualities and characteristics to their peers. Makes no connections to ethnic heritage or student's upbringing.	
Effective use of primary resources	Uses a range of primary sources to support all connections to ethnicity. Clearly analyzes and interprets all information for peers.	Uses primary sources to support most connections to ethnicity. Clearly analyzes and interprets most information for peers.	Uses few or no primary sources to support connections to ethnicity. Consistently unclear in analysis and interpretation of information for peers.	
Journaling	Consistently produces clear and thoughtful reflections. All points communicate the importance of ethnic cultures and values. Writing is grammatically correct.	Produces clear responses but a few lack in-depth reflection. Most points communicate the importance of ethnic cultures and values. Some of the writing needs further editing.	Produces responses that are not clear and lack depth. Few points communicate the importance of ethnic cultures and values. Most of the writing needs further editing.	
Layout and construction	Entire scrapbook is well organized and clearly presents ethnic connections or evidence. Pages are attractively designed and chronologically organized. They neatly showcase primary resources.	Most of the scrapbook is well organized although some pages do not effectively present ethnic connections or evidence. Most pages are in chronological order and effectively showcase primary sources.	Scrapbook is disorganized, incomplete. It lacks ethnic connections. Pages are not in chronological order. They lack primary sources.	
			Total	

Rubric Scoring Guide:

Exceeded the standards	10 to 12 points
Met the standards	7 to 9 points
Approaching the standards	4 to 6 points
Not met	3 points and below

Figure 9.7 The True Meaning of A.L.O.H.A.

Getting along with others is a skill that is not normally taught but acquired through experience as we interact with different people. Our success is measured through effectively building relationships and practicing social etiquette. Ultimately, friendships we develop have an impact on our personal growth, careers, support networks, and effective functioning in our daily lives. Knowing others and respecting our differences is just the first step in establishing acquaintances; it takes additional qualities to develop these bonds into valuable associations.

The Hawaiian word aloha is commonly defined as hello and goodbye. However, if you examine its true definition, aloha has additional meanings including love, compassion, mercy, and empathy. It is a term that embodies the Hawaiian culture and values. Since it is easily remembered, let's use it as an acronym to stand for critical personal qualities that we should demonstrate when interacting with others. For each of the Hawaiian terms below, list actions that you might perform to establish respectful and caring relationships with your classmates. List at least three points for each term.

Aulike To be kind	
Laulima To cooperate	
Olu olu To be polite	
Huikala To forgive all faults	
Ahonui To be tolerant	

Figure 9.8 The True Meaning of A.L.O.H.A. (Student Example)

Evaluation of Student Work: Sample exceeds the criteria. The student has thoughtfully reflected on the elements that make up the word aloha. She has provided at least three samples of actions that can be easily performed to demonstrate the qualities listed and promote the effective building of relationships.

Aulike To be kind	⚬ Help others who are in need. Assistance can be in the form of physical actions, donated goods, or words of encouragement. ⚬ Befriend new students on campus and take the time to show them around. ⚬ Be considerate of other people's feelings.
Laulima To cooperate	⚬ Work together in teams and share responsibilities evenly. ⚬ Be willing to work with new people. ⚬ Keep open lines of communication when working with others.
Olu olu To be polite	⚬ Always use words such as "please" and "thank you" to ask for help and express gratitude. ⚬ Take the time to smile and greet others. ⚬ Be aware of tone of voice and how your message is being conveyed when speaking. Also be careful when using email; avoid flaming and shouting at others (all caps).
Huikala To forgive all faults	⚬ People make mistakes; we must remember that not everyone is perfect. ⚬ When in error, admit your shortcomings and don't forget to apologize. ⚬ We each have different personalities and qualities. Weaknesses should never be the basis for judging another person.
Ahonui To be tolerant	⚬ People learn at different rates. We must be patient with those who need more time to grasp concepts. ⚬ Completing a project takes time. Rushing or pushing your teammates beyond their capability should never be an option. ⚬ Accept individual differences. A mature person is tolerant of differences among people.

Figure 9.9 Lei of A.L.O.H.A.

Every flower is unique and beautiful. Some have fragrances, bright colors, and many petals. Others are simple and fragile. In spite of their differences, they create a stunning lei when strung together. As a powerful metaphor for A.L.O.H.A., students will create a class lei comprised of "flowers" symbolizing their ideas for promoting citizenship, strengthening teamwork, and bridging diversity. The completed lei will serve as a visual reminder of the efforts and actions each of us must practice to build on our individual differences and work harmoniously in our community.

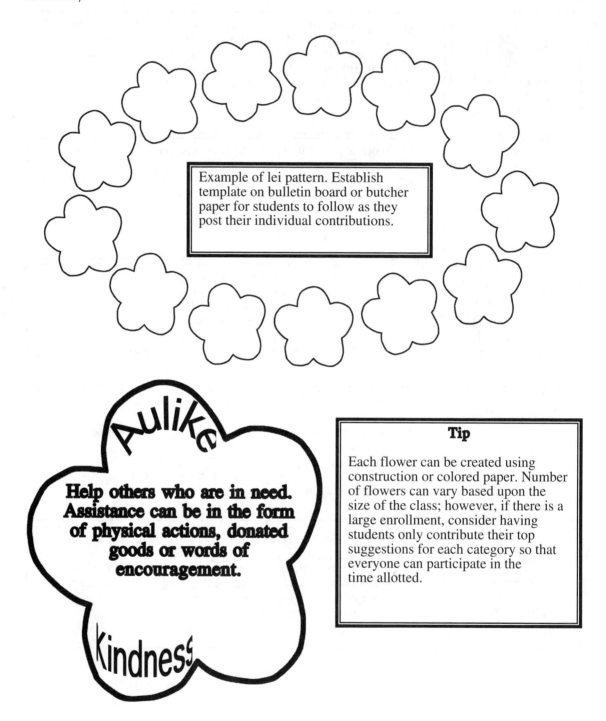

Example of lei pattern. Establish template on bulletin board or butcher paper for students to follow as they post their individual contributions.

Aulike

Help others who are in need. Assistance can be in the form of physical actions, donated goods or words of encouragement.

Kindness

Tip

Each flower can be created using construction or colored paper. Number of flowers can vary based upon the size of the class; however, if there is a large enrollment, consider having students only contribute their top suggestions for each category so that everyone can participate in the time allotted.

10 Voices Alive: Oral Histories Tell Us about Communities

COURSE: Social Studies, Language Arts
GRADES: 9-12
DURATION OF PROJECT: One semester
STUDENT OUTCOMES
  CONTENT GOALS:
    Students will conduct oral history research to understand how
    community members can provide valuable insight into our past.
    They will accomplish this by:

  - Practicing historical inquiry skills to understand how
    individual perspectives can enrich and influence people's
    view of the past.
  - Applying skills in interpersonal communication, decision
    making, and planning in their interviews.
  - Evaluating the information gathered for reliability,
    accuracy, and relevance.
  - Using various media formats to gather, record, and
    present information.

  PROCESS GOALS:
    Students will develop information literacy skills needed to foster
    complex and higher-order thinking.

DESCRIPTION OF PRODUCT OR PERFORMANCE

We are living history every day. Our perceptions, experiences, and knowledge of the events
and world around us are valuable records of history. Our stories and the stories of the people
around us are unique and provide important insight into the development, change, and
continuity of a community.

In order to preserve the personal experiences and historic perspectives of the
community, students will conduct oral history research and create multimedia presentations
based on their investigations. They will also have the opportunity to share their products with

community members. Ultimately, their presentations will be added to a repository of local history accessible through the school library media center. Students will be responsible for:

- Researching the history of the community through various resources.
- Identifying, contacting, and interviewing individuals from our community.
- Synthesizing, analyzing, and evaluating information and information sources.
- Placing information gathered in a historical context.
- Using various media formats to communicate information and ideas effectively to multiple audiences.

CONNECTION WITH STANDARDS

Standards from Social Studies, Language Arts, Technology, and Information Literacy are integrated in this project.

SOCIAL STUDIES

Standards addressed in this unit focus on specific skills within broad thematic standards that deal with time, continuity, and change; and individual development and identity. For more detailed information on the standards refer to <http://www.socialstudies.org/standards/>.

LANGUAGE ARTS

Standards addressed in this unit deal with using language to communicate with various audiences, conducting research on issues and interests, and using a variety of informational and technological resources. For more detailed information on the standards refer to <http://www.ncte.org/about/over/standards/110846.htm>.

TECHNOLOGY

Standards addressed in this unit deal with basic operations and concepts; social, ethical, and human issues; technology productivity tools; and technology tools for communication and research. For more detailed information on the standards refer to <http://cnets.iste.org/students/s_stands.html>.

INFORMATION LITERACY

Standards addressed in this unit focus on the access, evaluation, and use of information; excellence in information seeking and knowledge generation; social responsibility in dealing with information; and working positively and effectively in groups. For more detailed information on the standards refer to <http://www.ala.org/ala/aasl/aaslproftools/informationpower/InformationLiteracyStandards_final.pdf>.

OVERARCHING PROJECT QUESTIONS

- What is a community?
- How do individuals, events, and community landmarks shape and define a community's history?

- How has the past influenced present-day perspectives?
- How does oral history contribute to our understanding and appreciation of the past?

TIMELINE FOR PROJECT

Figure 10.1 Project Timeline

Time	Instructor's Tasks (LMS/T)	Student's Performance Tasks

Days 1–2	**CONNECT**
	• Arrange a field trip to a community landmark or location. (T)
	• Invite a local storyteller or historian to present interesting tales from the community's past. (LMS/T)
	• Facilitate discussion on group reaction to stories. (T)
		CONNECT
		• Listen to presentation by local historian or storyteller. As stories are told, make note of the following:
		  – Places
		  – People
		  – Events
		  – Practices, values, attitudes
		• As a class, discuss information gathered.

Day 3	**WONDER**
	• Have students discuss their reaction to the field trip and speaker. (T)
	• Link landmark or location to its place in the development of the community and lead discussion into what is a community. (T)
		WONDER
		• Discuss in groups:
		  – What did you learn on the field trip?
		  – What is a community?
		  – How would you describe our community?
		  – What do you know about our community's history, geography, and people?
		  – What else would you like to know?

Days 4–5	**CONNECT**
	• Explain that oral histories and other primary sources are means to learning more about the community. Discussion should include:
	  – What is oral history?
	  – What are primary sources?
	  – How are the resources used by historians?
	  – Why are primary sources important?
	  – How are oral histories created?
	  – How can primary sources and oral histories answer our questions? (T)
	• Show students a model of an oral history from:
	  – Past student projects
	  – Accounts from the files of community organizations
	  – Library of Congress' American Memory (T)
	• Explain project. (T)
	• Have students think about what they would like to learn about our community. Revisit responses from previous session. (T)
		CONNECT
		• Take notes on discussion of oral history.
		• Examine a past oral history project as a model.
		• Select a category of personal interest and gain general information about it using a variety of resources.
		• Respond to the prompt:
		  – What could oral histories tell us about our community?
		• Decide on a topic for further investigation.
		• Work in groups of three or four people, who are interested in the same topic.

continued

Time	Instructor's Tasks (LMS/T)	Student's Performance Tasks
Days 6-25	**INVESTIGATE** • Review various primary sources and provide instruction on analyzing these sources. (LMS/T) • Help students apply criteria for evaluating Web sites. (LMS) • Have students search for information relating to the community's past and present. (LMS/T) • Encourage development of additional questions for deeper investigation. (LMS/T) • Connect students with community resources relating to their topics. – Community organizations – Universities/colleges – State archives – Public library – Local newspapers – Museums – Historic societies (LMS) • Provide instruction on conducting interviews and using equipment if necessary. Be sure to cover: – Preparing for the interview – Creating questions – Conducting interviews – Videotaping – Administering the interviewee evaluation form – Explaining release/permission forms – Posting interviews (LMS/T/Tech coordinator) • Help students develop questions for interview. (T/LMS) • Have students evaluate their peers' questions. (T/LMS) • Model interview techniques. Have students practice interviewing skills with peers. (T/LMS) • Allot time for students to analyze information. (T)	**INVESTIGATE** • Use community questions generated from the previous session as a guide for research. Continue to develop queries for deeper investigation. • Select various primary sources (e.g., documents, photographs, songs) relating to the community and your topic. • Apply criteria for selecting and evaluating Web sites. • Find community resources relating to topic. • Use *Preparing for the Interview* worksheet. (See Figure 10.3) • Select and contact community individuals to interview. • Create interview questions relating to your topic. Use *What Should I Ask?* (See Figure 10.4) Group the questions based on their focus. Groups may include: – Biographical data – Events – Influential people – Activities – Geography • Exchange and review questions with the group. Modify if necessary. • Practice interviewing skills and using equipment. Use *Interview Checklist and Tips* as a guide. (See Figure 10.6) • Interview community members. *Note: Students will need additional time to complete interviews. Teachers should determine completion date based on their deadlines and student progress.*
	ASSESS • Provide instruction on analyzing information from interviews. (LMS/T) • Have student reflect on the interview by using the Community Interviewee Evaluation form. Remind students that interviews can be with more than one individual. Interviews can be re-done if necessary. (LMS/T)	**ASSESS** • Analyze interview using the *Analyzing the Interview* worksheet. (See Figure 10.8) • Review *Community Interviewee Evaluation* form with teacher. (See Figure 10.7) • Evaluate primary sources for relevance, accuracy, reliability, and impact. Select sources to be used in presentation.
	REFLECT • Conduct ongoing assessment to evaluate students' progress through conferencing, observations, and reflections. (LMS/T) • Provide coaching sessions, individual assistance, and guidance as projects develop. (LMS/T)	**REFLECT** • Respond to questions: – Did you meet your expectations with the interviews? Why or why not? – Did the interview verify what you already discovered in your research? – What other questions do you have as a result of the interview? – What would you improve on next time? – Have you encountered any difficulties finding information? How did you address this problem? – What are your next steps?

Time	Instructor's Tasks (LMS/T)	Student's Performance Tasks

Days 26-45	**CONSTRUCT**
	• Provide instruction and guidance on developing digital media.
	   – Highlight points with visual and audio features to support main ideas.
	   – Design and sequence your work for greater impact, focus, and efficiency. (Tech coordinator)
	• Provide instruction on using various editing and publishing tools (e.g., video editing, podcasting). (LMS/Tech coordinator)
	• Allot time to work on presentation. (T)
		CONSTRUCT
		• Evaluate primary sources collected for relevance, accuracy, reliability, and impact.
		• Compile all information. Then select most relevant segments to use in the presentation.
		• Design storyboard and layout information. Use *Production Layout* guide. (See Figure 10.10)
		• Create presentation.
		Note: Depending on media format chosen, students may need additional time for constructing projects.

	REFLECT • Conduct ongoing assessment to evaluate students' progress through conferencing, journals, and progress reports. (T/LMS/Tech coordinator) • Provide coaching sessions, individual assistance, and guidance as projects develop. (T/LMS/Tech coordinator)	**REFLECT** • Confer with instructors for feedback on project and action plan. • Provide progress reports on planning of project.
Days 46-48	**EXPRESS** • Organize schedule for presentations. Arrange for equipment if needed. (T)	**EXPRESS** • Present information to class.
	REFLECT • Provide feedback on project. (LMS/T)	**REFLECT** • Provide feedback on projects. Use *Multimedia Presentation Scoring Guide.* (See Figure 10.11) • View feedback and discuss with group how to address suggestions made.

Days 49-60	**CONSTRUCT**
	• Continue to allot planning time to refine the project presentation for a community audience. (T)
	• Have students assist in planning, preparing, implementing, and evaluating the event. Possible venues for the presentation include:
	   – School parent night
	   – Public library event
	   – Session with community organizations
	   – Local mall event (LMS/T)
		CONSTRUCT
		• Improve project with peer and student feedback.
		Note: Students may discover they have to go back to the initial CONNECT and WONDER phases as they refine the presentations.
		• Organize event to share presentations with the community and school.
		• Invite community members, who contributed and supported the project, to attend the presentation.

	REFLECT • Conduct ongoing assessment to evaluate students' progress through conferencing, journals, and progress reports. (T/LMS) • Provide coaching sessions, individual assistance, and guidance as projects develop. (T/LMS)	**REFLECT** • Confer with instructors for feedback on project and action plan. • Provide progress reports on planning of project.
Days 61-62	**EXPRESS** • Have students present to a community audience. (T) • Encourage community members to participate in assessing projects. (T)	**EXPRESS** • Present projects to community.

continued

Time	Instructor's Tasks (LMS/T)	Student's Performance Tasks
Days 62-63	**REFLECT** • Have students reflect on process and product. (T/LMS) • Allot time for sharing reflections. (T/LMS)	**REFLECT** • Share with class the results of the projects and reflections. — What do individual perspectives tell us about the history of our community? — Why are oral histories important to our understanding and appreciation of the past? — How have past events, people, and landmarks shaped our community today? — How do we feel about our community after completing this project?

ASSESSMENT CHECKPOINTS

Figure 10.2 Project Assessment Plan

Checkpoints in the process	What is assessed	Who assesses	Assessment tool
Connect	Student participation and content understanding	Teacher Library media specialist Student	Observation Written reflection
Wonder	Student participation and concept understanding	Teacher Library media specialist Student	Observation Written reflection
Investigate	Information seeking, access, and retrieval Effective and efficient use of information Evaluating information sources	Teacher Library media specialist Student	Observation Research questions Reflections *What Should I Ask?* (See Figure 10.4) *Interview Checklist* (See Figure 10.6) *Community Interviewee Evaluation* (See Figure 10.7) *Analyzing the Interview* (See Figure 10.8)
Construct/Express	Evaluation, synthesis, presentation of project and project implementation	Teacher Library media specialist Student	Observation Conferencing
Reflect	Assessment and evaluation of personal progress and modifications for continued improvement	Teachers Library media specialist Student	Reflection Peer Review *Community Interviewee Evaluation* (See Figure 10.7) *Analyzing the Interview* (See Figure 10.8) *Multimedia Presentation Scoring Guide* (See Figure 10.11)

RESOURCES USED IN THE PROJECT

American Memory. Washington, DC: Library of Congress, 2006. 2 Aug. 2007 <http://memory/lov.gov/ammen/index.html>.

Center for Oral History. Honolulu: University of Hawaii, n.d. 2 Aug. 2007 <http://www.oralhistory.hawaii.edu>.

Slopes, Linda. "Making Sense of History." *History Matters: The U.S. Survey Course on the Web*. New York: American Social Project/Center for Media and Learning, City University of NY, and Center for History and New Media, George Mason University, 2002. 2 Aug. 2007 <http://historymatters.gmu.edu/mse/oral/>.

The American Folklife Center. Washington, DC: Library of Congress, 2006. 2 Aug. 2007 <http://www.loc.gov/folklife/>.

Truedell, Barbara. *Oral History Techniques: How to Organize and Conduct Oral History Interviews*. Bloomington: Indiana University: Center for the Study of History and Memories, n.d. 2 Aug. 2007 <http://www.indiana.edu/~cshm/techniques.html>.

STANDARDS CITED

American Association of School Librarians, and the Association for Educational Communications and Technology. *Information Literacy Standards for Student Learning*. Chicago: American Library Association, 1998. 2 Aug. 2007 <http://www.ala.org/ala/aasl/aaslproftools/informationpower/InformationLiteracyStandards_final.pdf>.

International Society for Technology in Education. *National Educational Technology Standards: The Next Generation. National Educational Technology Standards for Students*. Washington, DC: Author, 2007. 2 Aug. 2007 <http://cnets.iste.org/students/s_stands.html>.

National Council of the Teachers of English, and International Reading Association. *Standards for the English Language Arts*. Urbana: International Reading Association, 1996. 2 Aug. 2007 <http://www.ncte.org/about/over/standards/110846.htm>.

Task Force of the National Council for the Social Studies. *The Curriculum Standards for the Social Studies*. Silver Spring: National Council for the Social Studies, 1994. 2 Aug. 2007 <http://www.socialstudies.org/standards/>.

SAMPLES OF STUDENT WORK

FIGURE 10.5: WHAT SHOULD I ASK? (STUDENT EXAMPLE)

Criteria for evaluation of student work:

- Addresses all components of the organizer
- Uses closed-ended questions appropriately for gathering information
- Uses open-ended questions to gain deeper insight into the topic

FIGURE 10.9: ANALYZING THE INTERVIEW (STUDENT EXAMPLE)

Criteria for evaluation of student work:

- Provides responses that accurately address the questions
- Reflects critical thinking in analyzing the interview
- Logically explains and supports the appropriateness of the interview

REFLECTION OF THE INSTRUCTORS

This project has been relevant and rigorous for our students. Through their work, students have made lasting contributions to their community. By completing their oral histories, students learned the value and importance of this form of research as a means to understanding the rich history of a place.

Different teacher teams at our school have effectively implemented this particular unit. Because we wanted to make the project meaningful for the students and for the community, we incorporated historic references, oral history interviews, and artifacts. While the final product was extremely important, the process employed by the students was equally critical. At different points in the project, students required more direction and construction time than initially anticipated. For example, we had to de-construct the interview process as students had no experience in this area. We had to teach them how to properly greet people, what to wear to an interview, and how to write thank you letters. The people interviewed were also asked to complete an evaluation form so students could obtain outside feedback regarding their interviewing skills. A few students ran into logistical and technical difficulties (transportation, parental approval, computer glitches) but overall the interview process went smoothly. Students were excited about creating the presentations and wanted more time to construct their videos and podcasts.

As library media specialists, we worked very closely with students to identify community resources for them. Information specific to our neighborhood was frequently difficult to locate. We often resorted to interlibrary loans and visits to the public library and state archives. We also wore many hats as the project moved along and we found that students needed various forms of assistance. Some of our roles included being video editor and taxi driver as well as consultants for the interviews.

TEMPLATES AND RUBRICS FOR VARIOUS TASKS

Figure 10.3 Preparing for the Interview

Oral histories collect information about the past from those who have lived through the events and activities. They are personal recollections that reflect individual feelings and values.

Preperation is the key to success. Here are tips for setting up an oral history interview.

6 **Practice, Confirm, Practice**
- o Stage a mock interview.
- o Confirm appointment.
- o Check equipment.
- o Practice again.

5 **Prepare Equipment**
- o Determine the equipment, supplies, and assistance you will need.
- o Practice setting up and using the equipment.

4 **Prepare questions**.
- o Create questions that are relevant to the interviewee.
- o Realize that questions need not be used but serve as a start and guide when needed.
- o Design questions that are open ended but focused.
- o Have someone read your questions to check for relevancy, clarity, and logic.

3 **Set up the interview.**
- o Contact individuals.
- o Explain the purpose of your project and your expectations for the interview.
- o Confirm appointments.
- o Learn something about your interviewees.

2 **Know your topic well.**
- o Consider what you already know.
- o Identify information that you need.
- o Think about where you might go to find this information.
- o Consider who you might interview to learn more about your topic.

1 **What is your goal?**
- o Clearly state what you hope to accomplish.
- o Identify what you hope to find out.
- o Be able to explain why your project is important.

Figure 10.4 What Should I Ask?

It is a good idea to prepare a list of questions for the interview. You don't need to follow the list exactly, but it is a starting point and a means to continue if the interview falls into a lull. In creating your questions, refer to the goals of your assignment on the *Preparing for the Interview* worksheet you previously completed. Consider the following tips as you work.

TIPS:

1. **Ask open-ended questions**. You want to get the best explanation from your interviewee.
2. **Ask questions with a single focus**. Don't confuse the person by asking too much at once.
3. **Remember that people's memories work well with a point of reference.** Examples: a typical day, event, or a specific person.
4. **Start with biographical questions.** Learn more about the interviewee.
5. **Don't ask very personal or probing questions.** Be sensitive to the person's feelings.
6. **Explain the goals of the interview to the interviewee and send an advance copy of the questions so he or she can prepare.**

TOPICS TO COVER:

Let's start! In the left column, list the focus for the questions. In the right column, create the questions.

Question Focus	Questions

Figure 10.5 What Should I Ask? (Student Example)

Evaluation of student work: This example successfully demonstrates the student's ability to ask relevant questions. She provides both closed-ended questions that are appropriate for the interview and a series of open-ended questions that allow her to probe for deeper information.

TOPICS TO COVER: SCHOOL, HOUSING, EVENTS, ACTIVITIES, GEOGRAPHY

Let's start! In the left column, list the focus for the questions. In the right column, create the questions.

Question Focus	Questions
Personal background	1. When and where were you born? 2. Who were your parents? Where were they born and raised? What jobs did they hold? 3. Could you tell me about your brothers and sisters (if you have any)? 4. What ethnic background are you? 5. What family events did you celebrate as a child?
Education	1. Where did you go to school? 2. What was your school like? 3. Which subjects did you enjoy? Dislike? Excel in? 4. How did teachers address behavior problems? 5. Can you describe any funny or memorable moments from school?
Housing	1. What was your house like? 2. Could you describe your neighborhood? 3. Who were your neighbors and what were they like? 4. How many houses were in your neighborhood? Were they all physically alike? 5. How has housing changed over time in your neighborhood?
Lifestyle	1. What did you do for fun growing up in this neighborhood? 2. How did neighbors in your community relate or connect to one another? 3. Are there any community practices or activities that stand out in your memory? 4. How has the lifestyle changed over time since you've lived here? 5. How have new people moving into the community influenced changes?
Geography	1. What was the community like when you were growing up? 2. What was the population like? 3. How did the ethnic composition influence the community? 4. What were the important landmarks in the community? 5. How has the area changed and developed through the last 30 years?

Figure 10.6 Interview Checklist and Tips

Interviewing can be very stressful but your pre-interview preparation can make it a pleasant and valuable learning experience. Below are some reminders to make your experience a success. Check off the items as you progress through the process.

PRE-INTERVIEW

- Contact the community member via telephone, email, or letter. Make sure you include an explanation of the project and purpose of the interview.
- Set up the date, time, and place for the interview.
- Create purposeful, thoughtful questions to guide your interview.
- Have someone read through your questions for feedback.
- Re-confirm the appointment prior to your interview date.
- Double-check all equipment and supplies. Bring along extra batteries, tapes, an extension cord, and necessary reference materials.
- Do not go alone to the interview. Take an adult or group member with you.
- Dress appropriately.

INTERVIEW

- Greet the interviewee and thank him or her for participating.
- Set up equipment. Examine the area for the best possible spot to conduct the interview.
- Break the ice. As you set up equipment, chat informally to establish rapport.
- Before asking questions, restate the goals and purpose of the project and interview.
- Have the interviewee read and sign a release permission form. Start the recording by stating your name, the date, location, and name of interviewee.
- Begin the interview with biographical and easy questions.
- Speak in a clear pleasant voice at a comfortable pace.
- Ask a question and provide interviewee "think time" to respond.
- Don't cut off or talk over an interviewee.
- Refrain from arguing or leading the interviewee with questions containing bias.
- Listen very carefully.
- Be aware of visual and nonverbal cues that indicate the subject is uncomfortable or tired.
- Jot down notes if necessary but don't let it be distracting.
- Don't end the interview abruptly. Converse informally to conclude the session.
- Thank the interviewee for participating in the project and invite him or her to the community presentation.

POST-INTERVIEW

- Immediately after the interview, make note of the topics covered and any follow-up you may need to do.
- Label tapes and recordings. Make a copy of the interview and store the master.
- Write a thank you letter.
- If you borrowed anything from the interviewee, make copies, and return materials.
- Analyze the interview. Verify facts.
- Create more questions if needed.

CONGRATULATIONS! YOU ARE DONE! GREAT JOB!

10.7 Community Interviewee Evaluation

Name of student: _____   Name of interviewee: _____

Title of project: _____

Thank you for participating in our Oral History Project. This project allows us to practice valuable life skills while learning about the community in which we live. Please help me to assess my performance by evaluating the quality of the interview. In the chart below, put check marks next to the descriptions that best match my work. If you have any other suggestions that might help me improve my skills, feel free to write your comments on the back of this sheet. If you have any questions, please call Mrs. Smith at (000) XXX-XXXX. Thank you very much.

Area	Excellent	Satisfactory	Needs Improvement
Setting up the interview	The student: • Politely asked to set up the interview. • Clearly explained the purpose of the project and interview expectations. • Called to confirm. • Sent me questions along with a release form.	The student: • Asked to set up a time for interview. • Needed to be asked about the purpose and expectations of the interview. • Called to confirm. • Sent me questions but not a release form.	The student: • Called at the last minute for interview. • Needed assistance in all phases of setting up the interview. • Did not call to confirm. • Did not send me questions or a release form.
During the interview	The student: • Never interrupted or rushed me. • Had questions that showed research on the topics. • Asked many relevant questions based on my responses.	The student: • Rarely interrupted or rushed me. • Asked one or two questions based on my responses. • Asked questions that indicated he or she didn't listen carefully to my responses.	The student: • Continually interrupted or rushed me. • Had vague questions that were hard to answer. • Did not ask any questions based on my responses.
Following the interview	The student: • Thanked me. • Collected the release form. • Invited me to the community presentation.	The student: • Thanked me. • Collected release form only after being reminded. • Invited me to the presentation when prompted.	The student: • Forgot to thank me. • Did not give me a release form. • Did not invite me to the presentation.

Signature of Interviewee _____   **Date** _____

Figure 10.8 Analyzing the Interview

While oral histories teach us much about the past, they are memories that are based on individual perspectives and recollections. These perspectives are valuable; however, they may be biased or factually inaccurate. All data should be critically examined before use. Complete the chart below to analyze the information you have gathered.

	Response
Who is the interviewee? • What is the interviewee's relationship to the events discussed? • What stake might he or she have in presenting a particular version of the event? • Would the interviewee's socioeconomic status or cultural background influence his or her version of the events?	
What was said during the interview? • Did the interviewee avoid answering any questions? • What might be the reason for this? • Were there any factual errors? • If so, explain. • How does the interviewee's story compare with other information you have collected?	
When did the events take place? • How long ago did the things discussed actually happen? • How might this have influenced what was shared?	
Where did the interview take place? • How did the location impact the interview? • Were others present? How might this have influenced what was said?	

Looking at your answers, do you believe this interview is appropriate for your purposes? Explain.

Figure 10.9 Analyzing the Interview (Student Example)

Evaluation of student work: The student was able to address all of the questions with reasonable explanations and details resulting from his interview. He was also able to justify why this interview was relevant and useful for his final product.

	Response
Who is the interviewee? • What is the interviewee's relationship to the events discussed? • What stake might he or she have in presenting a particular version of the event? • Would the interviewee's socioeconomic status or cultural background impact his or her version of the events?	*Ms. V has lived in this area for 60 years of her life. She is 72 years old and she is of Japanese ancestry. She came to Oahu after her family was released from the Poston Relocation Camp in Arizona after WWII. She was about 12 years old.* *They were imprisoned at Poston because her parents were born and raised in Japan. She worked for a small auto parts and repair shop for nearly 40 years. She had not missed a day of work for nearly 25 years. In 1989, her employer bought her a car as a thank you. Although she officially retired, she continues to work at the shop full time. Although not wealthy, Ms. V is a saver. She was able to purchase her own home for herself and her blind mother. She enjoys seeing familiar faces in the area where she has lived and worked most of her life.* *She is very family oriented and is the eldest of two brothers and five sisters. She is very healthy physically and mentally. She gets exercise by working in her garden on her days off.*
What was said during the interview? • Did the interviewee avoid answering any questions? What might be the reason for this? • Were there any factual errors? • How does the interviewee's story compare with other information you have collected?	*We started with biographical questions then moved to her childhood, teen, and adulthood. She didn't avoid answering any question and if she didn't know the answer she said so.* *The description of the area, people, and events correspond to the information that I found in my library research. There were minor errors when she tried to remember exact dates. Her memory of things revolved around important personal events.*
When did the events take place? • How long ago did the things discussed actually happen? • Could this have influenced what was shared?	*About 60 years had passed since she came to live here. This affected her ability to remember specific details relating to some of her recollections.*
Where did the interview take place? • How did the location impact the interview? • Were others present? Could this have influenced what was said?	*The interview took place at Ms. V's home. She was able to show me pictures of her family and what the area looked like, the houses and different people. Four of us were there: Ms. V, her sister, me, and Billy who was filming. Ms. V and her sister reminisced a bit during the interview. We captured this on film. If Ms. V didn't remember something she would ask her sister to help her.*

Looking at your answers, do you believe this interview is appropriate for your purposes? Explain.

The goal of this interview was to get a personal view from someone who lived in the area. We wanted to get an idea of what life was like over 40 years ago and how it has changed. Although Ms. V wasn't born in the area, we felt she would be a good interviewee. Her answers gave us a view from a female working class perspective. Most people in the area were working class. Like many other families, her family was large and had first and second generation immigrant roots. We don't feel her sister's presence impacted the interview in a negative way. It actually provided us with another perspective and more stories to use.

Figure 10.10 Production Layout

Before jumping into constructing your project, plan it. Laying out your information will allow you to see the focus and flow of your information and make the actual construction of the project much easier. The layout is not set in stone. You may find yourself having to rework certain steps to match your focus and objectives.

Directions	**Sample**

Step 1

Materials: Information gathered (e.g., notes, pictures, video)
Index cards 5x7
Poster paper

Team Blue
Project Focus: Development on the Leeward Plains from 1940-1970.
Topics Covered: Landscape, businesses, people in area, lifestyle, events, and activities
Objectives:
1. Give background on the geography from 1940-1970
2. Explain population in area
3. Describe housing, lifestyle of Leeward Plains
4. Discuss how development has brought change
5. Discuss future plans and predictions

Step 2

Write the following on an index card:
 • Group name
 • Focus of your project/title
 • Topic(s) covered
 • Objectives

Step 3

Create additional cards each containing one idea. The cards should include the following:
 • Main or title card
 • Why this story is important
 • Profiles of the important people in the story, the event, or the situation
 • History of the event or situation
 • Impact on the community
 • Acknowledgements and credits

Write the focus of this idea at the top. *Seq. #*

Sketch of your image or document

Description of shot/audio: _____

Image(s)/audio to be used: _____

Estimated time of clip: _____

Narration: Transition: _____

Step 4

Place your cards on the table or floor and arrange them in a possible sequence for your project.

Step 5

As a group, discuss arrangement of cards.
 • Is the order logical?
 • Did we address all our objectives?
 • Are the images/video appropriate and relevant?

Step 6

Once you've settled on the order of your cards, number the cards in the top right hand corner. Paste or tape the cards on the poster paper for reference during the construction stage.

10.11 Multimedia Presentation Scoring Guide

	4	3	3	1
Subject knowledge Score:	Knowledge is evident in entire presentation. Information is accurate and relevant. Details clearly support main idea.	Knowledge is evident in most of the presentation. Information is mostly correct and relevant. Most details support main theme.	Some knowledge is evident. Some information is confusing or irrelevant. A few examples and details support main theme.	Little knowledge is apparent. Information is inaccurate, irrelevant, and confusing. No details support main theme.
Organization of content Score:	Entire presentation is logically organized. The introduction is clear and relevant. Audience knows what to expect from presentation. Introduction sparks audience's interest.	Almost all of the presentation is logically organized. The introduction is clear and coherent. Audience knows what to expect from presentation. Introduction sparks audience's interest.	Parts of the presentation are logically organized. The introduction shows some structure but it does not interest most of the audience.	Presentation is not logically organized. The introduction does not explain what will follow. The main idea is unclear and does not appear relevant to the audience.
Copyright Score:	All sources are properly cited according to MLA style. Various resources have been used. Release forms for photos, interviews, and other sources are completed and filed.	Most sources are properly cited. Various sources have been used. Release forms for photos, interviews, and other sources are completed and filed.	A few sources are properly cited. A limited range of sources has been used. Release forms are not entirely completed or filed.	Information sources are not properly cited. Only one or two resources have been used. Release forms are not completed.
Technology Score:	Visual and technological aids creatively support the presentation and spark audience interest.	Visual and technological aids support the presentation.	Visual and technological aids support some parts of the presentation.	Visual and technological aids are vague and irrelevant to the presentation.
Total	**Rubric Scoring Guide:** **Exceeds standards – 14 to 16 points** **Meets standards – 11 to 13 points**		**Approaches standards – 7 to 10 points** **Does not meet standards – 6 points or less**	

11 Raising the Bar: New Sports For a Challenging Tomorrow

> **COURSE:** Physical Education, Language Arts, Social Studies
> **GRADES:** 9-12
> **DURATION OF PROJECT:** Two weeks
> **STUDENT OUTCOMES**
>   CONTENT GOALS:
>   Students will demonstrate their understanding of the historical as well
>   as current development of sports and athletic games by:
>
> - Identifying, defining, and analyzing sports and games.
> - Explaining rules and objectives that guide the playing of
>   the activity.
> - Studying current trends in athletic equipment and physical
>   conditioning that influence performance outcomes.
> - Adapting sports to continuously challenge today's
>   athletes.
>
>   PROCESS GOALS:
>   Students will develop information literacy skills needed to foster
>   complex and higher-order thinking.

DESCRIPTION OF PRODUCT OR PERFORMANCE

Since ancient times, sports and athletic games have played an important role in society. Over time, advancements in technology have transformed many of these traditional games into sophisticated action sports demanding higher levels of physical exertion using specialized gear. As a result, rules and objectives have become increasingly rigorous and athletes have been hard pressed to meet the challenge. Although some of the events still resemble those played generations ago, many sports now fall in the "extreme" category. We have also seen shifts from team to individual play, and games have been reinvented to push modern athletes to the limits of their physical abilities. These extreme sports have become the focus of current pop culture. Developed by athletes and sports enthusiasts, the games have gained an international following. Some of these events have even earned Olympic recognition and sanction. This project challenges students to conduct in-depth investigations of existing sports and create a new "extreme" version of one game. Students will be responsible for:

- Gathering, analyzing, and presenting information on existing sports and athletic games.
- Summarizing the historical development of these activities.
- Describing current trends (equipment, rules, training) that influence the sport.
- Developing a new version of a sport to challenge today's athletes.
- Presenting proposals for these new sports to developers and potential sponsors in the community, who are planning an extreme games event.

CONNECTION WITH STANDARDS

Standards from Physical Education, Language Arts, Social Studies, Technology, and Information Literacy are integrated in this project.

PHYSICAL EDUCATION

Standards addressed in this unit focus on the demonstration of movement patterns, physical activities, principles, strategies, and tactics; respectful and responsible behavior in physical activity settings; and promotion of physical activity for health, enjoyment, challenge, and self-expression. For more detailed information on the standards refer to <http://www.aahperd.org/naspe/publications-nationalstandards.html#list>.

LANGUAGE ARTS

Standards addressed in this unit deal with using language to communicate with various audiences, employing a range of writing strategies, applying language conventions, and conducting research using a variety of informational and technological resources. For more detailed information on the standards refer to <http://www.ncte.org/about/over/standards/110846.htm>.

SOCIAL STUDIES

Standards addressed in this unit focus on specific skills within broad thematic standards that deal with time, continuity, and change; science, technology, and society; and civic ideas and practices. For more detailed information on the standards refer to <http://www.socialstudies.org/standards/>.

TECHNOLOGY

Standards addressed in this unit deal with basic operations and concepts; social, ethical, and human issues; technology productivity tools; technology tools for communication and research; and technology problem solving and decision making. For more detailed information on the standards refer to <http://cnets.iste.org/students/s_stands.html>.

INFORMATION LITERACY

Standards addressed in this unit focus on the access, evaluation, and use of information; appreciation for all forms of creative expression; development of self-reflection skills in knowledge acquisition; and social responsibility in working with information. For more detailed information on the standards refer to <http://www.ala.org/ala/aasl/aaslproftools/informationpower/InformationLiteracyStandards_final.pdf>.

OVERARCHING PROJECT QUESTIONS

- How have sports and games impacted society throughout history?
- How have specific sports and games evolved over time?
- How have advances in technology and medicine influenced performance in sports and games?
- How can sports and games be adapted to challenge today's athletes and hold the interest of spectators?

TIMELINE FOR PROJECT

Figure 11.1 Project Timeline

Time	Instructor's Tasks (LMS/T)	Student's Performance Tasks
Day 1	**CONNECT** • Facilitate discussion regarding society's fascination with sports/games. Concentrate on the historical impact and influence they have had on society. (LMS/T)	**CONNECT** • Regroup into team huddles (groups of three to four). • Discuss as a team possible theories to answer the essential question: — How have sports impacted society throughout the course of history? • Share the ideas in a class discussion.
	WONDER • Review physical education skills that have been taught throughout the year. (T) • Distribute photographs of sporting events/athletes from past to the present. Drawing on the previous class dialogue, discuss how society has had an impact in the evolution of sports. Make connections to the rules of the games that were taught and how the sports have changed. (T/LMS)	**WONDER** • Remain in team huddles. • Review the photographs that were distributed. Look for similarities and differences among the sports as they were practiced in the past and today. • Complete the *Sports Then and Now* chart. (See Figure 11.3) List these differences on the chart. Formulate hypotheses or reasons related to the evolution of these sports. • Share the results with the class; welcome additions.
	CONNECT • List common ideas generated from the discussion. (T) • Categorize ideas under topic headings. Some suggestions include: — Technological advancements — Development of safety gear — Strength and endurance training — Health and physiology research — Societal acceptance — Modernization (T/LMS)	**CONNECT** • Build a list of common ideas generated from the discussion. • Suggest topic headings to organize the ideas. Within group huddles, brainstorm how each topic has had a significant impact on sports you have played in your PE class. Reflect on the following question: — How have specific sports and games evolved over time?

continued

Time	Instructor's Tasks (LMS/T)	Student's Performance Tasks
Day 2	**WONDER** • Focus on technology and strength/endurance training as the point for discussion. Because of advances in science, athletes are better conditioned to meet the rigors of their sport. This has led to changes in sports to make them even more challenging. (T) • Introduce the mini-research project, "Mapping the Milestones of Sports History." (T/LMS)	**WONDER** • Select a sport to research. Everyone should select a different sport. Use *Mapping the Milestones of Sports History*. (See Figure. 11.5) • Brainstorm possible answers to the following prompt: — How have advances in technology and medicine influenced performance in sports and games? • Use the responses from the brainstorming session to identify keywords or subjects to begin the research process.

Days 2-3	**INVESTIGATE**
	• Introduce different print and online resources. Reinforce the use of the library's online public access catalog, e-books, and online reference subscriptions. (LMS)
	• Review methods to evaluate the relevance of Web sites. Highlight the abundance of sport fan sites that inhabit the Internet and their inadequacy for use in research. (LMS)
		INVESTIGATE
		• Conduct research to examine factors that have influenced the development of your selected sport. Information should be organized under categories that include:
		  — Technological advancements
		  — Development of safety gear
		  — Strength and endurance training
		  — Health and physiology research
		  — Societal acceptance
		  — Modernization

Day 3	**CONSTRUCT/EXPRESS**
	• Assist students in constructing their Milestone Maps. (T/LMS)
	• Check student's information for accuracy, scope, and sequence. Encourage students to dig deeper (beyond utilizing a few sources) to uncover the data they need to showcase the development of the sport. (T/LMS)
		CONSTRUCT/EXPRESS
		• Use the information gathered and analyzed to construct the Milestone Map. The completed map should pose a visual representation of the essential questions:
		  — How have specific sports and games evolved over time?
		  — How have advances in technology and medicine influenced performance in sports and games?

Day 4	**REFLECT** • Coordinate the sharing of students' completed Milestone Maps. (T/LMS) • Post the maps on a collective memory board (e.g., bulletin board, tack board) in the room. (T/LMS)	**REFLECT** • Share Milestone Maps with classmates. • Highlight the important factors that have affected the development of different sports over time. • Post completed maps on the collective memory board.
	CONNECT • Introduce the concept of "extreme" sports. Highlight how technological advancements and modernization have been the catalyst for the development of many extreme activities. (T) • Show a video of "extreme" sport clips. Visually show students the range of games that have been created and the technological advances that influenced their development. (T) • Invite students to participate in the Mahalo X-Games Incorporated's quest to discover new X-Game designs for a local tournament. Distribute and explain the Request for Proposal. (T)	**CONNECT** • Discuss some of the sports highlighted as "extreme" and the technological influences that inspired them. Create a list of possible advancements that might be applied to the creation of other sports. • Build on the created list; think about sports currently being played. Are there changes that might be made to modernize the sport? Might several sports be combined to create a new sport that offers additional challenges for athletes? • Select a new game to develop. • Submit it as an entry to the Mahalo X-Games Tournament. Complete the *Extreme Games Request for Proposal*. (See Figure 11.7) The completed proposal should adequately address the following essential question: — How can sports/games be adapted to challenge future athletes and hold the interest of spectators/supporters?

continued

Time	Instructor's Tasks (LMS/T)	Student's Performance Tasks
Day 5	**INVESTIGATE** • Reintroduce the memory board. Throughout the project, students will be able to refer to it as a resource for inspiration and background information. (LMS) • Introduce print and electronic resources that will be useful for this project. (LMS) *Note: Few reliable reference sources have been published because of the currency of the topic. Highlight official organizations that offer credible information to assist in creating the sport.*	**INVESTIGATE** • Conduct research to build background information for the creation of your new sport. Information should include history, origin, objectives, rules, strategies, and examples of play. • Recheck information to verify that the sport that has been created is original.
Days 6-8	**CONSTRUCT/EXPRESS** • Review the proposal directions given by Mahalo X-Games Inc. Clarify any questions that students may have regarding the requirements. (T) • Review critical elements of technical writing. Familiarize students with the procedures for creating an instructional manual to explain their newly developed "extreme" sport. (T) • Assist students in drafting and editing their proposals and technical manuals. Provide assistance through coaching and conferencing. (T/LMS)	**CONSTRUCT/EXPRESS** • Using the data collected from research, develop a proposal for a new sport/game. • Include a technical manual to explain and teach your newly created "extreme" sport. Include all of the elements necessary to clearly explain how to play your activity to the Mahalo X-Games panel of experts and prospective participants. Use *Technical Writing Rubric*. (See Figure 11.10)
Day 9	**CONSTRUCT/EXPRESS** • Convene a panel for game selection and proposal review. Invite members of the community, e.g., sports professionals, business leaders, and fitness authorities to serve on the review panel. (T/LMS) • Evaluate and select proposals for inclusion in the X-Games Tournament. Use *Request for Proposal Panel Score Card* as a tool to award points. (See Figure 11.9) (Panel) • Assess proposals for technical writing skills. Use *Technical Writing Rubric*. (T/LMS)	**CONSTRUCT/EXPRESS** • Submit proposals to the Mahalo X-Game Inc. • Prepare for the possibility that the panel may call for additional information/explanation. • Ready a presentation to teach the sport that was designed. All winning entries will be announced and winners are expected to deliver instruction to the class.
Day 10	**REFLECT** • Announce the winning proposals to the class. (Panel) • Provide feedback on the proposals reviewed. Present critiques, observations, and overall impressions. Encourage students to resubmit proposals next year. (Panel) • Have students with selected proposals instruct the class on their winning sport. The objective of the presentations will be to prepare all students who might be interested in applying as Tournament athletes. (T)	**REFLECT** • Instruct the class on how to play the newly selected X-Games. • Train teams for possible entry in the X-Games Tournament. • Provide helpful feedback to creators of the sport regarding possibilities for improvement and development of strategies for play. Compile this feedback with the teacher's help.

ASSESSMENT CHECKPOINTS

Figure 11.2 Project Assessment Plan

Checkpoints in the process	What is assessed	Who assesses	Assessment tool
Connect	Student participation and content understanding	Teacher Library media specialist Student	Observation Group discussion
Wonder	Higher-order thinking and ability to make connections to prior experiences	Teacher Student	Observation Group discussion *Sports Then and Now Chart* (See Figure 11.3)
Investigate	Information retrieval and the efficient, effective use of resource materials	Library media specialist Student	Library research Observation Consultation Mapping the *Milestones of Sports History* (See Figure 11.5)
Construct/Express	Evaluation, synthesis, and presentation of data in a clear manner	Teacher Library media specialist Student	Observation *Extreme Games Request for Proposal* (See Figure 11.7) Sample of Extreme Sports Technical Manual (See Figure 11.8)
Reflect	Assessment and evaluation of personal progress and modifications for continued improvement	Teacher Library media specialist Student	Self-reflection *Request for Proposal Panel Score Card* (See Figure 11.9) *Technical Writing Rubric* (See Figure 11.10) Observation

RESOURCES USED IN THE PROJECT

American Sports Data, Inc. *Generation Y Drives Increasingly Popular "Extreme" Sports: Growth of New "Millennial" Pursuits Outpaces Traditional Activities. Sector Analysis Report.* New York: Author, 2006. 10 Aug. 2007 <http://www.americansportsdata.com/dev/pr-extremeactionsports.asp>.

Cave, Steve (Ed.). "The Life of X." *X Games History.* ESPN, 2003. 10 Aug. 2007 <http://skateboard.about.com/cs/events/a/XGamesHistory.htm>.

Checkmark Books. *The Book of Rules: A Visual Guide to the Laws of Every Commonly Played Sport and Game.* New York: Duncan Petersen, 1997, 1998.

Conoco Phillips. "Extreme Sports." *Teaching Tools.* 16 Feb. 2003. 10 Aug. 2007 <http://www.teachingtools.com/ThinkSmart/ExtremeSports.htm>.

Corbett, Doris, John Cheffers, and Eileen Crowley Sullivan (Eds.). *Unique Games and Sports Around the World: A Reference Guide.* Westport: Greenwood Press, 2001.

Craig, Steve. *Sports and Games of the Ancients.* Westport: Greenwood Press, 2002.

ESPN, and Walt Disney Company. *Play Your Way.* 2007. 10 Aug. 2007 <http://disney.go.com/playyourway/>.

Exploratorium. "Sport Science." *Exploratorium: Sport Science.* San Francisco: Author, n.d. 10 Aug. 2007 <http://www.exploratorium.edu/sports/index.html>.

EXPN. "The Life of X: A Brief History of the Games." *X Games*. 2003. 10 Aug. 2007 <http://expn.go.com/xgames/history/s/history.html>.

Hickok, Ralph. "Sports History." *Hickok Sports*. 18 June 2006. 10 Aug. 2007 <http://www.hickoksports.com/history/extremesports.shtml>.

Koeppel, Dan. *Updated Extreme Sports Almanac*. Lincolnwood: Lowell, 2000.

STANDARDS CITED

American Association of School Librarians, and the Association for Educational Communications and Technology. *Information Literacy Standards for Student Learning*. Chicago: American Library Association, 1998. 2 Aug. 2007 <http://www.ala.org/ala/aasl/aaslproftools/informationpower/InformationLiteracyStandards_final.pdf>.

International Society for Technology in Education. *National Educational Technology Standards: The Next Generation. National Educational Technology Standards for Students*. Washington, DC: Author, 2007. 2 Aug. 2007 <http://cnets.iste.org/students/s_stands.html>.

National Association for Sport and Physical Education. *Moving into the Future: National Standards for Physical Education*. 2nd ed. Reston: American Alliance for Health Physical Educational Recreation and Dance, 2004. 10 Aug. 2007 <http://www.aahperd.org/naspe/publications-nationalstandards.html#list>.

National Council of Teachers of English, and International Reading Association. *Standards for the English Language Arts*. Urbana: International Reading Association, 1996. 2 Aug. 2007 <http://www.ncte.org/about/over/standards/110846.htm>.

Task Force of the National Council for the Social Studies. *The Curriculum Standards for Social Studies*. Silver Spring: National Council for the Social Studies, 1994. 2 Aug. 2007 <http://www.socialstudies.org/standards/>.

SAMPLES OF STUDENT WORK

FIGURE 11.4: SPORTS THEN AND NOW (STUDENT EXAMPLE)

Criteria for evaluation of student work:

- Accurately collects information from observation, information recall, and group discussion
- Documents and compares critical details from the photographs
- Poses a hypothesis that is probable and supported by the proposed outcome
- Completes a worksheet that clearly communicates a sport's past and present practices

FIGURE 11.6: MAPPING THE MILESTONES OF SPORTS HISTORY (STUDENT EXAMPLE)

Criteria for evaluation of student work:

- Accurately interprets the data collected
- Lists milestones that have significantly impacted the historic development of the sport
- Completes a map that is comprehensive in its scope and sequence of historic events

FIGURE 11.8: EXTREME GAMES REQUEST FOR PROPOSAL (STUDENT EXAMPLE)

Criteria for evaluation of student work:

- Complies with the requirements, organization, and format specified in the *Request for Proposal*
- Presents a unique sport in manageable sections and uses a clean layout with clearly labeled graphics and illustrations
- Creates a sport that can easily be replicated because of clearly written instructions, detailed directions, and descriptive guidelines
- Has the potential to attract athletes and spectators because of its appeal and challenging design

REFLECTION OF THE INSTRUCTORS

As library media specialists, we pushed ourselves to think creatively in working with the physical education department on this project. The PE teachers wanted to design a unit that showcased their students' mastery of the PE standards. Together we brainstormed ideas for an innovative product that demanded critical thinking and tested students' recall of physical education skills learned throughout the year. The teachers admitted they were uncomfortable with integrating other subjects in their project, i.e., language arts and social studies. We served as coaches through the process and assisted the department in collaborating with the language arts instructors.

We wound up playing a greater role in formulating and executing this collaborative effort than we had originally envisioned. For example, we established a review panel to provide students with a realistic analysis of their assignment. Volunteers from community businesses and organizations (e.g., Rotary Club) evaluated the projects. Because students knew that external reviewers were looking at their work, they put additional effort into following the requirements specified in the *Request for Proposal,* thus elevating the quality of their final products.

TEMPLATES AND RUBRICS FOR VARIOUS TASKS

Figure 11.3 Sports Then and Now

Sports have undergone transformation and development since their initial creation. A sport is rarely played the same now as when it was first conceived. Over time rules, guidelines, and equipment design change for many sports. Take a look at pictures of sports taken many years ago and compare them with current photos. Note similarities and differences and list them in the blocks below. Reflect on your results and develop possible reasons that may have prompted the change. List your plausible hypothesis below. Be prepared to share your results with the class.

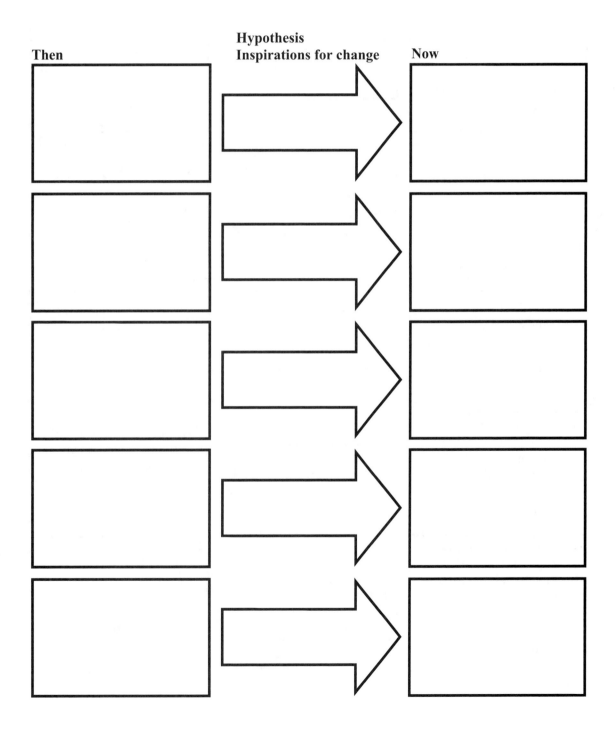

Then

Hypothesis
Inspirations for change

Now

Figure 11.4 Sports Then and Now (Student Example)

Evaluation of student work: This sample contains all of the observations and revelations that the student compiled after examining the photos of his particular sport. His responses are detailed and show definite differences that have occurred over the years. The completed organizer captures the evolution of the sport and lists possible reasons that might have influenced its development.

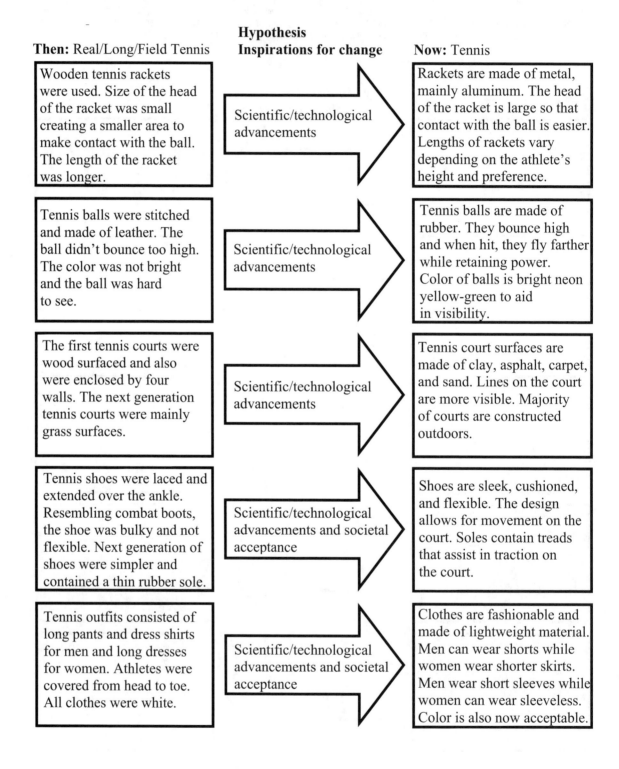

Then: Real/Long/Field Tennis	**Hypothesis** **Inspirations for change**	**Now:** Tennis
Wooden tennis rackets were used. Size of the head of the racket was small creating a smaller area to make contact with the ball. The length of the racket was longer.	Scientific/technological advancements	Rackets are made of metal, mainly aluminum. The head of the racket is large so that contact with the ball is easier. Lengths of rackets vary depending on the athlete's height and preference.
Tennis balls were stitched and made of leather. The ball didn't bounce too high. The color was not bright and the ball was hard to see.	Scientific/technological advancements	Tennis balls are made of rubber. They bounce high and when hit, they fly farther while retaining power. Color of balls is bright neon yellow-green to aid in visibility.
The first tennis courts were wood surfaced and also were enclosed by four walls. The next generation tennis courts were mainly grass surfaces.	Scientific/technological advancements	Tennis court surfaces are made of clay, asphalt, carpet, and sand. Lines on the court are more visible. Majority of courts are constructed outdoors.
Tennis shoes were laced and extended over the ankle. Resembling combat boots, the shoe was bulky and not flexible. Next generation of shoes were simpler and contained a thin rubber sole.	Scientific/technological advancements and societal acceptance	Shoes are sleek, cushioned, and flexible. The design allows for movement on the court. Soles contain treads that assist in traction on the court.
Tennis outfits consisted of long pants and dress shirts for men and long dresses for women. Athletes were covered from head to toe. All clothes were white.	Scientific/technological advancements and societal acceptance	Clothes are fashionable and made of lightweight material. Men can wear shorts while women wear shorter skirts. Men wear short sleeves while women can wear sleeveless. Color is also now acceptable.

Figure 11.5 Mapping the Milestones of Sports History

Objective: This exercise asks you to reflect on the development and evolution of different sports. Create a timeline by plotting out the milestones that have shaped the modern version of the game.

The Beginning: Describe your sport's origins. Who developed the game? When was it created? Where? Why? Provide important background information about the game's beginnings and the history behind its creation.

The Middle: How did the sport evolve over time? Identify key events and personalities that influenced major changes and adaptations of the sport. Focus on changes in the rules, equipment, and playing guidelines. Also make note of advancements made in technology, training, and science that have influenced change.

The Present: What are some of the notable achievements in recent times? List some of the current organizations, tournaments, and practices. Is the sport played nationally or worldwide? Evaluate and reflect upon the evolution of the game and the advancements still being made to challenge athletes and entertain fans.

Sport: _____

Start

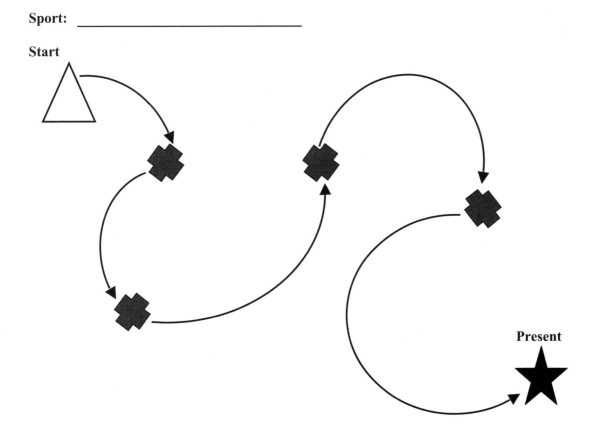

Present

Figure 11.6 Mapping the Milestones of Sports History (Student Example)

Evaluation of student work: This example meets the requirements for this assignment. The data collected are complete and show the development and evolution of the sport from its creation to the present. Information is accurate and the milestones cover the areas of influence that shaped and adapted the guidelines of play over the course of history.

Sport: Volleyball

Start

1895 Invented by William Morgan, physical director of the Young Men's Christian Association (YMCA) in Holyoke, Massachusetts. First created using a tennis net raised 6 feet 6 inches off the floor. Named mintonette due to its relationship to badminton, the sport was changed to volleyball to reflect its volleying nature. The sport gained popularity through the YMCA and ultimately spread worldwide.

1916 Rules issued jointly by the YMCA and the National Collegiate Athletic Association (NCAA). Philippines: Offensive passing (set and spike) developed.

1957 Volleyball designated as an Olympic Team sport. Included in the 1964 games.

1900 A special ball was designed and became the first Volleyball.

1917 Game changed from 21 to 15 points.

1897 Original rules published by Morgan in the *Official Handbook of the Athletic League of the Young Men's Christian Associations of North America.*

1955 Volleyball included in the Pan American Games.

1919 WWI American troops introduced the game to Europe.

1960 New techniques added that included the soft spike (dink), forearm pass (bump), blocking, and defensive diving and rolling.

1922 First nationwide tournament in the United States held by the YMCA in New York City.

1949 Women's Division was added (Senior women's division, 30+) added in 1977. Forearm pass introduced.

1964 Volleyball included in the Tokyo Olympics. New ball designed and adopted.

1998 End of side-out scoring. Rally point scoring adopted. First four sets played to a minimum of 25 points while the fifth set remained at 15.

Present: Volleyball is the 2nd most widely played sport worldwide. Three sets of rules govern the sport (NCAA, USAV, and the National Federation).

1928 The USA Volleyball Association (USVBA) was formed. [Now known as USA Volleyball (USAV)]

1998 Libero player is introduced. Officially adopted in 2002 by the NCAA, the player specializes in defensive skills.

Figure 11.7 Extreme Games Request for Proposal

Mahalo X-Games Inc.
2347 Maikai Way, Kapolei, HI 96707
Tel: 808-111-2222 · Fax: 808-111-3333

To: Extreme sports designers
From: Koa Leeward, Program Coordinator
Subject: Request for Proposal-Game Designs for Inclusion in the Mahalo X-Games
            Tournament

Background and Objectives

Mahalo X-Games Inc., a newly developed sports events planner, is interested in creating a local Extreme Games competition. To increase participation and interest, new game ideas are being solicited from interested designers. The selection committee seeks proposals that consist of team and individual play. Each proposal should be unique and not a sport already in existence. A technical manual explaining the objectives, rules, equipment, and guidelines must accompany the application. This document should be clearly written and understandable so that the committee can re-create and be knowledgeable about the sport.

Eligibility

Conditions of eligibility listed below will be strictly enforced. Proposals not following or meeting these criteria will be eliminated.
- Proposals must be complete, accurate, and clearly written.
- Proposals should be safe and not endanger the health and well being of participants. Safety equipment and precautions should also be designed to be worn if needed.
- Proposals requiring equipment for play should be readily available along with standard forms of sports gear. New inventions or apparatus designs will not be considered.

Content of Proposal

Proposals should address each of the items listed below under separate headings.
- Contact information: Applicants' names, home addresses, phone numbers and email addresses.
- Brief introduction/overview of sport: Provide a brief summary of proposed sport design.
- Complete technical manual: Describe the game, playing field, equipment, rules, guidelines, instructions on play, tactics, players' responsibilities, and criteria for winning.

Selection Process and Criteria

A panel of sports experts selected by Mahalo X-Games Inc. will review all proposals. All entries will be evaluated based upon the following criteria:
- Clear instructions and well-detailed technical manual.
- Ability to implement the game with the resources and equipment available to Mahalo X-Games Inc.
- Potential to attract athletes to participate in the event and spectators to view the event.

Schedule and Deadlines

See your school-based representative for exact due dates and notification of awards.

Figure 11.8 Extreme Games Request for Proposal (Student Example)

Evaluation of student work: This proposal contains all of the sections required by the Mahalo X-Games, Inc. in the *Request for Proposal*. It meets all of the eligibility requirements and is safe for athletes to play. The student has conducted background research and combined techniques from several games to create a challenging extreme sport. The resulting activity is original. The manual contains accurate details and clear instructions for the rules of play.

John Honu
43-210 Kuhio St.
Kapolei, HI 96707
(808) 444-8888

Mike Leeward, Program Coordinator
Mahalo X-Games, Inc.
2347 Maikai Way
Kapolei, HI 96707

Dear Mr. Leeward:

The following attachment is my official proposal for your X-Games Tournament. If you have any questions regarding the material please feel free to contact me at:

John Honu
43-210 Kuhio St.
Kapolei, HI 96707
(808) 444-8888
ihonu@malama.net

Thank you for your time and consideration.

Sincerely,

John Honu

John Honu

Extreme Volleyball Face-Off Technical Manual

Extreme Sport: Extreme Volleyball Face-Off

Introduction: Extreme Volleyball Face-Off is a fast-paced sport incorporating the rules, techniques, and skills from volleyball, dodge ball, and soccer. This sport is played with teams of 10 (six players starting on the court and the remaining four acting as substitutes). Using volleyball and soccer moves, players pass the ball and attempt to score a goal within three contacts. The goal is a soccer net located in the service area on the opposite side of the court. The objective is to be the first team to win three sets. Extreme Volleyball not only challenges the athlete's skills but his or her ability to be consistent in playing, to follow directions, and to execute control over the ball at all times.

Objective: To be the first team to win three sets. Each set needs 30 goals to win. If a fifth set must be played, the winner is the first team to reach 15 goals.

Equipment: 2 junior soccer goals with nets (width 5.20m x height 2.20m)
1 regulation sized volleyball (circumference 65-67cm/26in., weight 260-280g/9.5oz, pressure 0.30-0.325kg/sp.cm.)
Volleyball net (9.5m/31ft. long and 1m/3ft. wide)

Court/Field: Standardized volleyball court at least 59ft. long x 30ft. wide. Court should be lined with the centerline marking the half way division, boundaries of the playing area and attack-lines 10ft. parallel off either side of the centerline (creating an area of front and back zones). Similar to volleyball, the net is set up (height of 8 ft.) at the centerline. The sport can be played either indoors or outdoors.

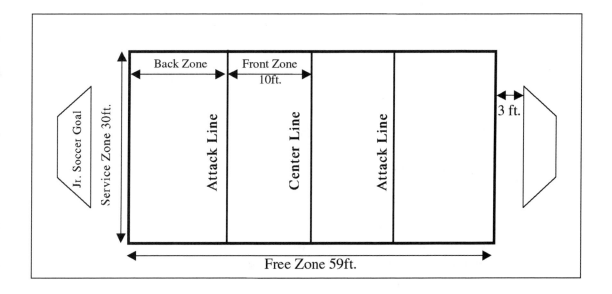

Officials: There are three referees who officiate the game. One serves as the head and is positioned at the centerline. His responsibilities: making final decisions on points, line calls, dead balls, and penalties. The other two referees are located in the service zone diagonally opposite from each other. They serve as both point and line judges. In addition, they assist the head referee by alerting him in calling penalties and dead balls.

Guidelines: **Teams.** Extreme Volleyball is a team sport consisting of 10 members; six are in active play while four remain available as substitutes. There are three positions that players can cover. The team leader is the setter, who determines strategy and sets up the attack. Two players complete the front zone by serving as outside hitters. They execute team strategies and score goals. The remaining three are back row specialists and goalies, who guard the goal (soccer net) and defend their team from the opponent's attacks.

Rotation. Each time a team wins control of the ball the players must rotate clockwise one position. Players must be in the rotated positions when the serves are made. Once the serve has been executed, a team can reorder members to effectively cover the court. However, each team must reset their players to the original positions before the next serve is made. Teams caught off rotation will be assessed a penalty that is charged to all of their players on the court.

Start of play. Team captains approach the head referee for the official coin toss. The winner may choose to serve or receive the first ball and decides the side of the court on which the team begins the game. Teams rotate serving from the second set. After the initial serve to start the set, the ball is live until it hits the floor, is out of bounds, or a goal is scored. As dead balls or goals occur, the opposing side gets to serve. Serving must be done within the service zone. The ball can be served or thrown; however, it must clear the net and land on the opponent's side of the court.

Passing the ball. Once the ball is served the receiving team has a maximum of three contacts to return the ball to the other side and attempt to score. The ball can be moved with techniques accepted in volleyball (bump, volley, and spike) and upper body moves in soccer (torso and head). At no time can the ball touch the floor or be caught/lifted using the players' hands. Players called for a lift or catch incur penalties.

Penalties. Once players receive three penalties they are removed from play for the duration of the set. Players are penalized for the following: bad sportsmanship, catching/lifting the ball, service error, net violation, double contact, game delay, service foot fault, incorrect team rotation, and intentionally grounding or causing a dead ball situation. In the case of a severe penalty, the head referee may remove a player (for one set or the entire game) after one offense. The team must continue to play without penalized athletes until the set is completed. Teams can continue to lose players due to penalties until only one member remains on the court.

Scoring. To earn a point, a team must get the ball into their goal (soccer net) located in the opposing team's service zone within three contacts. A point will not be awarded if the ball is deemed dead (touches the floor) before bouncing into the goal. Five sets make up a game. Sets 1 to 4 are 30 goals each. The fifth set is scored differently—it is a 15-point round (similar to volleyball). After the eighth point is scored, teams switch sides to finish the set.

Determining a winner. The winner is the first team to win three sets.

Rules:
- To score a goal on the opposite side of the court, a player must pass the ball over the net within the boundaries of the court.
- The ball can only be handled a maximum of three times before being returned to the other team's court or a goal attempt is made. A player may not touch the ball two times in succession. A penalty is assessed to the player that makes double contact.
- Players can only pass the ball using official volleyball and upper body soccer techniques. Using the leg or feet is acceptable as long as the ball does not make contact with the ground. If the ball hits the floor, play stops. If a player lifts, catches, or carries the ball, a penalty is assessed.
- If the ball goes out of bounds due to a bad pass, the ball is still in play. Players may go after and pass the ball back to the team's side of the court. At no time can the player cross into the opponent's side of the court.
- Players cannot come in contact with the net at any time. If a player makes contact, he is assessed a penalty and the referee stops play.
- Players cannot cross into the opposing team's court during play. If caught trespassing, a penalty is assessed and play stops.
- The team is in violation if players assume incorrect positions, fail to follow the order of rotation, or serve out of turn. Each active member on the court is assessed one penalty.
- When serving, a player must stay within the service zone. If the service line is crossed, a penalty is assessed for a foot fault and the team loses control of the ball to the opposing team.
- If players accumulate three penalties, they are disqualified and must sit out the rest of the set. The team must continue play with the remaining players.
- At any point in the match a substitution can be made. The team leader notifies one of the referees to make the switch. If a player has been disqualified due to penalties, he or she may not serve as a substitute.
- Each team gets two 30-second timeouts per set. The team captain must notify officials of intent to take the timeout before leaving the court.
- If there is a disagreement with a judge's call only the team captain may approach the referee. Once the plea is made the head referee has the right to overturn the call. The referee's decision is final.

Figure 11.9 Panel Score Card for RFP

Mahalo X-Games

Please review the proposal to determine eligibility

Criteria	Yes	No
Complete – Does the proposal include all of the requested information, parts, and documents?		
Deadline – Was the proposal received by the posted deadline?		
Originality – Is the proposed sport unique (it has not been invented yet)?		
Equipment – Are standard forms of sports equipment being used?		
Safety – Is the sport safe (it does not endanger the health or well being of participants)?		

 STOP! If you marked **NO** on any of the criteria above, the proposal is ineligible. Discontinue scoring. If qualifications are met please continue to the scoring sheet below.

Use this section to score the proposal and technical manual

Criteria	Points (10 max)
Comprehensive – Proposal contains all the pieces necessary to understand the sport. Includes background information on the game, playing field, equipment, rules, guidelines, playing instructions, tactics, players' responsibilities, and criteria for winning.	
Clarity – Instructions are clearly written, organized in manageable sections, and easy to understand. Content is clearly communicated to readers and is true to the vision of the creators of the sport.	
Details – Sports procedures provide enough detail and information for readers to comprehend and re-create the game. Includes necessary graphics and illustrations to explain elements of the competition.	
Accuracy – Details are accurate and clearly stated. Facts and figures presented throughout the proposal are consistent. Data presented within each section are reliable and reflect results of research.	
Staging – Proposed game can be easily held on the grounds of the community center where the event will be held.	
Ease of Play – Sport can be easily played, rules memorized, and guidelines implemented.	
Use of Equipment – Equipment required is familiar and easy for athletes to manage.	
Officiating – Referees/officiates can easily be trained and educated on the operation of the sport.	
Challenge – Sport is competitive and challenging to athletes.	
Popularity – Game has the potential to draw people. Athletes will be excited to participate while fans will want to attend matches.	
Total Points	

Proposal Information

Proposed Sport

Designer's Name

Contact Address/Phone Number

Contact Email Address

Scoring Guide

Grade	Points
Superior	10
Very Good	8-9
Good	6-7
Approaching (Not met)	5↓

Applications receiving scores of **Superior** and **Very Good** throughout the grading process will be reviewed again for possible inclusion within the X-Games tournament.

Judge's Corner

Judge's Name

Judge's Signature

Date

Overall Comments:

Figure 11.10 Technical Writing Rubric

Criteria	Exceeds (3)	Meets (2)	Approaches (1)	Score
Specifications	Follows specifications of the *Request for Proposal*. All information is complete and follows the application's format criteria.	Follows specifications of the *Request for Proposal* but some information is incomplete and some format criteria are not followed.	Does not follow specifications of the *Request for Proposal*. Most of the information is incomplete; format criteria are not followed.	
Organization	Proposal is organized in manageable sections that describe how the sport is played. All points of the activity are covered.	Proposal is organized in sections; however, some sections are too large to clearly understand how the sport is played. Although major points are covered there is confusion on how to play portions of the game.	Most of proposal is not organized in manageable sections; therefore, the sport is not easy to understand. It is confusing as to how the entire game is played.	
Directions	Each step of play is clearly described. Reader can easily interpret all game objectives, guidelines, and strategies. Writing is grammatically correct.	Most steps of play are clearly described. Reader can easily interpret most of the game objectives, guidelines, and strategies. Some of writing shows problems with grammar, spelling, and punctuation.	Most steps of play are not clearly described. Reader has trouble interpreting most of the game objectives, guidelines, and strategies. Most of writing shows problems with grammar, spelling, and punctuation.	
Graphics and illustrations	All of the graphics and illustrations add clarity to points being made. All items are neatly created, clearly labeled, and easy to interpret.	Most of the graphics and illustrations add clarity to points being made. Most of the items are neatly created, clearly labeled, and easy to interpret.	There are few graphics and illustrations. Those included offer little clarity. Most items are not neatly created, clearly labeled, or easy to interpret.	
			Total	

Rubric Scoring Guide:

Exceeded the standards	10 to 12 points
Met the standards	7 to 9 points
Approaching the standards	4 to 6 points
Not met	3 points and below

12 Do I Have to Like it? Understanding and Appreciating Art

COURSE: Art, Language Arts
GRADES: 9-12
DURATION OF PROJECT: Three weeks
STUDENT OUTCOMES
  CONTENT GOALS:
    Students will develop a greater understanding and appreciation of art
    by researching the influences that affect an artist's work. They will
    accomplish this by:

    • Learning about important artists through researching their
      lives and their impact on art.
    • Examining the historical, social, cultural, environmental,
      and personal influences on an artist's work.
    • Analyzing how art communicates ideas, emotions,
      knowledge, and experiences to others.
    • Applying art elements to describe, analyze, interpret, and
      evaluate an artist's work.

  PROCESS GOALS:
    Students will develop information literacy skills needed to foster
    complex and higher-order thinking.

DESCRIPTION OF PRODUCT OR PERFORMANCE

From prehistoric times, humans have communicated their experiences, feelings, and thoughts
through various forms of art including painting, sculpture, and pottery. When examining art,
we are viewing a piece through the artist's eyes and given insight into the artist's feelings and
ideas. We gain even richer appreciation of the art when we study the artist's work knowing
about his or her home life and family and the social norms and historical highlights of the
times in which the artist lived. Students will be responsible for:

  • Gathering and analyzing information on the life of a selected artist.
  • Examining the historical, social, cultural, and environmental milieu as
    well as the artist's personal experiences that might have influenced his or
    her work.

- Selecting a piece from the artist's collection that shows a major turning point or breakthrough in his or her career.
- Utilizing art terminology in analyzing and evaluating a work of art.
- Presenting a biographical profile of the artist's life and work.

CONNECTION WITH STANDARDS

Standards from Fine Arts, Language Arts, Social Studies, Technology, and Information Literacy are integrated in this project.

ARTS EDUCATION

Standards addressed in this unit include evaluating a range of artworks and relating them to history and culture. For more detailed information on the standards refer to <http://artsedge. kennedy-center.org/teach/standards.cfm>.

LANGUAGE ARTS

Standards addressed in this unit deal with using language to communicate with various audiences, employing a range of writing strategies, applying language conventions, and conducting research using a variety of informational and technological resources. For more detailed information on the standards refer to <http://www.ncte.org/about/over/ standards/110846.htm>.

SOCIAL STUDIES

Standards addressed in this unit focus on specific skills within broad thematic standards that deal with culture; individual development and identity; and individuals, groups and institutions. For more detailed information on the standards refer to <http://www. socialstudies.org/standards/>.

TECHNOLOGY

Standards addressed in this unit deal with basic operations and concepts; social, ethical, and human issues; technology productivity tools; and technology tools for communication and research. For more detailed information on the standards refer to <http://cnets.iste.org/ students/s_stands.html>.

INFORMATION LITERACY

Standards addressed in this unit focus on the access, evaluation, and use of information; appreciation for all forms of creative expression; development of self-reflection skills in knowledge acquisition; and social responsibility in working with information. For more detailed information on the standards refer to <http://www.ala.org/ala/aasl/aaslproftools/ informationpower/InformationLiteracyStandards_final.pdf>.

OVERARCHING PROJECT QUESTIONS

- What does it mean to "appreciate" art?
- How can I better grasp and appreciate a work of art?

- How might knowledge of an artist improve my understanding of an art piece?
- What influences and inspires an artist's creation of a work?

TIMELINE FOR PROJECT

Figure 12.1 Project Timeline

Time	Instructor's Tasks (LMS/T)	Student's Performance Tasks

Day 1	**CONNECT**
	• Select an art piece to grab students' attention. (T)
	• Lead discussion on the artwork. Use vocabulary and information from previous lessons to tap students' prior knowledge. (T)
		CONNECT
		• Study a selected art piece and discuss the following:
		  – What is your first impression of the piece?
		  – What was the artist communicating in this piece?
		  – How does it make you feel?
		  – What is it about?
		  – Can you guess when it was created?
		  – Can you guess who created it?

Day 2	**WONDER**
	• Review discussion from yesterday on reaction to the art piece. Have students share reflections. (T)
	• Lead discussion into the overarching questions. (T)
	Note: Let students know that art appreciation is more than just liking an art piece. It involves a deeper understanding of the work, the circumstances under which it was created, and the recognition of the message being conveyed through the artist's eye.
		WONDER
		• Share reflections regarding artist's message.
		• Discuss overarching questions.
		• Realize that artists are influenced by various factors including:
		  – Personal experiences
		  – Religion
		  – Culture
		  – War
		  – Historical events
		  – Current notions about society, politics, and other factors

Day 3	**CONNECT**
	• Explain project scenario to students. (T)
	• Using the art piece from Day 1, model how students can create a profile that centers on questions such as:
	  – What type of art form is this?
	  – What was your first impression when seeing it?
	  – What is it all about? Are there any recognizable images?
	  – What are the points of emphasis?
	  – What feelings or emotions do you get from the piece?
	  – Does the piece remind you of something?
	  – What techniques were used to create it? (T)
	• Monitor student understanding through observation and written response to the above prompts. Provide clarification or further instruction as needed. (T)
		CONNECT
		• Go over the following scenario:
		A film production company is planning a television show focusing on art and artists. The goal of the show is to increase public understanding and appreciation for art. As employees of the company you have been asked to suggest artists and their work to be used. The producers want written critical profiles of artists and their work, which they hope to use in their decision-making and as a companion resource for the show. In addition, you will present your profile to the producers to convince them to include your artist and his or her work in the program.
		• Go through steps with the teacher on how to create the artist's profile.
		• Based on the modeling done by the teacher using the piece of art from Day 1, respond to the following questions:
		  – Using my new knowledge of the artwork, what message was the artist trying to communicate?
		  – What is my impression of the piece now? How did piecing together information influence my impression?

continued

Time	Instructor's Tasks (LMS/T)	Student's Performance Tasks

Days 4-9	**INVESTIGATE**
	• Review assignment. (T)
	• Have students create key questions to guide their research. (T)
	• Encourage students to continue generating questions as research progresses. (LMS/T)
	• Briefly summarize the various art periods from which students might choose. (T)
	• Provide a list of possible artists and art pieces students might want to investigate. (T)
	   Note: The art teacher may want to restrict the historical art periods depending on the project time frame and curriculum focus.
	• Provide time to do a pre-search on possible topics. (T)
	• Explain how to complete the graphic organizer, *Viewing Various Artists.* (LMS)
	• Provide access to and instruction on a variety of possible print and online resources. (LMS)
	• Have student assess their informational needs as they review their questions. (LMS/T)
	
	ASSESS
	• Conduct ongoing assessment to evaluate students' progress through conferencing, observations, and reflections. Provide assistance where needed. (LMS/T)
		INVESTIGATE
		• Create key questions to focus the research. Organize questions into categories.
		• Continue to generate questions to provide in-depth information on:
		  – Home life/family
		  – Education
		  – Influences in the artist's life
		  – Work (e.g., specific pieces, style, technique, philosophy)
		  – Milestones in the artist's work
		  – Pictures of the artist's work that exemplify turning points or highlights of his or her career
		• Skim through various art books to find information on three possible topics.
		• Use the graphic organizer, *Viewing Various Artists,* to take notes. (See Figure 12.3)
		• Select an art piece and artist to research.
		• Gather information using print and online resources to answer questions. Create a working bibliography of resources used.
		
		ASSESS
		• Assess the status of your research by referring to your questions.
		  – Have all required areas been addressed?
		  – Is my information adequate to create a comprehensive profile of this art piece and artist?
		  – Are there any gaps in my research?
		  – What should I do next?

Days 10-15	**CONSTRUCT** • Have students gather all their information. (LMS/T) • Create a sample profile to use as a model or gather art catalogs for students to view. Discuss with students how they might develop their profiles using the *Art Critique Checklist* to guide them. (LMS/T) • Have students exchange drafts for editing. Provide the time needed for peer evaluations. (T) • Allot time to work on presentation. (T) • Monitor student progress through observation, peer edits, self, and peer reflection. (LMS/T)	**CONSTRUCT** • Gather all information (notes, pictures, bibliographies). • Draft profile. • Submit draft for peer evaluations. Evaluate at least two drafts from peers using the *Art Critique Checklist.* (See Figure 12.5) • Create and practice a short presentation of your research. • Monitor your own progress through conferencing and self-reflection.
Days 16-18	**EXPRESS** • Organize schedule for presentations. (T)	**EXPRESS** • Present to class. • Evaluate three classmates' presentations using the *Art Critique Checklist.*
Day 19	**REFLECT** • Discuss with students the wide range of influences that impact an artist's style, technique, ideas, and overall work.	**REFLECT** • Review the various influences that impact artists and their art. • Based on your research and the presentations respond to the question: – How can knowledge about artists help me better understand and appreciate the art they create?

ASSESSMENT CHECKPOINTS

Figure 12.2 Project Assessment Plan

Checkpoints in the process	What is assessed	Who assesses	Assessment tool
Connect	Student participation and content understanding	Teacher Library media specialist Student	Observation Group discussion Reflection
Wonder	Higher-order thinking and ability to make connections to prior experiences	Teacher Student	Observation Group discussion Reflection
Investigate	Information retrieval and the efficient, effective use of resource materials	Library media specialist Student	Question development Observation *Viewing Various Artists* (See Figure 12.3) Reflection Consultation
Construct/Express	Evaluation, synthesis, and presentation of data in a clear manner	Teacher Library media specialist Student	Observation *Art Critique Checklist* (See Figure 12.5) Consultation
Reflect	Assessment and evaluation of personal progress and modifications for continued improvement	Teacher Library media specialist Student	Reflection

RESOURCES USED IN THE PROJECT

Glastein, Jerry. *Formal Visual Analysis: The Elements of Principle and Composition.* *ARTSEDGE.* Washington, DC: The John F. Kennedy Center for the Performing Arts, n.d. 5 Aug. 2007 <http://artsedge.kennedy-center.org/content/3902/>.

Greenway, Shirley. *Art: An A-Z Guide.* New York: Franklin Watts, 1993.

National Gallery of Art. *Art for the Nation: Collecting for a New Century.* Washington, DC: The National Gallery of Art, 2007. 5 Aug. 2007 <http://www.nga.gov/feature/artnation/splash.shtm>.

Payne, Joyce. *Teaching Students to Critique.* *ARTSEDGE.* Washington, DC: The John F. Kennedy Center for the Performing Arts, n.d. 5 Aug. 2007 <http://artsedge.kennedy-center.org/content/3338/>.

Sayre, Henry. *Cave Paintings to Picasso: The Inside Scoop on 50 Art Masterpieces.* San Francisco: Chronicle Books, 2004.

Sotto, Theresa. *Art Critiques Made Easy.* *ARTSEDGE.* Washington, DC: The John F. Kennedy Center for the Performing Arts, n.d. 5 Aug. 2007 <http://artsedge.kennedy-center.org/content/3932/>.

Strickland, Carol. *The Annotated Mona Lisa: A Crash Course in Art History from Prehistoric to Post-Modern.* Kansas City: Andrews and McMeel, 1994.

STANDARDS CITED

American Association of School Librarians, and the Association for Educational Communications and Technology. *Information Literacy Standards for Student Learning*. Chicago: American Library Association, 1998. 2 Aug. 2007 <http://www.ala.org/ala/aasl/aaslproftools/informationpower/InformationLiteracyStandards_final.pdf>.

Consortium of National Arts Education Associations. *The National Standards for Arts Education. ARTSEDGE*. Washington, DC: Author, 1994. 7 Aug. 2007 <http://artsedge.kennedy-center.org/teach/standards.cfm>.

International Society for Technology in Education. *National Educational Technology Standards: The Next Generation. National Educational Technology Standards for Students*. Washington, DC: Author, 2007. 2 Aug. 2007 <http://cnets.iste.org/students/s_stands.html>.

National Council of Teachers of English, and International Reading Association. *Standards for the English Language Arts*. Urbana: International Reading Association, 1996. 2 Aug. 2007 <http://www.ncte.org/about/over/standards/110846.htm>.

Task Force of the National Council for the Social Studies. *The Curriculum Standards for Social Studies*. Silver Spring: National Council for the Social Studies, 1994. 2 Aug. 2007 <http://www.socialstudies.org/standards/>.

SAMPLES OF STUDENT WORK

FIGURE 12.3: VIEWING VARIOUS ARTISTS (STUDENT EXAMPLE)

Criteria for evaluation of student work:

- Collects accurate and relevant data from a range of credible resources
- Addresses all questions in the organizer

REFLECTION OF THE INSTRUCTORS

Traditionally our art classes did not use the library for research projects as often as other content areas. They tended to focus on content theory and application of art elements in their own classrooms. As library media specialists, we believed research could be incorporated in all content areas. Therefore, we were pleased to finally work with several art teachers on this project. In this instance, the teachers wanted students to apply knowledge of their content, not by creating an art piece but by appreciating art through cultural and historical prisms.

We worked together throughout the project. There were times when the art teacher took the lead if students had specific questions regarding art elements, techniques, styles, and movements. As library media specialists, we took the lead whenever students had to find background material on the art and the artist. This required all of us to be flexible so that we could move between the classroom and the library depending on students' needs.

Print materials were either scarce or at reading levels far above our students' abilities. We enlisted help from public libraries to secure more suitable resources from their juvenile collections. At times, we had to assist students with alternative subjects for research. For example, several students had trouble finding biographical information on Asian artists dating back 300 years. In these cases, we worked with them to find more recent artists to study.

TEMPLATES AND RUBRICS FOR VARIOUS TASKS

Figure 12.3 Viewing Various Artists

Pollack? Kahlo? Warhol? With so many artists, whom will you select to profile? Spend time viewing the library's collection of art resources to find the most intriguing and influential subject for your project. To help you, fill in the frames below with three possible art pieces. In each frame, write a brief description of the work. Put the title of the piece in the space under the frame. Provide additional information about the piece and artist on the right.

Art #1: _____

Art #2: _____

Art #3: _____

Figure 12.4 Viewing Various Artists (Student Example)

Evaluation of student work: This sample exceeds expectations. The student has gathered accurate information on three pieces of art. The organizer is complete with important details regarding three artists and their bodies of work.

A woodblock print (Ukiyo-e). It is a big wave about to crash on 2 boats. Mt. Fuji is in the background (very small). Shades of blue, white, and brown are used. It uses perspective to make the wave seem bigger and Mt. Fuji smaller. The main focus is the dangerous wave. Printed 1823-29.

Art #1: **Great Wave Off Kanagawa**

Katsushika Hokusai was a Japanese painter and wood engraver. He lived from 1760 to1849 in Edo, the capital of Old Japan. He is well known for his printmaking or Ukiyo-e. He learned from another artist, Katsukawa Shunsho. He did many book illustrations and color prints about the Japanese people, culture, and traditions. He used curved lives and spirals, large broken strokes, and somber colors. Among his best-known works are the 13-volume sketchbook *Hokusai Manga* and a series of block prints known as the *Thirty-Six Views of Mount Fuji.* He was appreciated more in the West than in Japan. He influenced many Western Impressionists.

Looks like splatters of black, white, and grey paint thrown at the canvas. On the bottom, yellow, blue, and red appear but are swirled into the other colors. Made from paint drippings, they look like swirls with tails. Made in 1953.

Art #2: **Greyed Rainbow**

Jackson Pollack was an American painter. Born in 1912 he died in 1956. He was the fifth son born to a Wyoming couple. He grew up in Arizona and California. He was encouraged to paint as a teenager. He studied at the Art Students League in New York. He was interested in Surrealism and became the leader of the American Abstract Expressionism or New York School. He was very interested in expressing emotions. He used sticks, trowels, and knives to paint, not brushes. His style is called Action painting. He often worked on large canvases on the floor or against a wall. He says he wanted to paint his emotions without his thoughts getting in the way.

A marble sculpture of a half open right palm. There are figures of a man and woman curled in a fetal position. The hand is detailed with tendons, muscles, and fingernails. It is not a "finished" smooth piece but very rough. It looks unfinished. It was made in 1898.

Art #3 **The Hand of God**

Francois-Auguste-Rene Rodin was born in 1840, the second son of a working family. He was shy and nearsighted, which affected his academic work as a child. Art was his interest at age 10. His father sent him to boarding school but he eventually enrolled at a government school for craft and design. He worked in Decorative Arts to support his family and did art at night. At one point, he attempted to join the monastery but left to sculpt. His work and popularity grew over the years and he was known worldwide for his sculptures of the human form. In his design, he often changed parts of the anatomy. He felt that true beauty was an inner state.

Figure 12.5 Art Critique Checklist

This checklist will be used in the creation, peer editing, and presentation of our critiques.

Critic: When developing your critique, please address all items in the checklist.
Peer Editor and Evaluators: Read each description and place a check in the box if the critique has addressed the item. Provide constructive feedback in the box below the checklist.

Description	Analysis	Interpretation	Evaluation
Biography • I profiled the artist's life. • I identified historical, cultural, environmental, and social influences on the artist. • I described how the artist's work was viewed during the artist's lifetime.	**Biography** • I analyzed major influences in the artist's life. • I explained the extent to which the artist was impacted by various elements.	**Biography** • I explained how major life events shaped the artist's perception and ideas. • I linked the historic, social, and cultural influences on the artist's work.	**Judgment** • I expressed my opinion on the success or failure of the artwork to communicate the artist's ideas. • I supported my personal reaction to the artwork with examples. • I used credible resources to support my evaluation. • I organized my ideas in a logical and meaningful way.
Artwork • I selected a work from the artist to study. • I explained what was happening in the art piece(s). • I noted when and where the work was created. • I noted other pieces by the artist (by theme, major turning points).	**Artwork** • I noted major elements in the work (e.g., space, light, color). • I identified the technical qualities of the work (e.g., tools, materials, stroke). • I explained how the work was constructed. • I explained the relationships between the subjects. • I used art terms to explain and analyze the above points.	**Artwork** • I described how people might respond emotionally to the artist's work. • I explained how the work reminded me of other things I experienced. • I used the other art pieces as examples to explain his artistic style, focus, and technique.	**Presentation only:** • I kept eye contact with my audience. • I spoke so that they heard me clearly. • I answered all questions asked by the audience.
Feedback:			

13 Censorship: Defending the Freedom of Expression

> **COURSE:** Language Arts, Social Studies
> **GRADES:** 9-12
> **DURATION OF PROJECT:** Two weeks
> **STUDENT OUTCOMES**
>   CONTENT GOALS:
>
>   Students will demonstrate their understanding of the societal
> influences and beliefs that lead to censorship and the impact
> of this issue on society by:
>
> - Defining the issue of censorship.
> - Studying artifacts and published works that have been
>   censored.
> - Identifying the reasons for censorship and recommending
>   actions to prevent censorship and encourage freedom of
>   expression.
> - Formulating thoughtful opinions on controversial subject
>   matter based on information gathered.
> - Using newly gained knowledge to produce anti-censorship
>   posters that are shared with peers and the community.
>
>   PROCESS GOALS:
>
>   Students will develop information literacy skills needed to foster
> complex and higher-order thinking.

DESCRIPTION OF PRODUCT OR PERFORMANCE

To understand the complex history of censorship, students will investigate key works that have been challenged over time. They will research specific pieces and gather background information on the artists and the challenges they faced. Although literature has been the predominant target of censors, this unit includes other forms of artistic expression such as drama, film and video, music and dance, and the visual arts.

    Using the information they gather during the research phase of the unit, students develop a poster campaign to make their peers aware of the consequences of censorship. They display their posters in the school library during Banned Books Week. A smaller sampling of the most effective posters will also be loaned to the public library for a special exhibit. Students will be responsible for:

- Gathering, analyzing, and presenting information that highlights the work, the artist's perspective, and the reasons for censure.
- Presenting the historical importance of the work, its contributions to the art community, and its impact on society.
- Developing a poster that highlights the positive contributions of banned works throughout history.
- Sharing the posters with peers and the community to deepen everyone's understanding of the First Amendment and the importance of free expression.

CONNECTION WITH STANDARDS

Standards from Language Arts, Social Studies, Technology, and Information Literacy are integrated in this project.

LANGUAGE ARTS

Standards addressed in this unit deal with using language to communicate with various audiences, employing a range of writing strategies, applying language conventions, reading a range of literature, and conducting research using a variety of informational and technological resources. For more detailed information on the standards refer to <http://www.ncte.org/about/over/standards/110846.htm>.

SOCIAL STUDIES

Standards addressed in this unit focus on specific skills within broad thematic standards that deal with culture; individuals, groups and institutions; global connections; and civic ideas and practices. For more detailed information on the standards refer to <http://www.socialstudies.org/standards/>.

TECHNOLOGY

Standards addressed in this unit deal with basic operations and concepts; social, ethical, and human issues; technology productivity tools; and technology tools for communication and research. For more detailed information on the standards refer to <http://cnets.iste.org/students/s_stands.html>.

INFORMATION LITERACY

Standards addressed in this unit focus on the access, evaluation, and use of information; appreciation for all forms of creative expression; development of self-reflection skills in knowledge acquisition; and social responsibility in working with information. For more detailed information on the standards refer to <http://www.ala.org/ala/aasl/aaslproftools/informationpower/InformationLiteracyStandards_final.pdf>.

OVERARCHING PROJECT QUESTIONS

- Why does censorship occur?
- What factors influence what is censored?
- Is censorship ever justified?
- How would society have been affected if censors were successful throughout history?
- How have existing conditions in a particular society affected what was censored?
- How might we combat censorship and protect the freedom to express ourselves?

TIMELINE FOR PROJECT

Figure 13.1 Project Timeline

Time	Instructor's Tasks (LMS/T)	Student's Performance Tasks
Prior to Day 1	**CONNECT** • Introduce the unit to the class. Explain that due to the sensitive nature of the material, students must respect each other's right to express an opinion and must display mature behavior. (T) • Distribute informational flyers for parents. Stress that if parents have strong objections or questions they must contact one of the instructors for more information. They may also request alternative assignments. (T) • Distribute the Banned Books reading list. Have students read different titles from the list prior to launching this unit. (T)	**CONNECT** • Ask questions to clarify objectives and expectations of the upcoming unit. • Agree to exercise mature behavior throughout the unit. • Discuss informational flyer with parents. • Read books from the Banned Books reading list and take notes on passages that have been flagged as controversial. • Share readings with the class. Discuss the passages that have been censored. • Form opinions on whether the ban was justified. Give reasons for your opinion based on evidence from the book itself.
Day 1	**WONDER** • Introduce the concept of censorship. Discuss the issues and facts behind the topic and its occurrence throughout the world. (T) • Highlight the differences between valid and invalid concerns. Consider: Is censorship ever justified? (T) • Facilitate discussion on concerns and motives that fuel censorship. Compile a list as students generate ideas. (T)	**WONDER** • Generate possible reasons for censorship. • Share responses with the class.

continued

Time	Instructor's Tasks (LMS/T)	Student's Performance Tasks

Days 1-2	**CONNECT**
	• List reasons for censorship generated from the discussion. Reasons should include but not be limited to:
	  – Strong sexual content
	  – Excessive violence
	  – Obscene or inappropriate language
	  – Unsuitable content for age group
	  – Graphics in bad taste or with nudity (T)
	• Go over the exercise *You Can't Say That!* (T)
	• Role-play a censor and model how to locate an article and eliminate "objectionable" facts from it. Discuss results with the class. (T)
		CONNECT
		• Build a list of reasons generated from the discussion.
		• Select an article from a newspaper resource. Use the generated list of reasons to role-play a censor. Cross out passages in the article that you consider controversial or "taboo." Use *You Can't Say That!* for this activity. (See Figure 13.3)
		• Throughout the process reflect on the following questions:
		  – Why does censorship occur?
		  – What factors influence what is censored?

Day 2	**REFLECT** • Have students share censored articles. (T) • Recap what students did and felt as censors. Highlight issues or concerns that fueled the censorship effort. (T)	**REFLECT** • Look over the censored article and determine how much information is still remaining. • Reflect on the negative impact censorship has on the sharing of information. • Share observations and findings with the class.
Days 2-3	**INVESTIGATE** • Distribute and explain the directions for the next assignment: *Would the World Be a Better Place?* For this task, students examine censorship throughout history. Have them select a work from one of the artistic genres that has been the target of censors. Focus their background research on the work itself, the artist's perspective, and grounds for objections. (T) • Introduce print and electronic resources that will be useful for this project. Resources may be scarce; look for historic books and Web sites that offer credible information to assist in research. (LMS)	**INVESTIGATE** • Conduct research to build background information for the art/piece and reasons for objections. Information should include history on the work itself, artist's perspective, and reasons for censure. Use *Would the World Be a Better Place?* for this activity. (See Figure 13.5)

	CONSTRUCT/EXPRESS
	• Allow students time to complete the organizer: *Would the World Be a Better Place?* (T)
	• Help students to formulate opinions, and hypothesize and answer the project's overarching questions. (T)
		CONSTRUCT/EXPRESS
		• Complete *Would the World Be a Better Place?* Based on data gathered, analyze and deduce the positive impact of the work on society. Using this information, hypothesize:
		  – How would society have been affected if censors were successful in banning items throughout the years?
		• Formulate an opinion on the issue of censorship based upon the completed research. Use the completed organizer to address the following:
		  – How have existing conditions in a particular society and period in history affected what has been censored?

Time	Instructor's Tasks (LMS/T)	Student's Performance Tasks

Days 4-5	**CONSTRUCT/EXPRESS**
	• Introduce the culminating activity, i.e., students creating posters to raise public awareness about censorship.
	• Instruct students on the use of different multimedia equipment for their projects. Technology should minimally include use of a digital camera, tripod, and scanner. (LMS)
	• Teach students how to utilize different software titles for their persuasive posters. These may include drawing, photo editing, and layout programs. (LMS)
		CONSTRUCT/EXPRESS
		• Apply the technology and software skills that were just learned.
		• Discuss effective methods to raise public consciousness about the dangers of censorship and the importance of freedom of expression. Seek answers to the following:
		  – How do we protect the freedom to express ourselves?
		  – What are possible solutions to overcome social stigmas and end censorship?
		• Brainstorm possible ideas for the poster campaign. Develop a plan to create posters using the software and technology introduced in class.

Days 5-7	**CONSTRUCT/EXPRESS** • Review *Ban Censorship Poster* guidelines. Ensure that students understand the objectives of the poster and the requirements that they need to fulfill. (T/LMS) • Allow time for students to design and construct posters. (T/LMS) • Provide feedback on posters through advising sessions. Check students' progress and redirect focus if needed. (T/LMS) • Provide comments for improvement and encourage students to provide constructive peer feedback. (T/LMS)	**CONSTRUCT/EXPRESS** • Create posters utilizing collected research data and new technology skills. Apply *Ban Censorship Poster* guidelines. (See Figure 13.7) • Seek feedback from peers and instructors to refine and improve posters. • Meet with teachers to provide update on progress and receive constructive comments for improvement.
Days 7-8	**REFLECT** • Collect and evaluate posters. Use *Poster Checkbrick* to assess and provide feedback for final improvements. (T/LMS)	**REFLECT** • Use *Poster Checkbrick* to assess work. (See Figure 13.9) • Submit posters for final improvements and evaluation. If changes are needed make adjustments and resubmit.
Days 8-9	**PRESENT/REFLECT** • Collect and submit posters to the school library for Banned Book Week. (T) • Publicize event and host visitors from the school and community. (LMS) • Solicit and collect feedback regarding the poster exhibit. (T/LMS) • Compile comments to share later with the class. (T) • Select posters to display at the public library. (T/LMS) • Submit posters to the public library staff for display as part of their censorship display. (LMS)	**PRESENT/REFLECT** • Submit posters to instructors for display in the school library. • Visit the school library to see posters on display. Observe public reaction to the exhibit and subject matter. • Submit selected posters to instructors for submission to the public library. • Visit the public library to see posters on display. Observe public reaction to the exhibit and subject matter.
Day 10	**REFLECT** • Share public feedback regarding the exhibits from both the school and public libraries. (T/LMS) • Facilitate and collect student feedback and compile list into suggestions for improvement and ideas for another campaign. (T/LMS)	**REFLECT** • Share collected observations with the class. • Discuss if the campaign successfully met the project's objectives. • Contribute to the discussion on improvements and possibilities for a future campaign.

ASSESSMENT CHECKPOINTS

Figure 13.2 Project Assessment Plan

Checkpoints in the process	What is assessed	Who assesses	Assessment tool
Connect	Student participation and content understanding	Teacher Library media specialist Student	Observation Group discussion *You Can't Say That!* (See Figure 13.3)
Wonder	Higher-order thinking and ability to make connections to prior experiences	Teacher Student	Observation Group discussion
Investigate	Information retrieval and the efficient, effective use of resource materials	Library media specialist Student	Library research Observation Consultation *Would the World Be a Better Place?* (See Figure 13.5)
Construct/Express	Evaluation, synthesis, and presentation of data in a clear manner	Teacher Library media specialist Student	Observation *Ban Censorship Poster* (See Figure 13.7)
Reflect	Assessment and evaluation of personal progress and modifications for continued improvement	Teacher Library media specialist Student	Self-reflection *Poster Checkbrick* (See Figure 13.9) Observation

RESOURCES USED IN THE PROJECT

American Civil Liberties Union. *What Is Censorship?* New York: Author, n.d. 12 Aug. 2007 <http://www.aclu.org/freespeech/censorship/26611res20060830.html>.

American Library Association. *ALA: What You Can Do to Oppose Censorship.* Chicago: Author, 2007. 12 Aug. 2007 <http://www.ala.org/Template.cfm?Section=basics&Template=/ContentManagement/ContentDisplay.cfm&ContentID=24792>.

American Library Association. *Intellectual Freedom and Censorship Q & A.* Chicago: Author, 2007. 12 Aug. 2007 <http://www.ala.org/ala/oif/basics/intellectual.htm>.

Blume, Judy. "Is Harry Potter Evil?" Editorial. *New York Times* 22 Oct. 1999, sec. Op-Ed. *Welcome to Judy Blume's Home Base.* 12 Aug. 2007 <http://judyblume.com/censorship/potter.php>.

Blume, Judy. "Judy Blume Talks about Censorship." *Welcome to Judy Blume's Home Base.* 12 Aug. 2007 <http://judyblume.com/censors.php>.

Burns, Kate. *Fighters Against Censorship: History Makers.* Farmington Hills: Lucent, 2004.

Foerstel, Herbert N. *Banned in the Media: A Reference Guide to Censorship in the Press, Motion Pictures, Broadcasting, and the Internet.* Westport: Greenwood Press, 1998.

Marzilli, Alan. *Policing the Internet (Point/Counterpoint).* New York: Chelsea, 2005.

MccGwire, Scarlett. *Censorship: Changing Attitudes 1900-2000.* Austin: Steck-Vaughn, 2000.

National Coalition Against Censorship. *National Coalition Against Censorship.* Ed. Jeanne Criscola. 12 Aug. 2007 <http://www.ncac.org/home.cfm>.

Public Broadcasting Service. *Culture Shock*. PBS, 2000. 12 Aug. 2007 <http://www.pbs.org/wgbh/cultureshock/index_1.html>.

Raskin, Jamin. *We the Students: Supreme Court Cases for and about Students*. 2nd ed. Washington, DC: CQ, 2003.

STANDARDS CITED

American Association of School Librarians, and the Association for Educational Communications and Technology. *Information Literacy Standards for Student Learning*. Chicago: American Library Association, 1998. 2 Aug. 2007 <http://www.ala.org/ala/aasl/aaslproftools/informationpower/InformationLiteracyStandards_final.pdf>.

International Society for Technology in Education. *National Educational Technology Standards: The Next Generation. National Educational Technology Standards for Students*. Washington, DC: Author, 2007. 2 Aug. 2007 <http://cnets.iste.org/students/s_stands.html>.

National Council of Teachers of English, and International Reading Association. *Standards for the English Language Arts*. Urbana: International Reading Association, 1996. 2 Aug. 2007 <http://www.ncte.org/about/over/standards/110846.htm>.

Task Force of the National Council for the Social Studies. *The Curriculum Standards for Social Studies*. Silver Spring: National Council for the Social Studies, 1994. 2 Aug. 2007 <http://www.socialstudies.org/standards/>.

SAMPLES OF STUDENT WORK

FIGURE 13.4: YOU CAN'T SAY THAT! (STUDENT EXAMPLE)

Criteria for evaluation of student work:

- Eliminates all potentially offensive actions or content from the document
- Clearly demonstrates censorship and the intent to block information
- Presents a biased point of view
- Includes all information requested on the worksheet

FIGURE 13.6: WOULD THE WORLD BE A BETTER PLACE? (STUDENT EXAMPLE)

Criteria for evaluation of student work:

- Provides comprehensive and accurate details on the banned work, artist's perspective on the work, and reasons for censure
- Details the positive impact of the work on society
- Concludes with plausible conjectures about what might have happened if the work had not survived censorship
- Includes all information requested on the organizer

FIGURE 13.8: BAN CENSORSHIP POSTER (STUDENT EXAMPLE)

Criteria for evaluation of student work:

- Satisfactorily meets the requirements for organization and format

- Communicates a clear and persuasive argument for freedom of expression
- Conveys its message in a visually arresting manner (e.g., attractive and uncluttered layout, eye-catching graphics and illustrations)

REFLECTION OF THE INSTRUCTORS

Censorship may be a timeless and universal issue; however, it is not on the list of "hot topics" among teenagers. As library media specialists, we wanted to arouse students' awareness of the importance of free expression and the First Amendment in a democratic society. Therefore, we volunteered to spearhead the planning sessions for this particular project. It was a challenging process because, although the goals of the lessons were clear, the activities created for this unit had to capture students' interest and stir action in them. Designing and preparing such activities took creative thought.

We were pleased to discover that our efforts paid off. Students readily identified with many of the censorship examples that we presented. One caveat: due to the sensitive nature of some of the controversial issues, students may formulate very strong opinions or be offended by the material presented. Be sure to notify parents about the unit's intent and objectives prior to beginning the project. If parents are concerned, advise them to contact the teachers involved for clarification or alternate assignments.

TEMPLATES AND RUBRICS FOR VARIOUS TASKS

Figure 13.3 You Can't Say That!

The United States Constitution and the Bill of Rights protect the rights of all Americans. These freedoms, however, are frequently taken for granted or forgotten. There are many countries where information is filtered and written with the intent to mislead readers. Throughout history censors have challenged material based upon different issues or beliefs. To understand the full ramification of how censorship can affect society, you will edit a document to delete controversial material. Pick a news article from a reputable source. Cite the article. Print two copies. Attach the first one to this worksheet for comparison. Use the second set as your working copy. Censure information based upon the following criteria:

- Objectionable language
- Violence
- Sexual content
- Racism/sexism

- Homosexuality
- Challenges to authority
- Anti-Christian sentiment
- Occult

Rewrite the article omitting the censored data. After you complete your work, reflect on how censoring the piece has changed the article and the information being presented. Include both the edited version of the article and your reflection below.

Original Article Citation:

Edited Version:

Reflection:

Figure 13.4 You Can't Say That! (Student Example)

Evaluation of student work: The student satisfactorily completed the assignment and all of its requirements. His edited version reflects thoughtful consideration of the material based upon the reasons discussed in class (e.g., violence, objectionable language, sexual content, racism/sexism). The student has omitted potentially objectionable references and the resulting article clearly presents a shallow and incomplete interpretation of events. His reflection verifies his understanding of how censorship limits the public's knowledge.

Original Article Citation:

Kocieniewski, Davie. "A Little Girl Shot, and a Crowd That Didn't See." *New York Times* 9 July 2007, Late ed.: A1. 12 Aug. 2007 <http://select.nytimes.com/gst/abstract.html?res=F0 0B16FA3B5A0C7A8CDDAE0894DF404482>.

Edited Version:

A seven-year-old girl was shot today and no witnesses have come forward. A woman who was standing 10 feet away had been too distracted by her young son to see who fired the shots. A man who was also in the courtyard told detectives he had been engrossed in conversation with neighbors and ducked too quickly to notice what had happened. At least 20 people were within sight but the case remains unsolved because not a single one will testify or describe what they saw to investigators.

Over the last decade silence has spread across the country as various gangs such as the Crips, Bloods, and Latin Kings have made witnesses scarce and unavailable to assist in criminal investigations.

Donations poured in to help pay for the victim's medical bills, send her to Disney World, and buy her a new bike. A Philadelphia businessman offered a $70,000 reward.

Reflection:

The original article was the equivalent of six typewritten pages. The major objection to this article was its graphic details of gang shootings and other acts of violence. There were also passages that might be interpreted as racist. In addition, there were also interviews detailing various crimes that the author used to sway readers to his point of view about gang violence.

By eliminating major portions of this article, I changed it from an article filled with critical detail to one that was a shallow and choppy recall of events. Although the original piece contained a lot of violence, it was necessary to understand the crimes being reported. Because I omitted this information, readers are robbed of the seriousness of the event and the injustices of gang warfare.

Figure 13.5 Would the World be a Better Place?

Works of artistic expression have been the targets of the censor throughout history. These masterpieces include representations from literature, film, video, music, dance, and the visual arts. If censors were successful in the removal of a piece, would the world be a better place? To draw a conclusion, one must research and study the work. Complete the following inquiry. Provide thoughtful and relevant information for all portions of the sheet below.

Title of piece:

Artist's name:

Art medium used:

Background information:

Why this piece was controversial:

What might have happened if the work had been eliminated because of censors:

Figure 13.6 Would the World be a Better Place? (Student Example)

Evaluation of student work: Information is accurate, comprehensive, and complete. The student successfully presents an overview of the artist's performance and reasons for censorship. He also provides plausible conclusions about what might have happened if the artist had not been allowed to perform.

Title of piece: "Hound Dog"

Artist's name: Elvis Aaron Presley

Art medium used: Music performance

Background Information: "Hound Dog"
Composers: Jerry Leiber, Mike Stoller
Year: 1953
Facts: Originally recorded by Big Mama Thornton in 1953 in a blues style.
Artist: Elvis Aaron Presley (January 8, 1935-August 16, 1977)

Elvis Aaron Presley began his singing career in 1954 with Sun Records (Memphis, Tennessee). In two years, Presley was a national sensation. His first hit single, "Heartbreak Hotel," sold over 300,000 copies in its first three weeks on the market and became number one on the pop (eight weeks) and country charts. He was known for his good looks, swinging hips, and dynamic vocal style.

Over the span of his career, Elvis starred in 33 films, appeared on television shows/specials, and toured the country many times. He sold over one billion records that earned him gold, platinum, and multi-platinum awards for over 150 different albums and singles. He was also awarded 14 Grammy nominations, three Grammy wins, and a Grammy Lifetime Achievement Award. The U.S. Jaycees recognized Presley as one of the Ten Outstanding Young Men of the Nation in 1970.

Why this piece was controversial:
Elvis's appearance on *The Milton Berle Show* on June 5, 1956, triggered national criticism and calls for censorship. Although Presley had already appeared six times on national television, his performance of "Hound Dog" with pelvis-shaking intensity, proved too much for the public. The performance spawned an outcry to ban Presley for his vulgarity, animalism, and appalling lack of musicality.

What might have happened if the work had been eliminated because of censors:
Presley's musical style was a combination of both R&B and country. He was at the beginning of his career. If his music had been successfully banned in 1956 with the performance of "Hound Dog," Presley's legacy would have taken a drastic turn. He would never have performed the music that earned him a historical niche in pop music history. I doubt that rock n' roll would have become such a unique musical genre without his dynamic presence.

Figure 13.7 Guidelines for Ban Censorship Poster Campaign

Do your part: **ban censorship!** Participate in our poster campaign to publicize Banned Book Week at our school library. We challenge you to design an eye-catching poster that will attract patrons and educate them on the serious implications of censorship. Use the information that you have researched and the technology tools that you have learned in class to create this poster. We will be displaying your posters in the library. The best of the posters will also be exhibited at the neighborhood public library to make the general public aware of the dangers of censorship. To participate, please follow these guidelines:

Know the purpose and rules of the campaign
- Purpose: Educate the public on the issue of censorship and publicize Banned Book Week.
- Research: Include reliable data on censorship and banned books.
- Dimensions, color, and resolution: Plan for 11x17 color posters. Use high resolution for possible enlargement.

Plan your poster
- Required information: Include the following information on the poster: Banned Book Week, name of the library, titles of banned books.
- Persuasive slogan/attention grabber: Select a gimmick that effectively draws attention to your poster and motivates the viewer to learn about the issue of censorship.
- Graphics: Brainstorm possible images that will effectively communicate your message and engage your audience.

Use the technology tools
- Digital photography: Take pictures using the appropriate resolution, focus, and lighting.
- Scanner: Replicate images digitally for incorporation into design.
- Software: Adjust and refine images, create graphics, and prepare a layout of your poster design.

Prepare your poster
- Layout/design: Arrange the poster using the above guidelines. Work on visual appeal.
- Readability: Use fonts that are legible and large enough to be seen from a distance.
- Clarity: Keep the layout simple, uncluttered, and logical. Be sure that your message is clear and effectively communicated.

Collect feedback on your project and make improvements
- Peer review: Ask colleagues for feedback. Use their comments to make improvements.
- Instructor consultation: Meet with your teachers and the library media specialists for clarification and feedback. Adjust the poster design as needed.
- Self-reflection: Review your work on an ongoing basis. Use these guidelines as your yardstick for thoughtful self-assessment.

Figure 13.8 Ban Censorship Poster Campaign (Student Example)

Evaluation of student work: This poster meets all of the specified requirements. Banned book week is publicized along with controversial literary titles. The layout is attractive, organized, and can clearly be read. The finished product reflects the use of technology and software skills that were introduced. Through the use of eye-catching graphics and information collected through research, the example presents a persuasive argument for freedom of expression.

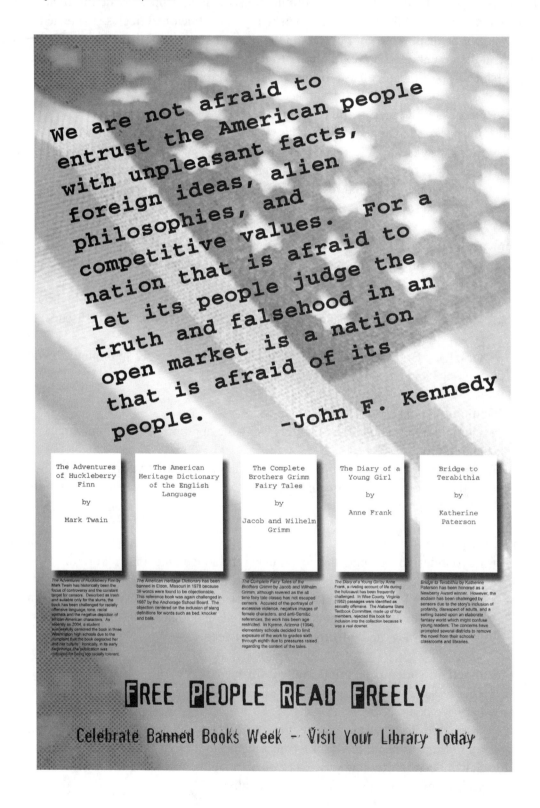

Figure 13.9 Poster Checkbrick

A *checkbrick* is a combination of a rubric and checklist. Use this checkbrick to assess your poster as you are working on it. It is a useful tool for both peer and self-critiquing. The instructors will also use it to evaluate your final product. How to use the checkbrick: mark the most appropriate rating for each criterion and provide constructive feedback regarding the strengths and weaknesses of the work. For more details on the criteria, refer back to the guidelines for the *Ban Censorship Poster Campaign*. The ratings are: Exceeds (3), Meets (2), and Approaching (1) standard.

FOLLOWS RULES AND OBJECTIVES

Criteria	3	2	1	Comments and Feedback
Purpose				
Research				
Dimensions, color, resolution				
Subtotal				

SHOWS CAREFUL PLANNING

Criteria	3	2	1	Comments and Feedback
Required information				
Persuasive slogan/attention grabber				
Graphics				
Subtotal				

USES TECHNOLOGY TOOLS

Criteria	3	2	1	Comments and Feedback
Digital Photography				
Scanner				
Software				
Subtotal				

DESIGNS EFFECTIVE POSTER

Criteria	3	2	1	Comments and Feedback
Layout/Design				
Readability				
Clarity				
Subtotal				

COLLECTS FEEDBACK AND RESULTS SHOW EVIDENCE OF ONGOING IMPROVEMENT

Criteria	3	2	1	Comments and Feedback
Peer review				
Instructor consultation				
Self-Reflection				
Subtotal				

TOTAL POINTS EARNED: **RECOMMENDED FOR PUBLIC LIBRARY EXHIBIT:**

14 Geometry: The Musical Formula

COURSE: Geometry, Music
GRADES: 9-10
DURATION OF PROJECT: One week
STUDENT OUTCOMES
    CONTENT GOALS:
        Students will understand geometric concepts and design a system for
        remembering formulas by:

        • Studying different formulas needed to calculate
          geometric computations.
        • Using music to aid in teaching and learning
          difficult concepts.
        • Researching different children's songs and analyzing
          lyrics and melodic phrases.
        • Composing math songs to remember complex
          geometry concepts.
        • Recording and sharing songs with peers through
          downloadable files.

    PROCESS GOALS:
        Students will develop information literacy skills needed to foster
        creative, complex, and higher-order thinking.

DESCRIPTION OF PRODUCT OR PERFORMANCE

In order to succeed in geometry, students must learn and apply math formulas to manipulate properties; measurement; and relationships of points, lines, angles, surfaces, and solids to solve problems. They often encounter difficulties in analyzing a problem, recalling the correct process, and applying the procedures in the right sequential order.

In this project, students will use music as a learning tool and uncover the potential of song lyrics to assist in learning equations and solution sequences. Students will research and collect familiar melodies. Selecting a geometric concept as a focus, they will put formula elements to music as a study aid for classmates. The completed songs will be recorded as an electronic file and made available for download from the class's Web page. Students will be responsible for:

- Learning and applying different geometric formulas
- Gathering different children's and popular tunes
- Analyzing lyrics and melodic phrases
- Composing new lyrics based upon geometric formulas
- Recording electronic files and sharing geometric songs with peers

CONNECTION WITH STANDARDS

Standards from Language Arts, Mathematics, Music, Technology, and Information Literacy are integrated in this project.

LANGUAGE ARTS

Standards in this unit addressed using language to communicate with various audiences, employing a range of writing strategies, applying language conventions, and conducting research using a variety of informational and technological resources. For more detailed information on the standards refer to <http://www.ncte.org/about/over/standards/110846.htm>.

MATHEMATICS

Standards addressed in this unit focus on geometric properties, shapes, and relationships. Students analyze and apply transformations, spatial reasoning, and modeling to solve mathematical problems. For more detailed information on the standards refer to <http://standards.nctm.org/document/appendix/numb.htm>.

MUSIC

Standards addressed in this unit foster composition, orchestration, variation, and improvisation to create original melodies and musical pieces. For more detailed information on the standards refer to <http://www.menc.org/publication/books/standards.htm>.

TECHNOLOGY

Standards addressed in this unit deal with basic operations and concepts; social, ethical, and human issues; technology productivity tools; and technology tools for communication and research. For more detailed information on the standards refer to <http://cnets.iste.org/students/s_stands.html>.

INFORMATION LITERACY

Standards addressed in this unit focus on the access, evaluation, and use of information; appreciation for all forms of creative expression; development of self-reflection skills in knowledge acquisition; and social responsibility in working with information. For more detailed information on the standards refer to <http://www.ala.org/ala/aasl/aaslproftools/informationpower/InformationLiteracyStandards_final.pdf>.

OVERARCHING PROJECT QUESTIONS

- What are unique properties and characteristics associated with geometry?
- How does music influence our ability to learn and grasp cognitive skills?
- How might music help us to understand and recall geometric concepts?

TIMELINE FOR PROJECT

Figure 14.1 Project Timeline

Time	Instructor's Tasks (LMS/T)	Student's Performance Tasks

Day 1	**CONNECT**
	- Provide information which would answer:
	  – What are unique properties and characteristics associated with geometry?
	  This information contributes to the understanding of the course work and leads to relevant, real-world applications of the formulas being taught. (T)
		CONNECT
		- Jot down notes to make connections between formulas and applications found beyond school.
		- Clarify questions that may arise regarding relevant applications of geometry.

	WONDER - Poll the class to see how many geometric formulas they can recall from memory. (T) - Facilitate a discussion on how students memorize information. Brainstorm different techniques to improve the number of equations that they retain. (T) - List different methods on a collective memory list at the front of the room. (T)	**WONDER** - Recall as many geometric formulas as possible. - Contribute to the discussion regarding strategies for memorizing information. - Share responses with the class.
	CONNECT - Review mathematic equations that were missed. (T) - Discuss the formulas that were remembered. Emphasize that memorization of the equations must also include the sequence in which to solve the problem. (T)	**CONNECT** - Complete notes to remember equations that were forgotten. - Ensure that the notes include the properties, characteristics, and problem-solving sequence needed to decipher geometric values.

continued

Time	Instructor's Tasks (LMS/T)	Student's Performance Tasks
Day 2	**WONDER** • Revisit the list of suggested memory techniques. (T) • Focus on items affiliated with rhymes, poems, and songs. (LMS/T) • Ask students to sing songs that they know from memory. Discuss the characteristics of the piece that allows the tune and lyrics to be memorable. (LMS/T)	**WONDER** • Perform songs remembered from childhood. • Analyze tunes for memorable features. Share findings with the class.
	CONNECT • View examples taken from various children's educational television programming: — *Between the Lions* — *School House Rock* — *Sesame Street* (LMS/T) • Facilitate a discussion on how music is strategically used as a helpful tool for learning. (LMS)	**CONNECT** • Examine samples of children's programs. Note spots featuring music and songs to teach different curriculum concepts. • As a class discuss the following: — How has music influenced our ability to learn and grasp cognitive skills? — How can music help us to understand and recall geometric concepts? • Contribute to the discussion regarding the power of music as a tool for learning. Cite evidence gathered from viewed samples along with knowledge gained from prior personal experiences. • Share conclusions with the class.
Days 2-3	**INVESTIGATE** • Distribute and explain the directions for the next assignment: *That Old Familiar Tune*. (LMS) *Note: For this task, students examine children's and popular songs throughout history.* • Have them select a piece that is familiar and contains a memorable tune. The song should be repetitive and contain a chorus and several stanzas. (LMS) • Introduce print and electronic resources that will be useful for this project. Be aware that lyrics may not be cited the same in different sources. Resources may be scarce; look for historic/cultural music books and Web sites that offer credible information to assist in research. Locate the original or traditional version of songs whenever possible to ensure the correct version of the lyrics is obtained. (LMS)	**INVESTIGATE** • Conduct research to build a list of potential songs to use in the composition phase of the project. Use *That Old Familiar Tune* worksheet. (See Figure 14.3) • Collect background information for the piece (country of origin, date of creation, and name of composer). • Find background and bibliographic information to cite the piece. • Include the lyrics of the piece. Be sure to type it out in sing-along format, noting verses, chorus and when to repeat.

Time	Instructor's Tasks (LMS/T)	Student's Performance Tasks
Days 3-4	**CONSTRUCT/EXPRESS** • Allow students to familiarize themselves with their selected tunes. (LMS/T) • Distribute and explain the directions for the next phase of the assignment: *Geometry Sing-Along*. (LMS/T) • Analyze each line of the lyrics for a breakdown in syllables. Have students list results in the space provided. (LMS) • Assist students in selecting a geometric formula to teach. Be sure that there is no replication among students. (T) • Encourage the class to highlight essential elements of the equation and the process used to arrive at its properties and values. This will serve as the foundation for the compositions. (T) • Help students to formulate lyrics to adequately teach geometric formulas. Be sure to match the number of syllables using the original lyrics and analysis as a guide. (T/LMS)	**CONSTRUCT/EXPRESS** • Practice singing and internalizing the selected song. • Analyze the lyrics for syllables and phrase breakdown. List findings on *Geometry Sing-Along* worksheet. (See Figure 14.5) • Select a geometry formula that will serve as inspiration for the composition. Note description of the function and the sequence for problem solving. • Use notes/details collected and compose new lyrics for the selected tune. Be sure to match syllable analysis and ensure that it serves as a teaching tool for the memorization of the formula. • Write out new lyrics in the correct sing-along format. Note verses, chorus, and places where repeats are needed. • Practice newly created song. Prepare for recording the piece.
Days 4-5	**CONSTRUCT/EXPRESS** • Instruct students on the use of different multimedia equipment for recording their compositions. Technology should minimally include use of a digital recorder and microphone. (LMS) • Teach students how to utilize different software titles for the editing of their media clip. These may include music editing programs. (LMS) • Upload finished songs onto the class Web page. Equip the page with a Web counter and guestbook to collect data on guests visiting the site and their downloading activity. (LMS/T)	**CONSTRUCT/EXPRESS** • Apply the technology and software skills that were just learned. • Record and edit newly created geometry song. • Upload finished project onto the class Web page with the assistance of the instructors. • Present and teach classmates the words to the new song. • Prepare to answer any questions that may arise in understanding and executing the formula. • Perform the new song as a class. • Encourage classmates to visit the page and download the music clip to aid them in learning and memorizing the geometric functions.
Days 6-7	**REFLECT** • Collect and evaluate music download data. Analyze traffic on the Web site and give updates to the class. Highlight the popular downloads and guestbook comments. (LMS/T) • Use *Music Composition Checkbrick* to assess and provide feedback for final improvements. (LMS/T)	**REFLECT** • Use *Sing-along Checkbrick* to assess work. (See Figure 14.7) • Provide feedback to classmates regarding their pieces. Through peer review, identify strengths and areas of growth so improvements can be made. • Incorporate feedback in improving the geometry tune. • Submit the finished product for uploading to the Web site and final evaluation.

ASSESSMENT CHECKPOINTS

Figure 14.2 Project Assessment Plan

Checkpoints in the process	What is assessed	Who assesses	Assessment tool
Connect	Student participation and content understanding	Teacher Library media specialist Student	Observation Group discussion
Wonder	Higher-order thinking and ability to make connections to prior experiences	Teacher Student	Observation Group discussion
Investigate	Information retrieval and the efficient, effective use of resource materials	Library media specialist Student	Library research Observation Consultation *That Old Familiar Tune* (See Figure 14.3)
Construct/Express	Evaluation, synthesis, and presentation of data in a clear manner	Teacher Library media specialist Student	Observation *Geometry Sing-Along* (See Figure 14.5) MP4 Recording
Reflect	Assessment and evaluation of personal progress and modifications for continued improvement	Teacher Library media specialist Student	Self reflection *Sing-Along Checkbrick* (See Figure 14.7) Web page download meter Observation

RESOURCES USED IN THE PROJECT

Keyes, Allison. "Using Hip-Hop to Teach Math." *The Tavis Smiley Show*. Washington, DC: National Public Radio, 2003. 12 Aug. 2007 <http://www.npr.org/templates/story/story.php?storyId=1551657>.

Public Broadcasting Service. *PBS Kids*. Washington, DC: U.S. Department of Education, 2007. 12 Aug. 2007 <http://pbskids.org/>.

Rath, Linda K. *Between the Lions: Get Wild about Reading*. Boston: WGBH, 2007. 12 Aug. 2007 <http://pbskids.org/lions/>.

"Schoolhouse Rock Lyrics." *Schoolhouse Rock*. 12 Aug. 2007 <http://www.schoolhouserock.tv/>.

Sesame Workshop: Sesame Street. New York: Sesame Workshop, 2007. 12 Aug. 2007 <http://www.sesameworkshop.org/sesamestreet/>.

"Using Music to Teach Math." *All Things Considered: Fixing Our Public Schools*. Southern California Public Radio. Pasadena: KPCC, 2005. 12 Aug. 2007 <http://www.scpr.org/news/features/2005/10/fixing_our_schools.html>.

STANDARDS CITED

American Association of School Librarians, and the Association for Educational Communications and Technology. *Information Literacy Standards for Student Learning*. Chicago: American Library Association, 1998. 2 Aug. 2007 <http://www.ala.org/ala/aasl/aaslproftools/informationpower/InformationLiteracyStandards_final.pdf>.

International Society for Technology in Education. *National Educational Technology Standards: The Next Generation. National Educational Technology Standards for Students.* Washington, DC: Author, 2007. 2 Aug. 2007 <http://cnets.iste.org/students/ s_stands.html>.

The National Association for Music Education. *National Standards for Music Education.* Reston: Author, 1994. 12 Aug. 2007 <http://www.menc.org/publication/books/ standards.htm>.

National Council of Teachers of English, and International Reading Association. *Standards for the English Language Arts.* Urbana: International Reading Association, 1996. 2 Aug. 2007 <http://www.ncte.org/about/over/standards/110846.htm>.

National Council of Teachers of Mathematics. *Principles and Standards for School Mathematics.* Reston: Author, 2007. 12 Aug. 2007 <http://standards.nctm.org/ document/appendix/numb.htm>.

SAMPLES OF STUDENT WORK

FIGURE 14.4: THAT OLD FAMILIAR TUNE (STUDENT EXAMPLE)

Criteria for evaluation of student work:

- Cites a song that is commonly recognized
- Includes original lyrics for the piece
- Formats song sheet in a sing-along format, effectively notating parts, chorus, and repeat sections
- Completes lyric analysis, correctly identifying multisyllable words
- Includes all information requested on the worksheet

FIGURE 14.6: GEOMETRY SING-ALONG (STUDENT EXAMPLE)

Criteria for evaluation of student work:

- Composes lyrics that teach the geometric formula selected
- Rhymes words at the ends of musical phrases
- Matches new lyrics to original rhythms within a song utilizing the correct number of syllables
- Includes all information requested on the song sheet

REFLECTION OF THE INSTRUCTORS

Educational television teaches children everything from math and reading to art and history. Many of these shows include musical snippets. With this in mind, the instructional team decided to use music as a device for students to learn math concepts through repetitive, catchy tunes. As library media specialists, we worked with teachers to adapt this teaching tool for secondary students.

The teachers were initially unsure about the incorporation of music in this integrative unit because none of them had any training in this area. However, one of the library media specialists had a degree in music education and took the lead. Knowing that students had previous experiences with poetry in the classroom, the team incorporated this important skill within the lyric composition aspect of the unit.

TEMPLATES AND RUBRICS FOR VARIOUS TASKS

Figure 14.3 That Old Familiar Tune

Are there times when you can't get a melody out of your head? Is there a song that you learned as a child that you still remember today? Let's find out what makes these tunes so memorable. Research children's and popular songs composed throughout history. During the process select a familiar catchy tune (do not replicate tunes that your classmates have chosen). Discover its history and its origin. Track down the original lyrics and list it below. Be sure to have it in sing-along format noting verses, chorus, and when to repeat. In preparation for the second part of this assignment, conduct a syllable breakdown of each word included in the lyrics. Write out your analysis in the space provided.

Song Title:

Composer:

Date Created (if the exact date or year is not known then list possible era/century):

Country of Origin:

Song Lyrics	Syllable Analysis

Figure 14.4 That Old Familiar Tune (Student Example)

Evaluation of student work: In this example the student was successful in selecting a familiar children's song and tracking its historic roots. Lyrics have been precisely recorded and are easy to follow as a sing-along. Syllable analysis is complete and accurate.

Song Title: London Bridge Is Falling Down

Composer: Traditional (composer not known)

Date Created (If exact date or year is not known then list possible era/century): c. 1659

Country of Origin: England (note: lyrics vary by region, the following is the most familiar)

Song Lyrics	Syllable Analysis
London Bridge is falling down,	2 1-1 2 1
Falling down, falling down,	2 1, 2 1
London Bridge is falling down,	2 1-1 2 1
My fair Lady.	1 1 2
Build it up with wood and clay,	1-1 1-1 1-1 1
Wood and clay, wood and clay,	1-1 1, 1-1 1
Build it up with wood and clay,	1-1 1-1 1-1 1
My fair Lady.	1 1 2
Wood and clay will wash a-way,	1-1 1-1 1-1 1
Wash a-way, wash a-way,	1-1 1, 1-1 1
Wood and clay will wash a-way,	1-1 1-1 1-1 1
My fair Lady.	1 1 2
Build it up with bricks and mortar,	1-1 1-1 1-1 2
Bricks and mortar, bricks and mortar,	1-1 2, 1-1 2
Build it up with bricks and mortar,	1-1 1-1 1-1 2
My fair Lady.	1 1 2
Bricks and mortar will not stay,	1-1 2 1-1 1
Will not stay, will not stay,	1-1 1, 1-1 1
Bricks and mortar will not stay,	1-1 2 1-1 1
My fair Lady.	1 1 2
Build it up with iron and steel,	1-1 1-1 1-1 1
Iron and steel, iron and steel,	1-1 1, 1-1 1
Build it up with iron and steel,	1-1 1-1 1-1 1
My fair Lady.	1 1 2
Iron and steel will bend and bow,	1-1 1-1 1-1 1
Bend and bow, bend and bow,	1-1 1, 1-1 1
Iron and steel will bend and bow,	1-1 1-1 1-1 1
My fair Lady.	1 1 2

Figure 14.5 Geometry Sing-Along

Now it's time to compose your own geometry song! Select a geometry formula or concept that you will teach through your song. Sketch out the problem solving method for the formula or concept. Highlight essential elements needed to arrive at the property and values. Follow the original rhyming pattern for your song and insert key geometry points into the lyrics. Use your syllable analysis from the *That Old Familiar Tune* organizer to keep the meter of each line the same. As you list your lyrics below, make sure to notate if there are repeats, different verses, and a chorus section. Remember, your composition should be mathematically correct and allow students to remember the formula you teach. Keep it simple, musical, and have fun!

New composition title:

Sing to the tune of (original song title):

Geometry sing-along:

Figure 14.6 Geometry Sing-Along (Student Example)

Evaluation of student work: This student's musical composition is an excellent sample of what can be taught using music as a medium for learning. The geometric formulas presented are correct and the problem-solving process is clearly conveyed. The tune chosen is familiar and easy for classmates to sing and remember. If there are chorus, repeats, and other musical notations, the parts are correctly labeled. The lyrics follow the syllabic pattern of the song, keeping its metric foundation and flow.

New composition title: Laws of Polygons

Sing to the tune of (original song title): Oh My Darling, Clementine

Geometry sing-along:

Oh my darling, oh my darling
Oh my darling polygon
You're a shape that's many sided
Oh my darling polygon

Area, what's the area
Of my darling polygon
Need to find the right formula
For my darling polygon

You're a square, you're a square
Where the sides are all the same
Square the value of its length
For the area that's the game

Rectangle and parallelogram
Finding area is not so hard
Multiply base times its height
And get an A on your report card

Triangle, it's a triangle
Three sides is all you've got
Half the value of base times height
Results in area on the spot

Trapezoid, here's a trapezoid
Draw a diagonal to split in two
Solve the area of two triangles
Add them together is all you do

Area what's the area
Know the shape for a start
Find the formula to get you going
Work the process and you're smart

Figure 14.7 Sing-along Checkbrick

A *checkbrick* is a combination of a rubric and checklist. Use this checkbrick to assess your song as you are working on it. It is a useful tool for both peer and self-critiquing. As you teach the tune to your classmates they will be utilizing this sheet to provide you with valuable feedback. The instructors will also use it to evaluate your final product. How to use the checkbrick: mark the most appropriate rating for each criterion and provide constructive criticism regarding the strengths and weaknesses of the work. The ratings are: Exceeds (3), Meets (2), and Approaching (1) standard.

CORRECTLY TEACHES GEOMETRIC FORMULA

Criteria	3	2	1	Comments and Feedback
Formula is accurately presented				
Problem-solving process is clear				
Steps to figure out values are clear and in chronological order				
All components, properties, and values are included				
Subtotal				

SELECTS AN APPROPRIATE CHILDREN'S OR POPULAR SONG

Criteria	3	2	1	Comments and Feedback
Song is a known children's or popular song				
Tune is catchy and easily recognizable				
Melody is memorable and easy to sing				
Subtotal				

COMPOSES APPROPRIATE LYRICS

Criteria	3	2	1	Comments and Feedback
Lyrics follow the syllabic analysis of the song				
Rhyming patterns are similar				
Metric meter of the phrases are identical to the original tune				
Words are appropriate and suitable for all audiences				
Subtotal				

INSTRUCTS THE CLASS SUCCESSFULLY IN LEARNING THE GEOMETRY SONG

Criteria	3	2	1	Comments and Feedback
Teaching is clear and understandable				
Students are able to sing the tune and understand the formula being taught				
Song is easily memorized by the entire class				
Subtotal				

TOTAL POINTS EARNED:

15 Dreams Work! Exploring Non-Traditional Careers

COURSE: Guidance/Career Development, Language Arts
GRADES: 9
DURATION OF PROJECT: One month
STUDENT OUTCOMES
CONTENT GOALS:
Students will explore and evaluate potential career options in relation to personal interests by:

- Identifying variables that impact career choices.
- Considering a range of occupations.
- Making thoughtful personal decisions about career choices.
- Recognizing that chance can play a role in making career decisions.

PROCESS GOALS:
Students will develop information literacy skills needed to foster complex and higher-order thinking.

DESCRIPTION OF PRODUCT OR PERFORMANCE

As adults, students will probably find themselves changing jobs more than once. New jobs will be constantly created to meet evolving community and world needs. Existing jobs will continue to be redefined by rapid technological advances. In this dynamic setting, students must ask critical questions about how the careers they choose might improve the quality of their lives. In most "career units," students go through the motions of researching careers that are traditional and easy to research. They rarely seize the opportunity to explore careers that might leverage their unique talents and ignite their dreams. In this unit, we challenge students to learn more about jobs that truly excite them. Their task is to seek information about such a job, design and present a slideshow on the job, and arrange for a speaker to share his or her career experiences at a "Dreams Work!" session for the class. Students will be responsible for:

- Gathering and analyzing information on exciting occupations suited to their specific interests and values.
- Interviewing people in such occupations.

- Discovering the factors that influence people's career decisions.
- Presenting information highlighting their findings and insights into these careers.

CONNECTION WITH STANDARDS

Standards from Career Development, Language Arts, Technology, and Information Literacy are integrated in this project.

CAREER DEVELOPMENT

Standards addressed in this unit focus on developing self-awareness and a positive self-concept, creating and managing career plans and goals, and using decision making as a component of career development. For more detailed information on the standards refer to <http://www.acrnetwork.org/ncdg/ncdg_framework.aspx>.

LANGUAGE ARTS

Standards addressed in this unit deal with using language to communicate with various audiences, employing a range of writing strategies, applying language conventions, and conducting research using a variety of informational and technological resources. For more detailed information on the standards refer to <http://www.ncte.org/about/over/standards/110846.htm>.

TECHNOLOGY

Standards addressed in this unit deal with basic operations and concepts; social, ethical, and human issues; technology productivity tools; and technology tools for communication and research. For more detailed information on the standards refer to <http://cnets.iste.org/students/s_stands.html>.

INFORMATION LITERACY

Standards addressed in this unit focus on the access, evaluation, and use of information; appreciation for all forms of creative expression; development of self-reflection skills in knowledge acquisition; and social responsibility in working with information. For more detailed information on the standards refer to <http://www.ala.org/ala/aasl/aaslproftools/informationpower/InformationLiteracyStandards_final.pdf>.

OVERARCHING PROJECT QUESTIONS

- What motivates a person to select a particular career?
- What factors influence a person's career decision?
- What do you need to know about yourself to make a good career choice?
- How might you use your unique talent or interest in your chosen career?

TIMELINE FOR PROJECT

Figure 15.1 Project Timeline

Time	Instructor's Tasks (LMS/T)	Student's Performance Tasks
Day 1	**CONNECT** • Write the following prompt on the board. – What job do you see yourself in at age 25? 35? 50? (T) • Discuss answers with students. List jobs on chalkboard. Facilitate discussion on "traditional" and "non-traditional" jobs. (T) • Have students take an interest/value inventory. Discuss results of interest inventory. (T) • Lead into a discussion on how personal interests can influence career decisions and how "thinking outside the box" might present exciting possibilities. (T) • Share a biography of a successful individual who capitalized on his or her personal interest and used it to secure a successful career and livelihood. Possible individuals: – Carey Hart (extreme athlete/ entrepreneur) – J.K. Rowling (author) – Tony Hawk (athlete/entrepreneur) – Bruce Lee (martial artist/actor) – John Grisham (attorney/novelist) – Martha Stewart (homemaking advocate/entrepreneur) – Jacques Cousteau (naval officer/ underwater explorer/author/ filmmaker) (LMS/T)	**CONNECT** • Respond to question prompt. • Follow up with these questions: – Which jobs would you consider to be traditional types of jobs? Non-traditional? Why? – Are your job choices traditional or non-traditional? • Complete an interest/value inventory. • Cluster interests into categories. • Discuss the following: – How did you group your interests? – How are these interests reflected in your personal life? – Can you see yourself continuing these interests into adulthood? • Read a biography of someone who turned an interest into a career. • Discuss the following: – What motivates a person to select a particular career? – What factors influence a person's career decision? – What do you need to know about yourself to make a good career choice? – How might you use your unique talent or interest in your chosen career?
Day 2	**WONDER** • Arrange for a field trip to a business that employs workers with varied interests and job descriptions including non-traditional jobs. (LMS/T)	**WONDER** • Participate in a field trip. Take note of the following: – Various jobs observed – Nature of the work – Training/education needed – Career paths of speakers

continued

Time	Instructor's Tasks (LMS/T)	Student's Performance Tasks
Day 3	**CONNECT** • Debrief with students regarding the field trip. (T) • Revisit student responses from Day 1. (T) • Introduce project. Place students in teams of three to four based on interests. (T) *Note: Teams may need to be adjusted according to interest areas, numbers of students, and other factors.*	**CONNECT** • Respond to the following: – What jobs did you learn about? – What interests do you think these jobs addressed? – How did these people select their current jobs? • Categorize these jobs according to our previous discussions about traditional and non-traditional jobs, and interests and values that might be critical. • Based on the results of your personal interest inventory, identify an interest that you might incorporate into a future job. • Organize in teams of three to four members based on interests. • Complete both parts of this research project: – Part 1: Research several careers that incorporate the interest areas reflected in your group. You will prepare slide presentations to share with the class. – Part 2: Select one job from your career cluster. As a team, invite a community member who has that particular job to speak to the class.
Days 4-6	**INVESTIGATE** • Introduce various print and online career information materials. (LMS) • Reinforce the use of the library's online public access catalog and school's online career/post-high school resources. (LMS) • Have students browse through various materials to select occupations. (LMS) • Assist teams in finding a community speaker for their career clusters. (LMS)	**INVESTIGATE** • Browse through various resources and select three or four non-traditional occupations that incorporate your interest area. • Research the selected jobs for the following: – Nature of work – Work conditions – Education and training – Skills – Salary – Job outlook – Related occupations • Find a person with one of the jobs researched.
	ASSESS • Assess students' progress in finding needed information. Provide informal conferencing. (LMS/T)	**ASSESS** • Confer with instructors on progress with the research.

Time	Instructor's Tasks (LMS/T)	Student's Performance Tasks

Days 7-12	**CONSTRUCT**
	• Have class create questions that highlight a career and a speaker. (T)
	• Teach students the following steps in working with a guest speaker:
	  – Write a request letter or script for a phone call.
	  – Follow up with reminders, questions to address, directions to school, and the schedule.
	  – Send a thank you letter. (T)
	• Set up schedule for guest speakers. (T)
	• Review the *Slide Presentation Rubric* with students. (T)
	• Provide time for students to create presentation. (T)
	• Collect completed presentations. (T)
		CONSTRUCT
		• Share team's questions with the rest of the class. Focus on questions with which you need additional help.
		• Create general questions that can be used for each guest speaker. Use *Career Inquiry Worksheet.* (See Figure 15.3)
		• Contact potential speakers. If they can make it, proceed with scheduling them. Be sure to ask speakers to address the following:
		  – Educational and career paths they traveled to get to this point in their careers.
		  – Personal interests that have been critical factors in their success.
		• Using research information collected, create a slide presentation that provides an overview of the guest speaker's job. Include an explanation of the types of people that might be suited for this particular job and why. Use the *Slide Presentation Rubric.* (See Figure 15.5)
		• Submit slide presentation to instructors.

	ASSESS/REFLECT • Conduct ongoing assessment through observation and conferencing. (T/LMS) • Provide coaching sessions, individual assistance, and guidance as projects develop. (T/LMS) • Review students' presentations and provide feedback for improvement. (T/LMS)	**ASSESS/REFLECT** • Confer with instructors for feedback on contacting the speaker and refining the slide presentation.
	CONSTRUCT • Return presentations to student teams one week prior to speaker's date for final improvements. (T)	**CONSTRUCT** • Confirm speaker's schedule and go over points to address. • Revise presentations as needed.
Number of sessions will vary	**EXPRESS** • Allot time for presentations. (T) • Review the general questions created by the class that can be used with all speakers. (T) *Note: If time permits, work with the technology teacher to convert presentations into enhanced podcasts for Web posting.*	**EXPRESS** • Present slides to class one day prior to speaker's visit. • Listen to speaker's presentation. Ask questions.

After presentations	**REFLECT**
	• Debrief on the presentations and effectiveness of the speakers. (T)
	• Lead discussion on the overarching questions of this project. (T)
		REFLECT
		• Revisit the overarching questions and share answers with the class.
		  – What motivates a person to select a particular career?
		  – What factors influence a person's career decision?
		  – What do you need to know about yourself to make a good career choice?
		  – How might you use your unique talent or interest in your chosen career?
		  – How has this project influenced your thinking about possible careers?
		  – To what extent are you expanding your career options beyond your original job choices?

ASSESSMENT CHECKPOINTS

Figure 15.2 Project Assessment Plan

Checkpoints in the process	What is assessed	Who assesses	Assessment tool
Connect	Student participation and content understanding	Teacher Library media specialist Student	Observation Discussion/reflections Interest inventory
Wonder	Higher-order thinking and ability to make connections to prior experiences	Teacher Student	Observation Written reflection
Investigate	Information retrieval and the efficient, effective use of resource materials	Library media specialist Student	Observation Informal conferencing
Construct/Express	Evaluation, synthesis, and presentation of data in a clear manner	Teacher Library media specialist Student	Observation Conferencing Drafts of speaker contact letter *Career Inquiry Worksheet* (See Figure 15.3) *Slide Presentation Rubric* (See Figure 15.5)
Reflect	Assessment and evaluation of personal progress and modifications for continued improvement	Teacher Library media specialist Student	Reflection

RESOURCES USED IN THE PROJECT

Beyer, Mark. *Demolition Experts: Life Blowing Things Up*. New York: Rosen, 2001.

Bureau of Labor Statistics. *BLS Career Information Home Page*. Washington, DC: U.S. Department of Labor. 6 Aug. 2007 <http://www.bls.gov/k12/index.htm>.

Goldberg, Jan. *Careers for Patriotic Types & Others Who Want to Serve Their Country*. New York: McGraw-Hill, 2006.

Lee, Richard S., and Mary Price Lee. *Careers for Car Buffs & Other Freewheeling Types*. New York: McGraw-Hill, 2004.

Mannino, Stephanie. *Cool Careers Without College for People Who Love Crafts*. New York: Rosen Pub., 2004.

Reeves, Diane Lindsey, and Lindsey Clasen. *Career Ideas for Kids Who Like Adventure and Travel*. New York: Ferguson, 2007.

Thornburg, Linda. *Cool Careers for Girls as Crime Solvers*. Manassas: Impact Pub., 2002.

U.S. Department of Labor. *Occupational Outlook Handbook*. Indianapolis: Jist Works, 2006.

STANDARDS CITED

American Association of School Librarians, and the Association for Educational Communications and Technology. *Information Literacy Standards for Student Learning*. Chicago: American Library Association, 1998. 2 Aug. 2007 <http://www.ala.org/ala/aasl/aaslproftools/informationpower/InformationLiteracyStandards_final.pdf>.

International Society for Technology in Education. *National Educational Technology Standards: The Next Generation. National Educational Technology Standards for Students.* Washington, DC: Author, 2007. 2 Aug. 2007 <http://cnets.iste.org/students/s_stands.html>.

The National Occupational Information Coordinating Committee. "The National Career Development Guidelines Framework." *America's Career Resource Network.* Washington, DC: National Training Support Center, 1989. 6 Aug. 2007 <http://www.acrnetwork.org/ncdg/ncdg_framework.aspx>.

National Council of Teachers of English, and International Reading Association. *Standards for the English Language Arts.* Urbana: International Reading Association, 1996. 2 Aug. 2007 <http://www.ncte.org/about/over/standards/110846.htm>.

SAMPLES OF STUDENT WORK

FIGURE 15.4 CAREER INQUIRY WORKSHEET (STUDENT EXAMPLE)

Criteria for evaluation of student work:

- Generates required number of questions
- Produces logical questions that are appropriate for each category

REFLECTION OF THE INSTRUCTORS

As library media specialists we often attend workshops to keep abreast of the latest curriculum trends and strategies and to deepen our knowledge of various content areas. We attended a workshop on the local fisheries industry that provided us with a fascinating opportunity to explore how seafood is caught, processed, marketed, and used. The biggest a-ha of the day was our realization that the people employed in this field were as varied in education, training, background, experience, and skills as the varieties of fish we had discussed at the session.

We returned to school wanting to share our excitement with students. We asked ourselves, how could we get students motivated to look beyond the "traditional" jobs they usually research in their career units? We posed this challenge to our guidance teachers and found that they were equally enthusiastic about breaking away from their traditional career research projects.

When we implemented this unit, we were delighted that many students were genuinely motivated to explore unusual jobs. They wanted to contact local speakers with unique occupations. Although we tried to help them find their speakers, students were not always successful in securing their first choices. In the future, we plan to expand our efforts beyond local speakers: using web cams, we want to connect our students to resources via the Internet. Instructors will need to be flexible in scheduling these virtual speakers, i.e., juggling classroom assignments and working around school activities. Although this is still in the discussion stage, we hope to make this an ongoing project where students' slide presentations are archived on the school's Web site as enhanced podcasts. Not only would this allow students to share their presentations with the entire school community, but it would also allow them to build on work done by previous classes and contribute to an online repository of career-related resources.

TEMPLATES AND RUBRICS FOR VARIOUS TASKS

Figure 15.3 Career Inquiry

Create questions in the following three critical categories for career explorations: personal background, job-related information, and reflections. This will help you focus and organize your research. Take note of the following guidelines:

- Write questions and answers that are short, simple, clearly stated, and unambiguous.
- Avoid writing questions that have several parts to answer. It's better to have several separate items rather than one item that requires several answers.
- Read questions out loud to a peer for feedback. Check for clarity.

Create at least five questions (more if possible) for each category below. An example is given for each area.

Personal Background	Job-Related Information	Reflections
• Where are you from?	• What difficulties have you encountered on this job?	• How personally satisfied are you at this job?

Figure 15.4 Career Inquiry (Student Example)

Evaluation of student work: This example satisfactorily meets the assessment criteria. Questions are clearly stated and appropriate for each of the categories. Some of the questions can actually fit in more than one category.

Personal Background	Job-Related Information	Reflections
• Where are you from? • *What schooling and training have you had?* • *Who were key people that have influenced your life?* • *What are your interests?* • *What special talents or skills do you have?* • *What factors in your life influenced your decision to take this job?*	• What difficulties have you encountered at this job? • *What other jobs have you had?* • *How did you find this job?* • *Is this position your dream job?* • *What are your major responsibilities?* • *What skills and attitudes are essential for this job?* • *What benefits do you see with this career?* • *How much do you get paid?* • *How do you deal with conflict on the job?* • *What does the future look like for this occupation?*	• How personally satisfied are you at this job? • *If you weren't in this job, what do you think you'd be doing?* • *For what reasons would you leave this job?* • *Where do you see yourself in the next five years?* • *What is the best part of this occupation?* • *How do you stay motivated?* • *Do you consider yourself a success?*

Figure 15.5 Slide Presentation Rubric

Criteria	Exceeds (3)	Meets (2)	Approaches (1)	Score
Coverage	Provides in depth information on key aspects of the topic.	Provides adequate information on key aspects of the topic.	Lacks information on many key aspects of the topic.	
Writing	The text is concise and clearly written. There are no errors in mechanics, grammar, and usage.	The text is clearly written. There are few errors in mechanics, grammar, and usage.	The text is unclear. There are many errors in mechanics, grammar, and usage.	
Content	Identifies key aspects of the job and supports all of them with accurate, detailed information.	Identifies key aspects of the job and supports most of them with accurate supporting data.	Identifies key aspects of the job but fails to support many of them with sufficient data.	
Sources	Uses a variety of print and online sources. Cites them correctly.	Tends to rely on one type of resource rather than a range. Cites them correctly.	Uses only one or two resources. Cites them incorrectly.	
Presentation	The presentation is logical, clear, and easy to follow. All of the slides are well designed and attractive.	The presentation is logical, clear, and easy to follow. Most of the slides are well designed and attractive.	The presentation is disjointed and difficult to follow. Most of the slides are overwhelming, distracting, or hard to see.	
			Total	

Rubric Scoring Guide:

Exceeded the standards	12 to 15 points
Met the standards	10 to 11 points
Approaching the standards	6 to 9 points
Not met	5 points and below

INDEX